HTML & CSS
QuickStart Guide®

HTML & CSS

QuickStart Guide®

The Simplified Beginner's Guide to
Developing a Strong Coding Foundation,
Building Responsive Websites, and Mastering
the Fundamentals of Modern Web Design

David DuRocher

Editors: Bryan Basamanowicz, Marilyn Burkley
Cover Illustration and Design: Katie Poorman, Copyright © 2020 by ClydeBank Media LLC
Interior Design and Graphics: Katie Poorman, Copyright © 2021 by ClydeBank Media LLC, Audrey Hardenburg

First Edition – Last updated: June 14, 2023

ISBN-13: 9781636100005 (paperback) | 9781636100012 (hardcover) | 9781636100029 (eBook) | 9781636100036 (audiobook) | 9781636100234 (spiral bound)

Publisher's Cataloging-In-Publication Data
(Prepared by The Donohue Group, Inc.)

Names: DuRocher, David, author.
Title: HTML and CSS QuickStart Guide : the simplified beginners guide to developing a strong coding foundation, building responsive websites, and mastering the fundamentals of modern web design / David DuRocher.
Other Titles: HTML and CSS Quick Start Guide
Description: [Albany, New York] : ClydeBank Technology, [2021] | Series: QuickStart Guide | Includes bibliographical references and index.
Identifiers: ISBN 9781636100005 (paperback) | ISBN 9781636100012 (hardcover) | ISBN 9781636100234 (spiral bound) | ISBN 9781636100029 (ePub)
Subjects: LCSH: HTML (Document markup language)--Handbooks, manuals, etc. | Web site development--Handbooks, manuals, etc.
Classification: LCC QA76.76.H94 D87 2021 (print) | LCC QA76.76.H94 (ebook) | DDC 005.72--dc23

Library of Congress Control Number: 2020952160

Author ISNI: 0000 0004 9330 7502

For bulk sales inquiries, please visit www.go.quickstartguides.com/wholesale, email us at orders@clydebankmedia.com, or call 800-340-3069. Special discounts are available on quantity purchases by corporations, associations, and others.

OVER 850,000

READERS **LOVE** *QuickStart Guides.*

Really well written with lots of practical information. These books have a very concise way of presenting each topic and everything inside is very actionable!

— ALAN F.

The book was a great resource, every page is packed with information, but [the book] never felt overly-wordy or repetitive. Every chapter was filled with very useful information.

— CURTIS W.

I appreciated how accessible and how insightful the material was and look forward to sharing the knowledge that I've learned [from this book].

— SCOTT B.

After reading this book, I must say that it has been one of the best decisions of my life!

— ROHIT R.

This book is one-thousand percent worth every single dollar!

— HUGO C.

The read itself was worth the cost of the book, but the additional tools and materials make this purchase a better value than most books.

— JAMES D.

I finally understand this topic ... this book has really opened doors for me!

— MISTY A.

Contents

PART II – DIGGING IN

| 14 | BOOTSTRAP

PART IV – THE WORK ENVIRONMENT

| 15 | WORKFLOW

| 16 | GIT

| 17 | WHAT'S NEXT?

BEFORE YOU START READING,
DOWNLOAD YOUR FREE DIGITAL ASSETS!

 HTML Starter Template

 All Source Code from Examples

 Online Resource Library

TWO WAYS TO ACCESS YOUR FREE DIGITAL ASSETS

Use the **camera app on your mobile phone** to scan the QR code or visit the link below and instantly access your digital assets.

SCAN ME or **go.quickstartguides.com/htmlcss** **VISIT URL**

Introduction

Congratulations on your decision to learn HTML and CSS! These languages are used daily by billions of people on web pages and apps and in countless other forms. Whether you're planning to build websites, wish to have an informed conversation with a developer, or just want to have a better understanding of the world around you, this book is a great start!

HTML and CSS Are Everywhere

It is nearly impossible to go about your day without encountering HTML and/or CSS. These languages lurk behind every web page, most application screens, television and video game console interfaces, and even the screen of your new smart fridge. You are continually consuming the results of this code but probably rarely stop to think about what's under the hood. That's about to change.

My Story

Hello! My name is David. I grew up in a small town outside of Rochester, New York. I spent countless hours of my childhood exploring the beautiful outdoors of upstate New York, Vermont, and New Hampshire via the plentiful hiking trails and campsites.

I didn't have a computer in my home, but that wasn't unusual at the time. My interest in technology started early, and video games helped fuel this passion. Once I had access to a computer, I began to teach myself coding in a programming language called BASIC. In high school, I moved on to HTML, CSS, and JavaScript.

When I was deciding what path to take, I considered computer science, software engineering, and other tech-heavy options. I eventually decided to pursue a degree in information technology, which I saw as a bridge between the computer and the human side of tech. I attended the Rochester Institute of Technology and was able to learn from some fantastic professors, many of whom came from non-computer-related backgrounds. They became teachers when the skills they had learned developed into a new industry. These professors helped me to see that sharing skills I have learned can take many forms.

In 2008, after moving to New York City and working in my field for several years, I was offered a position as an adjunct professor at the CUNY City College of Technology, where I rounded out the web design curriculum by introducing different web technologies I used in my everyday life on web development projects. Since then, I have moved on to other schools where I teach a wide variety of classes covering HTML and CSS, JavaScript, PHP, and WordPress. I enjoy the process of teaching, seeing new students' confidence grow as they feel more comfortable with new ideas, and watching the "light bulb" blink on when they see how they can use their newfound knowledge.

Outside of teaching, I work for Adobe as a technical account manager supporting the Adobe Experience Cloud collection of products. I still do plenty of freelance web development projects, and when I'm not building things online, I disconnect through hiking or camping on our local trails or in the mountains of Vermont and New Hampshire. At home, I dabble in woodworking and beekeeping. My wife and I work with various animal rescue organizations and are restoring our 1897 Shingle Victorian house in the northwest corner of Connecticut (figure 1).

fig. 1

Source: Illustration by Audrey Hardenburg

On-the-job learning has always been a part of my life. Though my education gave me a wide range of skills, the technology industry is continually changing. The number one skill I have developed is learning how to learn. I always find myself researching and learning new tools, techniques, and strategies for the work that I do.

In the spirit of continued learning in an ever-changing landscape, I wanted to write this book to create a quick but comprehensive guide to the tools I see as most valuable and most used in my experience as a web developer.

Why Learn HTML and CSS?

There are numerous reasons why you might have picked up this book. You may be interested in coding and someone suggested that you start with HTML and CSS. Your company may need to build or revamp a website. You may wish to start a web design firm. Or, like me, you might simply have an insatiable desire to learn.

Regardless of your motivations, HTML and CSS are a great place to start learning how to code. The languages require only a text editor and a web browser—two things you already have on your computer. And HTML and CSS offer instant gratification. You can put a few lines of HTML into a text file, save it, then open the file in a browser and immediately see your results.

The instant feedback of writing HTML can be appealing and satisfying to those who do not consider themselves computer experts. Results appear with a few straightforward instructions. Even a basic understanding of how to use these tools can give you a sense of moving from computer "user" to "superuser." While it's not technically programming, writing frontend markup in languages like HTML and CSS allows you to provide direction to the computer to display content in the precise way you desire.

Q: Is HTML a programming language?

Technically, HTML is not a programming language. HTML stands for "hypertext markup language." A *markup language* "marks up" text with instructions for display—in this case, via a web browser. Programming languages, on the other hand, use logical control statements to direct the flow of the program's execution. Programs take input and produce output, whereas HTML and related markup languages format existing content. Both are called coding, but there is a subtle difference.

WordPress

WordPress excels at blog and website creation but removes some of the control you have over HTML and CSS code. It's simple to add a page or blog post, but customizing the overall look and feel of the website, or creating a new website theme, requires knowledge of HTML and CSS. Even if you use WordPress, knowing HTML and CSS will transform your WordPress data entry skills into those of a full-fledged WordPress web developer.

Wix and Squarespace

Wix, Squarespace, and other website-building tools are excellent platforms for building a website. Their easy-to-use interfaces allow you to create a simple site with no knowledge of HTML. Both Wix and Squarespace allow for customization, but some custom HTML, CSS, and JavaScript isn't possible inside their platforms. Moreover, the website you build cannot be downloaded and used on other web servers. You must continue to purchase their services to maintain your site.

Who Can Benefit from This Book?

Any professional who uses the internet and technology can benefit from knowing HTML and CSS. In the process of writing this book, one of our editors lamented that roadblocks he had encountered in a previous position could have been avoided had he been able to make changes to website code himself. The IT staff and programming team had to handle his requests, slowing down his workflow and creating a more significant burden on the IT department.

Students of Web Development

Are you learning to build websites? This book will give you the foundation you need to understand the two core components of modern web design.

Educators

Will you be teaching web development? This book will help you get ahead of the most common questions your students will ask. It provides step-by-step guidance that will help you bring your students through the learning process with ease.

Science, technology, engineering, and math (STEM) initiatives are proliferating in elementary, middle, and high schools throughout the world. Many educators are pushing the boundaries of their knowledge to bring technology education to students at younger ages. This book works as a guide for students of all ages and can be used to assist teachers who are not highly experienced in the field of web development.

Adjacent Professionals

Perhaps your job doesn't require you to code websites, but you work with a developer or team that does. Understanding the process will enable you to have informed conversations and be able to advocate for your needs. If you have to hire a web designer, you'll have a leg up in the interview process, allowing you to make a better hiring decision.

Marketers and graphic artists frequently interact with web designers. Knowing HTML and CSS will benefit your project(s) and enable you to provide more value to your organization.

Professionals Looking for a Quick Reference/Primer

With easy-to-follow examples and plain-speak guidance, this book is excellent as a quick reference or refresher for a tool you don't use often or for someone getting back into the game.

Web Hobbyists

Many people build websites for their own enjoyment, as a passion project or hobby. This guide will provide a footing to begin building your sites from the ground up.

Employment Roles that Benefit from HTML/CSS Knowledge

If your overall goal is to become a programmer or developer, HTML/CSS is an excellent place to start.

There is a definite benefit in learning HTML and CSS, even if becoming a developer is *not* your ultimate goal. Since many of our daily activities involve a computer of some sort, it makes sense that more employees are expected to have a basic understanding of how computers display data. Even office managers and assistants are sometimes responsible for modifying web pages, so knowing how to do this gives you a clear advantage over other applicants.

Let's take a closer look at some of the workplace roles that utilize HTML/CSS:

Artist / Graphic Designer

Since HTML and CSS are essentially a method for displaying content, it makes sense that graphic designers would benefit from having a full understanding of these technologies to showcase their work. Knowledge of the HTML and CSS code necessary to display graphical content on the web gives the designer a tremendous advantage.

Marketer

Marketers often need to generate new materials for sales initiatives. Landing pages and email marketing messages are excellent ways to showcase your product and call customers to action, and these pages use HTML and CSS code. Basic HTML/CSS knowledge will enable you to respond quickly to marketing opportunities.

Writer / Content Provider

In the (not-so-distant) past, reporters and journalists would type their articles then hand them off to others for print layout. Now, with the growth of the internet and blog-driven content, writers often are asked to format their work in a nearly internet-ready format. Even though many publications use content management systems like WordPress, it is often necessary to make edits to the HTML code to ensure proper display.

Social Media Manager

While managing likes, shares, comments, and retweets may make up a large part of a social media manager's schedule, sourcing and delivering engaging content is vitally important. Knowing how to use links and basic HTML and CSS code will enable the social media guru to better format posts and linked content, giving them a leg up on the competition.

Entry-Level Quality Assurance Engineer

Many quality assurance (QA) professionals are responsible for testing software and websites. Understanding the display code behind the user interface gives a quality assurance engineer an advantage when crafting tests and preparing reports.

Modern QA testing has evolved toward automatic testing procedures. Often, configuring these systems requires knowledge of HTML and CSS.

Nonprofit

Nonprofit organizations have many of the same needs as larger companies, with one significant difference: they typically lack the budget to hire full-time developers. If you are an employee at a nonprofit, you can strengthen your organization by learning HTML and CSS. With web design knowledge, you can build and maintain your organization's website, design email marketing campaigns, and fully take advantage of social media.

Entrepreneur / Small Business Owner

If you are starting your own business, you already know firsthand that everything costs money and technical skills and know-how are particularly expensive. Knowing how to build your website could save you a fortune!

Even if you can't design the entire site yourself, providing a mockup of your ideas will save your designer time. And knowing HTML and CSS will help you make better hiring decisions with your technical staff and contractors.

How the Book Is Structured and How You Will Learn

With each chapter, I'll introduce new concepts via explanation, illustrations, and stand-alone examples. I'll provide context for each topic, so you'll know why it will be useful. Where relevant, I will add specifics from my own professional experience.

To add to the learning experience, we'll be providing you with an actual website that you'll be working on intermittently throughout the book. The website will be presented to you in need of a whole lot of tender love and care. But by the time you finish this book and have completed all the exercises, you'll be well on your way to delivering a high-quality, fully functional web product—see "Accessing the Coffee Shop Website" later in this section for download instructions and more details on this ongoing exercise.

Our objective is to have you finish this book with a solid understanding of HTML and CSS. We'll accomplish this through a combination of resources, including the book itself, the development of the downloadable Coffee Shop website, and an array of other helpful and educational resources.

Take a moment to visit go.quickstartguides.com/htmlcss and access your Digital Assets. We'll be referring you back here for access to various resources throughout the book. For now, though, take a few minutes and watch the short video titled "Using Our GitHub Repository."

In addition to Digital Assets, we're also hosting several essential resources on the ClydeBank Media GitHub page. Go to www.github.com/clydebankmedia. Find the "htmlcss-quickstartguide" repository and click to open. Inside you will find all of our source code for this book.

This social code-sharing platform (GitHub) uses the popular Git *source code management* system. Using Git is helpful if you're on a team, and it offers benefits for single-developer projects, but using the site's greater functionalities isn't essential at this stage of your learning. We'll cover Git in detail in part IV of the book. For now, just jump right into our GitHub site and explore. You can't break anything.

The source code inside the "htmlcss-quickstartguide" repository is organized by chapter and "Snippet number." It should be easy to locate any snippet of code found in the book. Moreover, you are free to use any of our coding examples for your own website projects (figure 2).

fig. 2

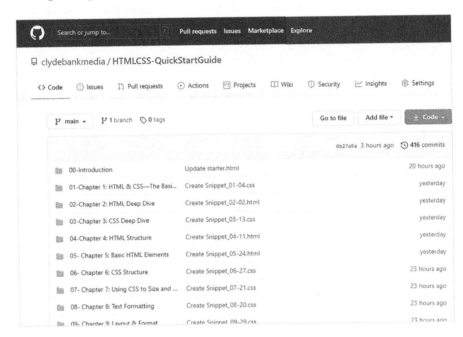

Use our htmlcss-quickstartguide repository on GitHub to easily copy and paste any code featured in this book.

By the way, a lot of the "On Your Own" exercises you encounter in this book can be aided by a basic HTML template. We have created a "Webpage Starter Template" that can be found in the HTML & CSS QuickStart Guide Digital Assets both in the "00-Introduction" folder in GitHub and in its own downloadable file, `starter.html` at clydebankmedia.com/htmlcss-assets.

starter.html

```
<!DOCTYPE html>
<html lang="en">
<head>
    <meta charset="utf-8">
    <meta name="viewport" content="width=device-width,
initial-scale=1, shrink-to-fit=no">
    <title>Starter Template</title>
</head>
<body>
        <!-- CONTENT GOES HERE -->
</body>
</html>
```

Setting Up Your Workspace

One of the great things about working with HTML is that getting started requires nothing more than a text editor and a web browser. From a beginner's perspective, it doesn't matter which text editor and *web browser* you choose, but if you're serious about your HTML training, you may want to acquire a few specific tools. I'll mention some tools in asides or callouts, but for now, let's begin with the basics.

The Importance of Folder Structure

Before you begin writing any code, it's a good idea to create a folder or directory on your computer where all your website files will live.

While it is certainly possible to put all your files in one folder, this technique will get messy very quickly. Making good choices regarding site organization will save you time and frustration as your site grows. A small site, at a bare minimum, will have a directory for the HTML files (at least an index.html file), and a folder for CSS files and images.

fig. 3

CSS

images

index

An HTML file, CSS folder, and image folder

You may end up with far more files in your main directory. Moreover, if your website has multiple subsections, you will likely end up with specific directories for each subsection.

Choosing a Text Editor

HTML files are simply text documents saved using the file extension `.html` rather than `.txt`. Any browser will display HTML files. Since HTML code is completely text-based, basic programs such as Notepad on Windows, TextEdit on Mac, or gedit on Linux are perfectly valid options for an HTML coder (figure 4).

fig. 4

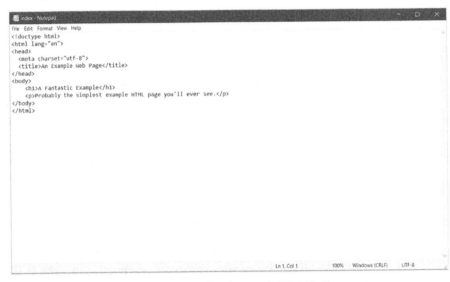

Windows Notepad with a simple HTML file

However, to make life easier, I recommend obtaining a good *code editor*. Code editors are text editors specifically designed for laying out HTML code (and other programming languages) in an organized fashion. They employ color coding, indentation, and a host of other features that aid coders in writing and maintaining code.

Again, none of these tools is required to get started, but if you find it difficult to follow or read code in a standard text editor, give one of these programs a try.

Here are the most popular text editors as of the time of publication. Many are free/open-source or available for a small price.

- » Visual Studio Code
- » Notepad++
- » Vim
- » Emacs
- » Sublime Text

Each of these editors has its pros and cons, but if you're having trouble deciding, I'd suggest installing both Visual Studio Code and Notepad++. It may seem strange to employ two editors, but I use Notepad++ for quick, single-file edits and the fully-featured Visual Studio Code for managing larger sites. Either can suit both scenarios, but these are my recommendations. At the end of the day, a coder's choice of a text editor is a matter of personal preference, and most any option will be fine. If you want a clear-cut recommendation, then I'd say get Visual Studio Code text editor, as most examples and exercises in this book will depict that text editor in action (figure 5).

fig. 5

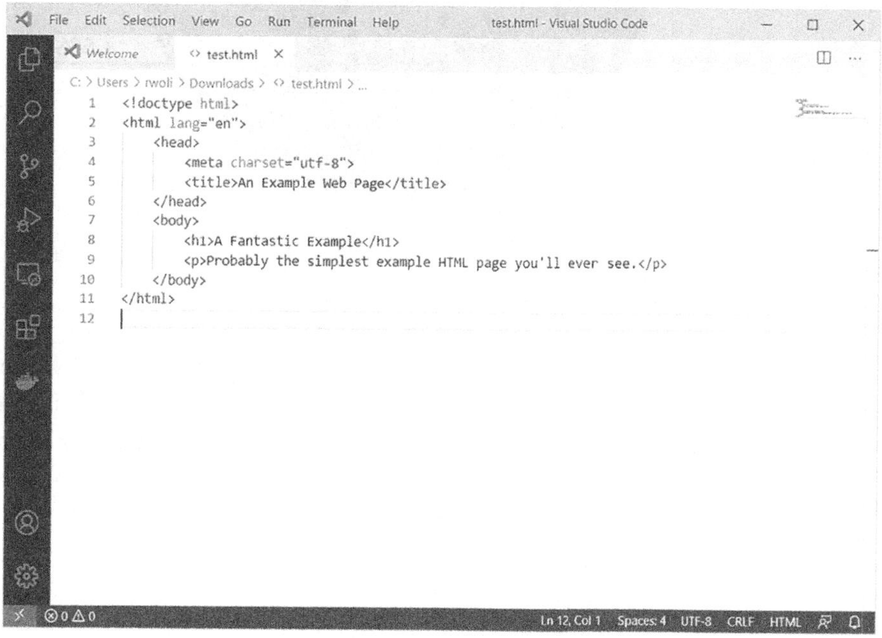

Visual Studio Code with the same HTML file as in figure 4. Note the file browser tabs, syntax highlighting, and other advanced features not found in Windows Notepad.

Popular Web Browsers

It's hard to be a *web designer* without a web browser. Fortunately, all major operating systems include one. For Windows, the default is Edge;

for macOS, it is Safari; and most Linux distributions include Firefox. At the time of publication, Google Chrome has the majority of the browser market share (figure 6).

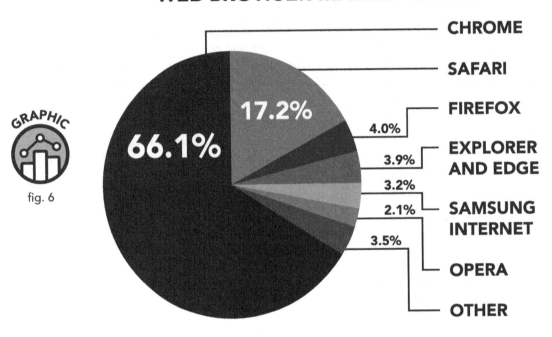

WEB BROWSER MARKET SHARE

CHROME — 66.1%
SAFARI — 17.2%
FIREFOX — 4.0%
EXPLORER AND EDGE — 3.9%
SAMSUNG INTERNET — 3.2%
OPERA — 2.1%
OTHER — 3.5%

GRAPHIC

fig. 6

Browser market share as of October 2020

Source: gs.statcounter.com

You can use any browser to get started, but it is essential to understand that different browsers may render content differently. When building a website, it is a best practice to test your results in multiple browsers to ensure that content renders according to your expectations. Some browsers allow a wider variety of coding styles for the sake of compatibility. In other words, they are more "forgiving" than others (as in, they allow you sloppier code and try to guess as to what you meant). Other browsers are stricter and require code to be structured in a precise way to display correctly.

If you do not want to spend time comparing different browsers, the easiest and safest pick at the time of publication is Google Chrome. Chrome is probably the best browser to work with at the moment because it firmly adheres to established web design standards. All of the browsers featured in figure 6 are available for free download.

Image Editing Software

You are probably familiar with image editing software, from Adobe's signature Photoshop to the very basic Microsoft Paint. You may not know, however, that image editing software is an essential component of your HTML workspace. Even if you are not planning on embarking on any significant graphic design work, you will still need to edit images so they will render optimally on the internet.

Sizing: Image size is one of the essential considerations when editing images. Image files must be downloaded from the web by a browser, so failing to optimize your images can lead to slow load times for your website. Images captured on a camera or smartphone are too large to display on a website and must be resized by image editing software.

Format: Many web browsers accept a wide array of image files, but .jpg, .png, and .gif are the most common. JPEG (.jpg) files are great for photos, while .png and .gif files work well for illustrations or smaller graphics. In cases where an image you want to use is not in the format you desire, image editing software helps you convert it to the desired format.

Image editors range widely in price and complexity. GIMP (the GNU Image Manipulation Program) is a free and open-source alternative to Adobe Photoshop. Both Photoshop and GIMP can be very complicated to use, and if you are not a graphic designer, they can be a bit unwieldy. Microsoft Paint, Paint.net, and Paint++ are more basic choices that offer a simple but efficient set of features.

ACCESSING THE HORRIBLE COFFEE SHOP WEBSITE

The initial ClydeBank Coffee Shop website is terrible and needs a lot of love. We designed it this way on purpose so you would gain experience working with an existing website.

Go ahead and download the sample "ClydeBank Coffee Shop" website, selected examples, images, and related files. They can all be downloaded easily from our GitHub account—www.github.com/clydebankmedia. Look for the repository called "ClydeBank-Coffee-Shop" and click to open.

As previously noted, you will be given opportunities to steadily incorporate your newfound HTML and CSS knowledge into improving this website as we go along. Look for the green "↓ Code" icon, where you can download the ZIP file containing all code and graphic assets for the site. If you're having trouble, see the walk-through in appendix V.

Believe it or not, you've already learned enough about HTML to get started with a simple hands-on exercise. In the directory you've downloaded, you'll find a multitude of files: several `.html` files, a `.css` file, and some images. Each `.html` file represents a website page. You'll recognize the names of standard pages, such as "contact" and "events." The `index.html` file serves as the home page. The web server looks for an `index.html` file as the default page to serve when a user navigates to the website (figure 7).

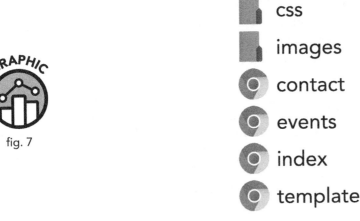

GRAPHIC

fig. 7

The images used on the website and the .css files are placed in their own directories. Note that your browser icons may be different if Chrome is not your default browser.

If you open the `index.html` web page in your browser and click on the "about" link, you'll notice its destination conspicuously missing. That means it's referenced in the `index.html` file but the `about.html` page cannot be found. Let's fix that now.

In your main website directory, you will find a `template.html` file that can be copied to create your `about.html` file. You will be developing this page later as you continue further down your path to HTML/CSS mastery.

Go ahead and copy the `template.html` file and name it `about.html`. It should be in the same directory as the `index.html` file. If you're able to complete this exercise on your own, great. If you're having trouble, don't worry. Once you grasp some core concepts, you'll be fine. At the end of this book in appendix V, "ClydeBank Coffee Shop Solutions," you'll find walk-throughs for all of our coffee shop exercises, including this one.

Your Essential Toolkit

You don't need much to code a website. Unlike with other programming, the barrier to entry is remarkably low. A text editor is the only requirement for coding HTML and CSS. As discussed in "Setting Up Your Workspace," we'll be using Visual Studio Code.

If you have a laptop or desktop with a single monitor, you can drag the Visual Studio Code editor window to the left or right and split the screen with a web browser. If you would rather have each in a full screen, you can simply use ALT+TAB to cycle between them. If you are using multiple monitors, you can place your text editor and web browser on two different screens.

In either case, we recommend having the *HTML & CSS QuickStart Guide* beside your computer for easy reference. If you're reading the e-book version, you can either ALT+TAB to it for reference or place it on a separate screen on a multi-monitor system (figure 8).

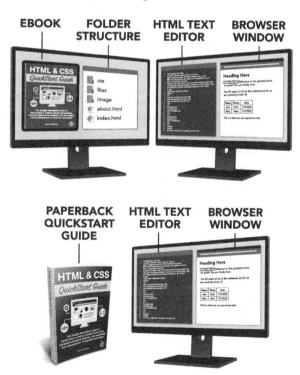

fig. 8

Your essential toolkit: a file explorer, text editor, web browser, and your copy of this book

A Quick Tour of Visual Studio Code

Visual Studio Code is a powerful code editor that provides a wide array of features for both beginners and experts. While it's extremely useful for web design, it can also work with other languages like JavaScript, PHP, Python, Ruby, and more. Let's download it and explore it together.

The interface is divided into four sections. Not all sections are immediately visible upon launch. Notice that in figure 9, the index.html file of the ClydeBank Coffee Shop website is loaded in the large right pane. The HTML is colored to make the various elements in the code easy to see.

The thin left pane shows a display of the current files in the current working folder. This pane is called the Explorer and is not shown when you start the editor. If you wish to see your working folder of files, go to File >> Open Folder to open the folder with the HTML files of your choice. You may want to open the folder containing the ClydeBank Coffee Shop website files that you downloaded in this chapter.

FILE EXPLORER

MENU

fig. 9

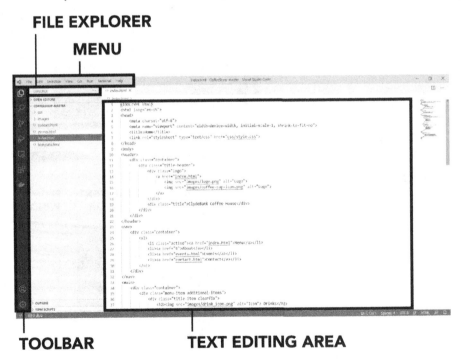

TOOLBAR   **TEXT EDITING AREA**

The Visual Studio Code editor

NOTE

You don't have to use the explorer pane, but it makes it easy to switch between multiple files.

On the far left side you'll see a dark toolbar with various icons. The explorer icon at the top of this bar toggles the file explorer pane. The search icon (displayed as a magnifying glass) toggles a pane to search through your website's files. The remaining icons focus more on source control (Git, discussed in chapter 16) and debugging features that don't pertain to HTML and CSS.

The final portion of the editor is the menu at the top of the application. Many of the various functions inside the editor are found in the menu, including the Open Folder command in the File menu. I encourage you to browse through the menu items to further explore the editor. Even if you don't need all of the functions at the moment, it's good to know where they are.

There are various themes and extensions you can activate in Visual Studio Code to change its appearance and add functionality. You can access these and other configuration options with the settings icon (displayed as a gear in the bottom left corner of the screen on the toolbar).

Visual Studio Code is not limited to code files. You can also use it as a text editor. It is far more powerful than Notepad and can save you a lot of time. As you gain experience with the editor and explore its features on your own, you'll feel more comfortable editing HTML and CSS.

Visual Studio Code has many color themes and extensions that will make your web development even more enjoyable. Click on the gear icon in the bottom left-hand side menu and select Extensions to see what's available. To explore the wide variety of color themes, click the funnel icon above the Extensions search bar and click Category, then Themes. You can also click Most Popular on the funnel icon to see the most-used extensions.

Getting the Most from This Book

Learning HTML and CSS requires patience and commitment. No one's learning path in this subject is identical to anyone else's. In this book we've done our best to present a sensible pathway for you, but you will undoubtedly learn a great deal from your own ingenuity and experimentation.

We'd like to recommend three specific tips to aid your reading and learning experience:

1. If you are struggling to fully understand a concept presented in this book, leave it be for a while. Skip ahead and move on. The book is laid out in such a way that you are sure to encounter one or more subsequent examples of the topic (often in the same section) that will help clarify the main point. Many elements in HTML depend on one another. This makes HTML somewhat challenging to teach in a linear fashion, but patient and persistent students will nibble away at the peripheries of complex topics until the bigger picture gradually comes into full focus.

2. At times, you will likely be tempted to veer off in a tangent of exploration inspired by a particular topic during the course of your reading. I recommend that you (a) go for it! Jump down the rabbit hole for a while and indulge your curiosity, but (b) don't wander for too long. Set a time limit for yourself, after which you'll return to the book and proceed with our prescribed learning structure.

3. I advise testing every HTML and CSS code example you see in this book. As stated before, you can access all source code for this book in the GitHub repository for the *HTML & CSS QuickStart Guide*: www.github.com/clydebankmedia/htmlcss-quickstartguide.

Congratulations! You have started your journey toward becoming a master of HTML and CSS. I look forward to helping you get started in the exciting world of web design.

Did you choose and download all the tools you need to edit and display HTML/CSS? We recommend that you have a file explorer, text editor, and web browser window open as you proceed to part I.

PART I

SETTING THE STAGE

| 1 |

The Basics and the Bigger Picture

Chapter Overview
» HTML and CSS power the web.
» HTML, CSS, and JavaScript are frontend languages.
» You must understand your audience.

HTML, or hypertext markup language, is the markup language that makes the web work. In other words, all web pages on the internet use HTML. When you access a web page, your web browser is interpreting a text file written in HTML that contains a set of instructions for formatting the content of the page so a human can read it. The earliest web browsers could *only* read HTML. In fact, the very earliest ones did not even have a graphical component; they were text-only and could be viewed only in command-line-based operating systems. Obviously, much has changed since the early days of command-line operating systems and HTML-only web pages. HTML now lives in a broader online ecosystem with other languages, online content management systems, and website search engines and aggregators. Let's explore this ecosystem in more detail.

HTML and CSS Basic Structure

No matter how complicated or fancy a website looks, at its core is HTML. In your web browsing experience, you may have (either accidentally or intentionally) clicked on a button that allowed you to view the source of a website's code. That code may have looked like gibberish to you then, but by the time you finish this text, you will be able to identify elements of HTML and CSS within code. Although we will cover HTML and CSS syntax in much greater detail later, it is important for now that you be able to identify the basic building blocks of both HTML and CSS, as we will be referring to these features quite often. Let's get a sneak preview of what HTML and CSS look like on some simplified web pages.

HTML Structure

HTML defines the basic structure of a web page. It provides additional formatting and organization information about the content of a website, no matter if that content is text, images, videos, tables, or data entry forms. Much of this process involves giving instructions to the browser, such as "this is a header," "this is a paragraph," "this is a link," etc. (figure 10).

IMAGE

fig. 10

HTML written in a text file

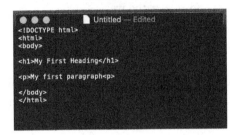

The same HTML interpreted by a browser

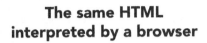

My First Heading

My first paragraph

Think in Terms of Elements

Each browser instruction written in HTML takes the form of an element. An *element* is the basic building block of HTML; it is fair to think of elements as the basic building blocks of any web page (figure 11).

GRAPHIC

fig. 11

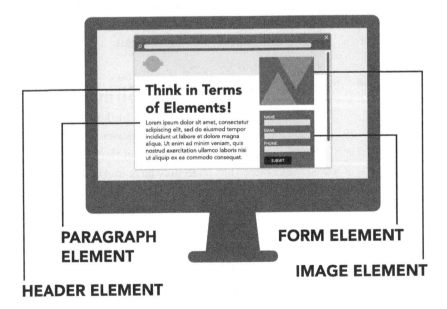

PARAGRAPH ELEMENT

FORM ELEMENT

IMAGE ELEMENT

HEADER ELEMENT

Each element begins with an opening tag and ends with a closing tag. The *tag* performs two key functions: it defines the starting point and stopping point of each element, and it defines the element type.

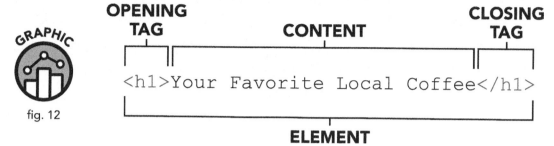

The basic structure of an HTML element

In figure 12, we can see that the tag `<h1>` defines a heading. All tags are encased in angle brackets `<>` with the closing tag having a forward slash `/` to denote the end of the element. All text inside these tags is considered part of that element.

CSS Structure

As you know, most web pages, when viewed through a browser, include much more than basic text. Modern websites employ creative formatting, color, navigation menus, and more. The look and feel of the internet are guided by an additional set of instructions handed to the browser, which tell it how to display the text formatted by the HTML. These instructions have been given by a different but dependent language: *CSS*, or Cascading Style Sheets. CSS tells the browser to display not only the basic structure of the content, but how to format it to make it look visually appealing and, most important, usable.

Consider this example of HTML and its result in the browser in figure 13.

```
<!DOCTYPE html>
<html>
  <head>
  <style>
    body { margin: 0; }
    .header {
      color: white;
      background-color: darkgray;
      padding: 20px;
```

```
        text-align: center;
    }
  </style>
  </head>
  <body>
    <div class="header">
      <h1>My First Heading</h1>
    </div>
    <p>My first paragraph.</p>
  </body>
</html>
```

fig. 13

```
<!DOCTYPE html>
<html>
  <head>
  <style>
    body { margin: 0; }
    .header {
      color: white;
      background-color: darkgray;
      padding: 20px;
      text-align: center;
    }
  </style>
  </head>
  <body>
    <div class="header">
      <h1>My First Heading</h1>
    </div>
    <p>My first paragraph.</p>
  </body>
</html>
```

My First Heading

My first paragraph.

On the right-hand side of figure 13 we can see our HTML example being displayed in the browser. We will explain the HTML and CSS code in depth in later chapters, but for now, the main purpose of this example is to show that the CSS code between `<style>` and `</style>` provides additional formatting for one of the HTML elements, the header. Note that the CSS code only provides structure for existing HTML elements.

If we take a closer look, we will see that CSS has a structure similar to that of HTML (figure 14).

CSS uses a piece of code called a selector to choose what HTML element to modify. It then describes the modification process in another piece of code, the declaration. The declaration consists of one or many properties (such as text color, centering, etc.). These properties are similar to the format controls in any word processor. You can apply a certain value to each property, such as bold, italics, or text alignment. CSS selectors will be described in more detail later. For now, it's sufficient for you to be able to differentiate CSS structure from that of HTML.

```
<style>

                body { margin: 0; }
SELECTOR ──[ .header {
                color: white;
                background-color: darkgray;
DECLARATION ──[ padding: 20px;
                text-align: center; }

</style>
```

PROPERTY ─
VALUE ─

fig. 14

The Relationship Between HTML and CSS

In the earlier days of the web, HTML stood pretty much on its own. Styling was built into the language, and any formatting that needed to occur would be applied directly to each element in the text via HTML coding. Incorporating styles right into individual elements worked fairly well, at least for small websites. However, when working with a large amount of web content, using this HTML-only approach was highly inefficient. Adding styling to a page required inserting the same piece of code repeatedly throughout an entire website—a time-consuming and error-prone process. Furthermore, HTML code could become very bloated. For each line of code that was written, the file size would increase, resulting in slower loading of web pages.

Demand grew for more robust web designs; a system was needed with which one could create a simple set of rules or instructions that could be stored in one place but would cascade across the entire site. In response to this problem, CSS offered sets of style instructions that allowed web designers to make changes across their entire website with only one small piece of code in a CSS file, resulting in cleaner code and huge time savings.

Instead of adding styles directly to each header tag, like this . . .

```
<header style="background-color: #f1f1f1; padding: 20px;
text-align: center;">
```

01-02.html

. . . we define this style *once* in our CSS file:

01-03.css

```css
.header {
    background-color: #f1f1f1;
    padding: 20px;
    text-align: center;
}
```

And now, *all* our `<header>` tags on the site will adopt this styling.

While HTML and CSS are technically two different languages, we use them together, as they are dependent on each other for the web to exist as we know it. CSS requires HTML, but HTML can, theoretically, stand on its own. A web browser can read and interpret a web page written in pure HTML with no problem at all. CSS, by itself, will do nothing. Loading a CSS file into a browser will produce a result that is meaningless to an end user (figure 15).

fig. 15

The home page of our website with CSS turned on   **The same home page with CSS turned off**

Existing websites can be viewed with all CSS turned off. This demonstrates the vast improvements CSS brings to web page design.

The difference between building a page with HTML alone and building one with CSS is the difference between building a house all by yourself and hiring a construction team. With a construction team, you can provide some universal guidelines, such as: "The house should have wooden floors, except for the bathrooms, which should be outfitted in tile" or "Paint all the bedroom walls blue except the master bedroom, which should be an eggshell white." If you were building a tiny house, perhaps you would not need the "CSS building team." However, if you were building a mansion, some general guidelines for design consistency would save you a lot of time and keep your house from looking like it was designed by an eccentric millionaire. You have probably encountered some websites with bizarre styling choices. More likely than not, those websites have inadequate or nonexistent CSS.

HTML and CSS are designed to be compatible with each other. HTML helps to identify the function of any piece of content on any given page, and CSS determines how it looks and works with the other pieces of content and with the page as a whole. If we think of HTML as a series of building blocks, CSS gives us the ability to change the shape, color, size, etc., to fit our needs. With the instructions provided by CSS, that simple set of building blocks takes on new shapes and sizes without affecting the integrity of the underlying structure. The two languages have become dependent on each other. In fact, most advancements in HTML are specifically intended to facilitate CSS's ability to make ever more granular and useful changes to the look and feel of web content.

You may have associated websites with certain website-generating software such as Wix, WordPress, or SiteBuilder. Site-building tools may be used to generate content in many different ways and from many different sources, but in the end, what is sent to the browser is HTML, usually formatted with CSS.

Comparable and Complementary Languages

If all we ever wanted was static content on a web page, HTML, CSS, and a few other tools would be sufficient. However, very few web pages display only static content. For example, think of the last time you looked up a web page for a restaurant, only to find very basic contact information, background music that you could not turn off, and a few scanned images of the restaurant's menu that had not been updated for a year. How helpful was that website? We have grown to expect much more from online content, including up-to-date inventory information, online purchasing and delivery services, and our own user accounts with customizable settings. All these items cannot exist on the frontend, or client-facing, part of a website that is designed by HTML and CSS. The extra functionality we expect requires a host of servers, databases, and other utilities on the backend that we as end users do not interact with directly (figure 16).

Think of a restaurant kitchen. The backend is where orders are organized and food is prepared. The frontend, including the wait staff, tables, and register, is where the customer interacts with the restaurant. Just as the waiters and maître d' don't cook the food, HTML and CSS cannot interact with databases and server processes. The backend requires its own programming languages that interface with the frontend languages to provide content we can see on our computers and mobile devices.

FRONTEND LANGUAGES

BACKEND LANGUAGES

fig. 16

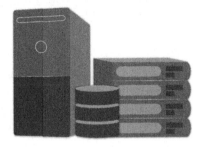

HTML, CSS, Javascript

PHP, Java, C++, Python, Node.js, Go, Ruby

Frontend Languages

Frontend languages are those which are interpreted by the "client," or the web browser. These languages have a direct impact on the user's sensory experience and dictate how information is displayed on computers and mobile devices. While the information displayed may have originated from backend sources, frontend languages act as a showcase and can present that information in a variety of ways.

Beyond HTML and CSS, the most prevalent frontend language on the web is JavaScript. JavaScript is a frontend programming language used for a variety of purposes but principally to provide some interactive elements on web pages, including form validation, pop-up windows, and animations. During the development of HTML5, JavaScript was formally integrated into HTML and, since then, has been fully supported to some level in all major web browsers.

Backend Languages

Backend languages address the need for accurate, dynamic, up-to-date content. Behind many frontend interfaces, there is a backend system with its own programming language that connects a website to databases, file servers, and other digital resources. Backend languages tend to fall in and out of popularity, with some websites switching backends completely or employing a combination of different backends to attain the desired functionality.

A website may use more than one programming language. Some of the most popular websites, which offer a multitude of features, employ several backend languages. Figure 17 provides a rundown, compiled and published by Wikipedia.

GRAPHIC

fig. 17

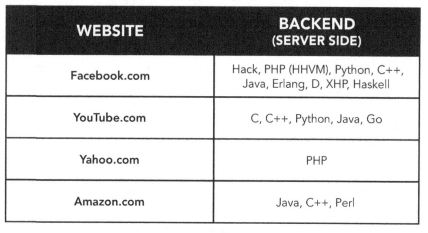

WEBSITE	BACKEND (SERVER SIDE)
Facebook.com	Hack, PHP (HHVM), Python, C++, Java, Erlang, D, XHP, Haskell
YouTube.com	C, C++, Python, Java, Go
Yahoo.com	PHP
Amazon.com	Java, C++, Perl

A table of popular websites and their backend technologies

As a website's functionality increases, so does the need for additional languages to handle new features.

Backend languages have related *frameworks*, such as Symfony (PHP), Laravel (PHP), CodeIgniter (PHP), and Django (Python), providing additional functionality and an easy-to-use code structure for the developer.

Content Management Systems

When you think of building a website, HTML coding may not be the first thing that comes to mind. To many people, building a website is a matter of downloading a website-building software package, choosing a template, and then uploading the results to a hosted site. Website-building tools are an example of *content management systems* (CMS). CMSs are software programs that allow non-coders to build, update, and modify websites (figure 18).

GRAPHIC

fig. 18

Popular content management systems

More than a third of all web pages on the internet are created in WordPress, which is a free, ***open-source*** CMS.

While any CMS system will generate a frontend page, each software package has different capabilities when it comes to providing backend programming and database support.

As we've previously discussed, WordPress and other content management systems are excellent tools, but knowing HTML and CSS transforms you from being a *user* of WordPress to a *designer* who uses WordPress. With custom CSS entries, you can achieve a look and feel far beyond any standard WordPress theme, and with HTML you can edit the header, footer, and even the sidebar without having to rely on widgets. Instead of depending on the creativity of theme designers, you can make a WordPress website look any way you want with a good working knowledge of HTML and CSS.

Understanding Our Online Audience

When making the transition from being a *consumer* of web content to being a *creator*, we must take a step back and think about who is looking at our site. Our goal is to provide information and content that can be consumed with minimal effort. In order to do this effectively, we need to create our content with all potential consumers in mind. Will they be able to read it? Will they be able to understand it? Can they find the information they need without assistance?

When designing websites, we typically think of creating them for someone very much like ourselves. Most people read web pages in the same way—it's a visual experience. How complicated could it be? In most cases, it's okay to take the approach of imagining ourselves as the reader of the site. However, it is extremely important to remember that every person (or thing!) reading a site does not process information the same way we do.

Search Engines / Spiders

Some of the visitors to your website will not even be human! Search engines and other online aggregation services employ an army of autonomous programs, often called "spiders" or "bots," which "crawl" through the web finding new pages to categorize and rank. These spiders do not experience the web in the same way as their human counterparts. Search engines such as Google use spiders to improve their search algorithm and increase the relevance of their search results. This improvement process has three main tasks: crawling, indexing, and ranking. Crawling attempts to discover new websites, and indexing attempts to understand the contents of a website. The ranking process then determines the relevance of a website to potential search terms. For example, the website of a local business would be deemed much more relevant to someone searching from the same geographical location as the business (figure 19).

GRAPHIC

fig. 19

CRAWLING

Bots "crawl" through the web, taking links to new pages and sites and saving the HTML code of what they find.

INDEXING

Customized programs sift through text and images from pages in order to understand them.

RANKING

Search engines use specialized strategies called algorithms to determine the results and order of pages returned from search queries.

Web developers generally want their sites to be as discoverable as possible, so it's important to have an understanding of *how* search engines discover and rank websites. There are ways to optimize a website for all three of the processes previously mentioned. Search engine optimization (SEO) is the art of creating website content or structure in a way that ensures the website is highly ranked (that is, it appears in the first few results or pages) within a given search engine in order to drive traffic to the site. SEO techniques could fill a book by themselves, and many marketing departments employ people specifically for their expertise in SEO.

EXAMPLE

A beautiful web page is created with many pictures of rare gemstones and hardly any text. While human consumers may clearly see the value of the web page, a spider may be unable to assess the page's value without the presence of text associated with the images.

In many situations, it is important for web developers to add text and other meta content that may be unviewable to the end user but viewable to the search engine spider. Maintaining an awareness of how spiders access and index data will help developers ensure their sites are given optimal placement in search engine results.

Online Accessibility Standards

According to figures released by the US Census Bureau on July 25, 2012, 8.1 million Americans (3.3 percent) have a vision impairment. In order to use the internet, many people use screen readers to relay the content. Screen readers are software programs that employ text-to-speech capabilities, in combination with knowledge of a program's common buttons and operations, to provide an audio-powered alternative to navigating the internet via point-and-click on a screen. Text-to-speech is not perfect, so a little forethought in web design goes a long way in accommodating people with vision impairments who may want to access your website. There are methods to ensure that web content can be read by screen readers. Moreover, HTML has built-in structures and features that can automatically handle screen reader accessibility.

In the United States, federal agencies are required by law to make all information on their websites accessible to people with disabilities. Regardless of whether it's a requirement for a specific website, it is a good idea to make it a habit to design accessible sites. An added perk is that good accessibility improves SEO performance.

More information about US federal requirements for websites can be found on the Americans with Disabilities website: www.ada.gov/pcatoolkit/chap5toolkit.htm.

There are many more protocols, web technologies, and internet standards than can be covered in this book. As mentioned previously, topics like search engine optimization can fill entire books by themselves. This text will stick to HTML and CSS web development as much as possible but will also identify other relevant topics and jumping-off points so that readers can follow their interests accordingly.

Chapter Recap

» HTML/CSS are markup languages that direct the display and layout of content on a web page.

» HTML is text content contained in elements. These elements are generally named after their purpose, such as `<p>` for paragraph and `<header>` for header.

» CSS is text markup that describes how the elements should look.

» JavaScript allows you to add interactive functionality to a web page.

» Content management systems (CMSs) like WordPress allow you to construct large websites with less HTML/CSS code.

» Search engines like Google crawl web pages and rank each site according to the content it contains.

» Search engine optimization (SEO) is the art of optimizing your HTML and content to rank higher in search engine results.

» Accessibility standards describe how web designers can aid site visitors with disabilities.

| 2 |
HTML Deep Dive

Chapter Overview

» HTML is a markup language originating at CERN.
» Web servers deliver HTML to a web browser.
» HTML is an evolving standard.

The concept of "markup language" predates the internet or even computers. Markup refers to a series of notes as instructions for how to handle textual content in a document. Markup existed in the early days of the printing press as a system developed by editors to communicate with the typesetter. The production editor would make a series of markup notes on a document to provide instructions to the typesetter pertaining to size, font, and other formatting concerns. As manual typesetting was replaced by more sophisticated machines and computers, the complexity of markup language increased as well.

HTML behaves in the same manner as manual markup, except that the instructions provided are not interpreted by a person but by a web browser. As with any programming language, a machine interpreter does not have the intelligence or discretion of a human typesetter, so the instructions are always interpreted the same way regardless of the intent of the programmer. This chapter will give a brief overview of the inception of HTML, its development, and how it operates with web servers and web browsers. Although readers with an existing familiarity with HTML may already know this information, this chapter can serve as a good refresher.

A Brief History of HTML

HTML originated at the Conseil Européen pour la Recherche Nucléaire (more commonly known as CERN, the European Council for Nuclear Research). CERN is most known for particle physics experiments such as the Large Hadron Collider. CERN needed a method by which to share and access digital documents internally across their intranet. Originally called SGML (standard generalized markup language), HTML functioned initially as an index system, including what today we would call "hyperlinks" that allowed the researchers to easily cross-reference documents.

When HTML was created, web browsers were purely text-based. HTML offered a few basic markup tools, known as tags, to format text on a page and create a few links to other pages. An average user could learn HTML 1.0 in the course of an afternoon. It soon became possible for developers to add a few other elements to web pages, such as images and other forms of media. Some of the community's additions to HTML have been retained for decades (such as iframes, a way to embed an HTML document inside of another HTML document), while others, such as "blink" (a rather annoying feature that made text flicker on the screen), were soon jettisoned due to lack of popularity.

HTML evolved rapidly as a result of competition from large browser companies. This competition initially splintered the language, as different web browsers had varying degrees of support for new and evolving HTML features. Eventually, as web browsers themselves came and went, HTML was further consolidated and standardized until it reached the form we experience today. While there are still some variations "under the hood" in how different browsers handle HTML, these differences are minimal, and all browsers generally provide a similar experience to the user.

Current Use

HTML is used on a broad array of devices. Pretty much any computing device you can think of—desktop and laptop computers, smartphones, tablets, and other mobile (and stationary) devices—use HTML in some way.

While web browsers are the primary venues for rendering HTML, the markup language is also used by many popular email readers, such as those hosted through web-based services like Gmail.

NOTE

HTML is often used in the displays found in stand-alone service kiosks in places such as airports, supermarkets, and libraries.

While most HTML was originally written by hand, it is now typically generated by various backend languages that work through CMSs to create dynamic content. HTML has gone through several versions, but the vast majority of what worked in HTML 1.0 is still functional.

How It Works

To help explain how HTML works, let's break it down into its parts. HTML, as defined earlier, stands for hypertext markup language. "Hypertext" simply refers to text that includes what we call "hyperlinks" or more often "links," which are simple instructions that tell a web browser to move to a new page. "Markup" is text with HTML tags applied to it, such as **bold** or *italicize*. HTML, like other languages, has predefined keywords that mean something specific to the web browser.

HTML files themselves are simply text files named with a specific extension; usually it's `.html` (though there are a few other extensions that are acceptable, we will mainly be using the `.html` extension in this book).

When a file is saved with this extension and then loaded into a web browser, the page will display as formatted according to the instructions in the markup.

Here is a little experiment you can do right now in less than five minutes to demonstrate how simple it is to generate a basic web page. You will need your essential toolkit computer and Visual Studio Code for this task. You can also use another text editor like the Notepad application that comes with Windows. Open a new text document and enter the following text:

02-01.html

```
<!DOCTYPE html>
<html>
    <body>
        You can put any text you like in this section!
    </body>
</html>
```

When you have finished typing, click "Save As" and name the file "test.html" and save it somewhere on your computer. When you are done, navigate to the file and open it. Your newly created HTML file should open in your default web browser. Congratulations! You have just created a web page. Obviously, this is a very rudimentary design and won't be breaking the internet any time soon, but you can quickly improve it using the methods explained in this book. Stick around!

Web Servers

Websites on the internet are hosted on servers called ***web servers***, which are computers that are hooked up to a network and make content available to users upon request. Web pages are served (delivered from host to end user) over a protocol known as HTTP (hypertext transfer protocol), by which a user, through the use of a web browser, makes a request to the server (using an HTTP request) and the server replies by sending an HTTP response to the web browser (figure 20).

WEB SERVER AND BROWSER INTERACTION

GRAPHIC

fig. 20

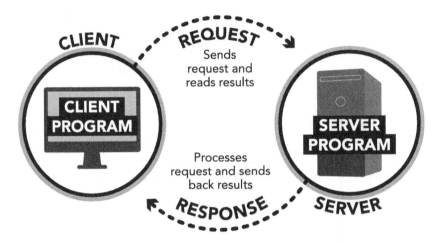

NOTE

When you create your own HTML file and open it in a browser, you are essentially becoming your own web server. If you look at the address bar of the browser, it will show the file location on your computer. You can learn more about web hosting in appendix I, "Web Hosting."

Web Browsers

At this point, you are probably familiar with the concept of a web browser and understand that web browsers read HTML, CSS, and JavaScript (figure 21). What you may not know is that every web browser approaches this process a bit differently. All web browsers contain an engine that takes the instructions provided in the markup (along with the locations of media, image files, video files, etc.) and generates a readable, integrated display that conforms to the instructions. But just like car engines that vary wildly in size, power, and design, the engines of web browsers can be "tuned" to provide different functions. Google Chrome, for example, runs a separate version of the browser for each browser tab you open. This prevents one bad page from crashing all your other tabs. Mozilla

Firefox claims to have the most extensive API, or ability to create custom applications that run within the browser. Microsoft Edge claims to be the most energy-efficient browser.

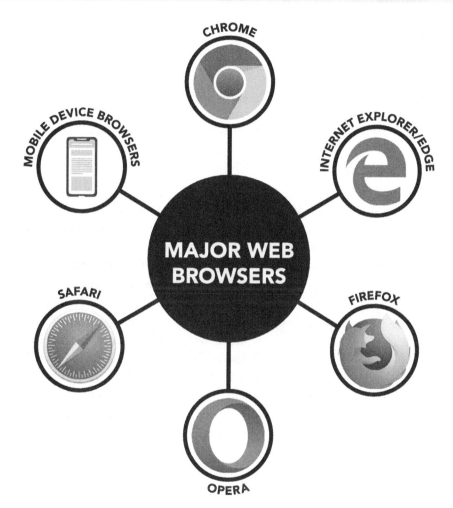

GRAPHIC

fig. 21

The HTML Itself

HTML code is essentially just text. As we demonstrated in our preview of HTML structure in chapter 1, markup elements always appear within brackets, beginning with "<" and ending with ">". The entire web page lives within the element `<html>`. That is to say that almost all the code for any given web page will be bookended by the following two tags: `<html>` and `</html>`. HTML page structure is normally divided into two major sections. The "head," which is labeled `<head>` and `</head>`, includes all metadata about a site—a series of instructions to be given to the web browser. Everything that is visible on the page appears inside `<body>` and `</body>`, which define (you guessed it) the body of the text.

02-02.html

```
<!DOCTYPE html>
<html>
    <head>
    </head>
    <body>
        The content of the body element is displayed in your
browser.
    </body>
</html>
```

Major Changes and Updates

HTML has gone through several major changes during its ever-evolving life cycle. These changes have followed a two-pronged strategy: increasing native HTML support for new features, and steadily shifting the responsibility of text and paragraph formatting over to CSS.

For example, multimedia elements, such as `<audio>`, which defines audio content, and `<video>`, which defines video content, have been added to HTML, while some legacy elements that defined fonts and alignment directly within the HTML have been removed and shifted to CSS.

As mentioned previously, HTML was initially developed for internal document management. Eventually, as networks spread beyond the confines of singular institutions, the driving force of HTML development came from web browser developers. Each web browser would interpret HTML very differently.

Eventually, the creators of HTML realized that a standardized process and a group to oversee that process was needed, and the World Wide Web Consortium (W3C) was formed in October of 1994 (figure 22).

WORLD WIDE WEB CONSORTIUM (W3C)
TIMELINE

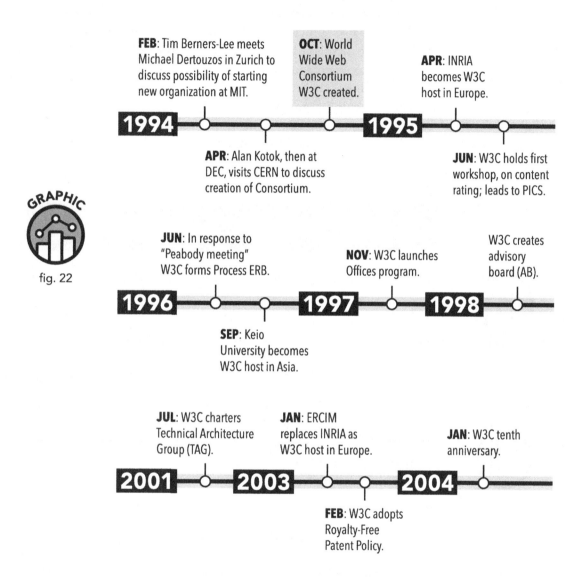

FEB: Tim Berners-Lee meets Michael Dertouzos in Zurich to discuss possibility of starting new organization at MIT.

OCT: World Wide Web Consortium W3C created.

APR: INRIA becomes W3C host in Europe.

1994

1995

APR: Alan Kotok, then at DEC, visits CERN to discuss creation of Consortium.

JUN: W3C holds first workshop, on content rating; leads to PICS.

GRAPHIC

fig. 22

JUN: In response to "Peabody meeting" W3C forms Process ERB.

NOV: W3C launches Offices program.

W3C creates advisory board (AB).

1996

1997

1998

SEP: Keio University becomes W3C host in Asia.

JUL: W3C charters Technical Architecture Group (TAG).

JAN: ERCIM replaces INRIA as W3C host in Europe.

JAN: W3C tenth anniversary.

2001

2003

2004

FEB: W3C adopts Royalty-Free Patent Policy.

HTML5

Each version of HTML added new features to the specification, but versions 4 and 5 added a whole new wave of functionality to the language. The biggest change with HTML5 is the standardization and demarcation of different roles within web development. Whereas in the past CSS and HTML tended to overlap, HTML5 enforces design and content separation.

JavaScript, which was for years the unofficial programming language of the web (and was used in conjunction with HTML), became the formally accepted standard with the advent of HTML5.

HTML5 also provides better multimedia support than did its predecessors, so there is no longer a need to use third-party plugins (for instance, Flash Player) to render videos or music. Also included within HTML5 is a wide range of user-submitted form enhancements and compatibility features to make writing web pages much easier.

HTML5 gives certain elements a friendlier name. Elements like "header," "footer," "section," "article," etc., are directly defined in HTML5, negating the need to create and assign names to a placeholder element known as a `<div>` (figure 23).

fig. 23

TYPICAL HTML4	TYPICAL HTML5
<div id="header">	<header>
<div id="menu">	<nav>
<div id="content">	<section>
<div id="article">	<article>
<div id="footer">	<footer>

Though the notation for basic elements became more simplified with HTML5, the `<div>` element was certainly not made obsolete. As you continue your study in HTML and CSS you will learn the importance of the `<div>` element.

Future Development

Like many technologies, HTML is a fluid specification with new advancements occurring on a regular basis. But though the language changes, many of the original principles remain the same. At the time of this book's publication, HTML5 represents the most current iteration of the language, but most past elements of HTML still exist within HTML5 and are regularly used. Elements of the language do not, for the most part, become obsolete. Considering this trend, what we have sought to achieve in this book is to provide an evergreen tutorial resource for HTML, one that can be used as a reference and teaching aid for years to come.

Some readers may wonder about the next iteration of HTML—presumably HTML6. The answer to that question is, as of now, unclear. There may not be an HTML6, at least not for quite a while. According to an influential standards-setting and monitoring community known as the Web Hypertext Application Technology Working Group (WHATWG), HTML is best treated as a "living standard." WHATWG recommends that interested tech communities continually monitor the way people use HTML and seek to modify it slowly but responsively as usage evolves and new needs arise. Because of this incremental "living standard" approach to development, there may never be another formal release of a comprehensively overhauled language that warrants the title HTML6. Then again, only time will tell.

As a coding language, HTML may remain quite unchanged for some time. Changes that occur to web development are more likely to relate to implementations of other languages, such as CSS and JavaScript.

Chapter Recap

» The W3C organization maintains and improves the HTML standard.

» Web browsers request web pages from web servers, and those servers then send a response back to the web browser, whose engine renders the HTML in a visual presentation.

» HTML can be thought of as a "living standard"—evolving in response to new technological developments and user needs.

» A solid understanding of HTML will reduce the time and effort needed to keep up with new HTML innovations.

| 3 |
CSS Deep Dive

Chapter Overview
» CSS styles HTML elements.
» Styles can be applied to all, some, or just one element.
» Not all browsers identically render styled content.

As we mentioned earlier, HTML is a tool to organize, categorize, and structure content. CSS provides the ability to change the appearance and shape of that structure in order to provide a better visual experience. While HTML creates the backbone of the *information* on a web page, CSS styles flesh out the content and improve the user experience.

Let's return to our analogy of visualizing a web page like a house. HTML allows us to define how many rooms, how many stories, and how much furniture the house has. CSS lets us define the style and shape of each room, the organization of the furniture within the rooms, and the colors and styles of everything from walls to floors. HTML labels the elements, and CSS applies a set of styling rules to elements with those labels.

As we learned in chapter 1, CSS stands for Cascading Style Sheets. CSS allows us to create global rules to style all elements of a certain type. For example, we can create a rule for paragraphs to have a certain indentation and font size, and this style will "cascade" through every paragraph in the document. CSS allows us to set general rules for our various styles and to set exceptions to those rules when needed. We will be exploring CSS in much more detail later, but for now, let's expand on the concept by continuing with our house analogy.

Let's say you have decided that all windows in the house will be three feet wide and four feet tall, with white trim. You can specify this information in a global style sheet for windows. However, you may have some exceptions to these rules. For instance, bathroom windows will only be two-and-a-half feet wide and will have gray trim. You can provide a set of instructions that says, "Apply this alternate style to all windows that are *also* bathroom windows." Now imagine there is a single window that you want to be tinted green;

you need to specify this information about that one individual window. CSS allows you to apply style rules both broad and narrow in scope to any of the content created in your HTML documents.

All web browsers have a set of built-in rules for how to interpret instructions provided in CSS files. For the most part, they handle this information in the same way. However, there is some variation in certain areas. Not all CSS rules are supported by all browsers. When using CSS, it's always a good idea to ensure that any unique or fancy effects you employ are supported by the browsers your site visitors are most likely using.

Background

In the early days of HTML and internet browsers, it was up to the browser to determine how to organize and lay out HTML code. As a result, all browsers would display websites differently. Simple things like font, text size, and color, if not explicitly defined in the existing HTML, would be determined by the browser and not the author of the web page. Web page creators had complete control over their content, but not their layout, graphic style, etc.

While it was possible to style content in the early forms of HTML, doing so often required the awkward use of various tags (such as `<font>` and `<center>`) within the page to specify layout. Reliance on these HTML tags resulted in code that was overly busy and difficult to read. It also led to inconsistencies in the pages of the website. Sites with any significant magnitude and breadth (comprising multiple pages) were apt to have certain pages using entirely different methods for styling content. The resulting websites had a disjointed look and feel and were burdened with overcomplicated HTML code. Moreover, variations among browsers exacerbated the problem, and the process of making site changes or updates was extremely time-consuming and error-prone. Major design updates to change the look and feel of a website often required recreating all the content. On top of the painstaking nature of making changes, pages ended up being extremely large, inflating load times.

Inspired by the desire to format web pages like traditional print media, the producers of various internet browsers began to publish "style sheets." Web designers, when designing for a specific browser, could employ these style sheets and effectively and efficiently exert more uniform and global control over their website's layout. Eventually, all major browsers used style sheets, and by consensus a standard emerged that became known as CSS.

How It Works

If HTML provides the building blocks of our web page, CSS allows us to shape the way these blocks look, work, and interact with the blocks around them. As HTML provides the structure for the content, CSS provides a set of rules that allows us to define how these structures appear on the page. CSS selectors are part of this rule set and help us select the HTML elements we want to style (figure 24).

fig. 24

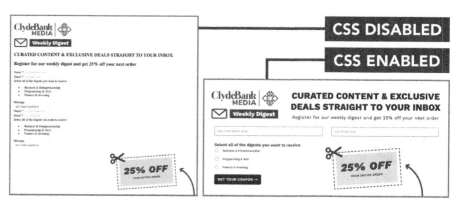

A portion of the ClydeBank Media website with CSS disabled (left) and enabled (right)

As mentioned earlier, the C in CSS stands for "cascading," meaning that the styling rules we provide will cascade throughout the site. Pure CSS is displayed as a named selector (such as "p" for paragraph) followed by a list of properties that will be assigned to this selector, such as the width, font, etc.

fig. 25

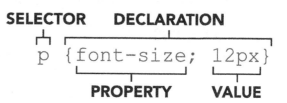

There is an important concept in CSS called "inheritance." To understand how inheritance works, we need to look at the structure of our HTML code. In HTML, structures are "nested." Outer elements are "parents" that contain other elements within them called "children." When CSS is applied, child elements inherit all the defined properties of their parent (typically font face, size, and color), but child elements can, at the CSS coder's discretion, be overridden with a set of rules distinct from those governing the parent elements.

In figure 26, `<div>` is the parent element and `<img>` and `<p>` are the child elements. We haven't gone over any of these elements yet, so don't worry about their function—for now, we're focused on the structure. The child elements are completely contained within the parent. The child element inherits all the properties from the parent, so the (img) image and the (p) paragraph are styled according to the (div) parent element unless the child element overrides them with its own selectors.

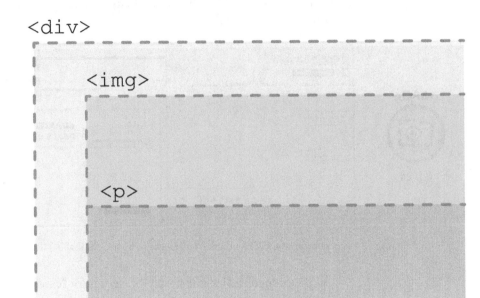

fig. 26

Let's look at the three approaches for incorporating CSS into HTML and the advantages and disadvantages of employing each method.

Inline CSS

Inline CSS styles are added inside individual HTML elements. Inline CSS bears the closest resemblance to previous versions of HTML, where each element was styled using HTML tags such as `<center>`, `<font>`, and `<u>`. This method of applying CSS has the smallest scope and impact, because it affects only the HTML element that contains it (figure 27).

The disadvantage of using inline CSS can be inferred from the very definition of CSS: *cascading* style sheets. Since inline CSS embedded into an HTML element affects only that element, this method misses out on the purpose of using CSS to begin with: to apply universal styling rules to a document that cascade throughout the document (or multiple pages) so that each element doesn't have to be individually styled.

```
<!DOCTYPE html>
<html>
<body>

<h1 style="color:darkgrey;font-size:50px;text-align:center;">This is a heading with inline CSS</h1>
<p style="color:black;font-size:20px;text-align:center;">This is a paragraph with inline CSS.</p>

    <h2>This is a heading without inline CSS</h2>
    <p>This is a paragraph with plain html and no inline CSS.</p>

</body>
</html>
```

fig. 27

This is a heading with inline CSS

This is a paragraph with inline CSS.

This is a heading without inline CSS

This is a paragraph with plain html and no inline CSS.

Inline CSS affects only the HTML element it inhabits.

Internal CSS

Internal CSS is CSS that is added to a selection of HTML elements within a single individual HTML page. Usually this is done by placing a set of `<style></style>` tags (normally inside the `<head></head>` element) in an HTML page. This approach is most likely to be used if there is only one page to be styled; it quickly loses its effectiveness if a website has multiple pages.

```
<!DOCTYPE html>
<html>
<head>
<style>
body {
  background-color: grey;
}

h1 {
  color: white;
  Text-align:center;
}
</style>
</head>
<body>

<h1">The style for h1 is defined in the style header</h1>
<p>This is a paragraph</p>

</body>
</html>
```

fig. 28

The style for h1 is defined in the style header

This is a paragraph

Internal CSS is placed in the <style> element within the HTML page.

```html
<!DOCTYPE html>
<html>
  <head>
    <style>
      body { background-color: gray; color: black; }
      h1 { color: white; text-align: center; }
    </style>
  </head>
  <body>
    <h1>This style for H1 is defined via CSS in the head.</h1>
    <p>Example paragraph.
  </body>
</html>
```

IMAGE

This style for H1 is defined via CSS in the head.

Example paragraph.

fig. 29

REMEMBER

Digital (copy & paste-able) access to all of the code samples in this book can be accessed in our GitHub account: github.com/clydebankmedia/htmlcss-quickstartguide.

External CSS

With external CSS, styles are added to multiple pages at once. This method of applying CSS is most commonly used for more complex web pages. External CSS uses CSS code in a separate, unique file called a style sheet that is used as a reference by all the HTML files. The CSS file is referenced, or "called," within the `<head>` tags of the HTML file(s) (figure 30).

CSS: (make sure it is named style.css in the CSS folder)

SNIPPET

```css
body { background-color: black; color: white; }
h1 { color: gray; text-align: center; }
```

03-02.css

HTML: (name it index.html, and note the css/style.css href in the link element since you created the style.css file in the CSS folder)

```html
<!DOCTYPE html>
<html>
  <head>
    <link rel="stylesheet" href="css/style.css">
  </head>
  <body>
    <h1>This style for H1 is defined via CSS in the head.</h1>
    <p>Example paragraph.
  </body>
</html>
```

fig. 30

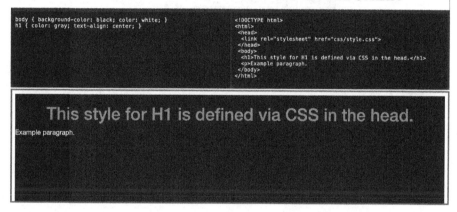

External CSS is placed in its own style sheet that is then referenced in the HTML page.

fig. 31

The style.css file in the CSS folder on the explorer pane of Visual Studio Code

Coders are not limited to any one of these methods for applying CSS to HTML. When mixing methods, however, it is important to realize that a hierarchy will be in play. Browsers will first apply any external CSS files, and these files will be applied in the order in which they are called on the page. Next, the browser will apply any styles listed directly on the page inside the `<style>` element. Finally, the browser will apply inline styles.

Applying Styles to Elements

There are three means by which we can apply styles to elements: element selectors, class selectors, and id selectors. Recall that CSS rule sets must first use selectors when identifying what is to be modified (figure 32).

ELEMENT SELECTOR   p {color: blue; }
SELECTOR

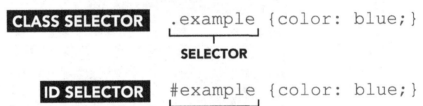

CLASS SELECTOR   .example {color: blue; }
SELECTOR

ID SELECTOR   #example {color: blue; }
SELECTOR

GRAPHIC

fig. 32

Element Selectors

Element selectors identify the type of the element (body, p, a, etc.), select every instance of that element, then apply the rule to it.

For demonstration purposes, let's look at the `<body>` element. This element contains all the viewable content within an HTML page. We often use it to set some "default" styles for the page.

SNIPPET

03-04.css

```
body { color: blue; }
```

In this example, we are selecting the element "body" on the HTML page. These rules are being applied to everything that exists within `<body></body>` on the page.

After the selector, we open a set of curly brackets {} that will hold our property declarations.

Each property declaration identifies a property (in this case, color). Then, following the colon, the desired setting for that property (in this case, blue) is identified. We use a semicolon at the end of each property declaration.

The result of this small CSS snippet would be to change the color of the visible text on the page to blue.

Use of the semicolon is required. If left out, both the property missing the semicolon and the one that follows it are unable to be processed and will be ignored by most browsers.

Class Selectors

Sometimes we want to apply a style to a subset of elements. For example, we may want to apply a style to a certain paragraph (or set of paragraphs) without affecting the others. To accomplish this, we need to establish a "class" of paragraphs. Elements can be assigned to a class using the class attribute in HTML.

`<p class="callout">` signals the beginning of a paragraph that will be defined by the "callout" class; the term callout is selected by the user. You can name a class whatever you please. CSS code will be used to define the stylistic attributes of this class. Consider the following HTML code:

03-05.html

```
<p>
    Lorem ipsum dolor sit amet, consectetuer adipiscing
elit. Aenean commodo ligula eget dolor. Aenean massa. Cum
sociis natoque penatibus et magnis dis parturient montes,
nascetur ridiculus mus. Donec quam felis, ultricies nec,
pellentesque eu, pretium quis, sem.
    </p>

    <p class="callout">
    Etiam rhoncus. Maecenas tempus, tellus eget
condimentum rhoncus, sem quam semper libero, sit amet
adipiscing sem neque sed ipsum. Nam quam nunc, blandit vel,
luctus pulvinar, hendrerit id, lorem. Maecenas nec odio et
ante tincidunt tempus.
    </p>
```

```
    <p>
    Nam pretium turpis et arcu. Duis arcu tortor, suscipit
eget, imperdiet nec, imperdiet iaculis, ipsum. Sed aliquam
ultrices mauris. Integer ante arcu, accumsan a, consectetuer
eget, posuere ut, mauris. Praesent adipiscing. Phasellus
ullamcorper ipsum rutrum nunc. Nunc nonummy metus.
    <p>


    <p class="callout">
    Etiam rhoncus. Maecenas tempus, tellus eget
condimentum rhoncus, sem quam semper libero, sit amet
adipiscing sem neque sed ipsum. Nam quam nunc, blandit vel,
luctus pulvinar, hendrerit id, lorem. Maecenas nec odio et
ante tincidunt tempus.
    </p>
```

Q: Lorem who?

Answer: The "Lorem Ipsum . . ." dummy text sequence has long been used as placeholder text in the printing industry. It provides a somewhat realistic layout of paragraph text for demonstration purposes. There are extensions in Visual Studio Code that will generate Lorem Ipsum.

Paragraph elements with the "callout" class will inherit its styling, whereas content between the regular `<p>` elements without this class definition will be rendered in a default manner or inherit the styling of the containing element.

To style the paragraphs with the "callout" class, we use a class selector in our CSS file. The class selector begins with a period and is followed by the class name, an open bracket, and an ensuing list of specific attributes:

03-06.css

```
.callout{
    color: gray;
    font-style: italic;
    margin-left: 20px;
}
```

As you can see, each attribute is formatted as follows: `[attribute type]: [attribute detail];` and then the selector is concluded with an end-bracket.

When applied, our class selector would result in output like that shown in figure 33.

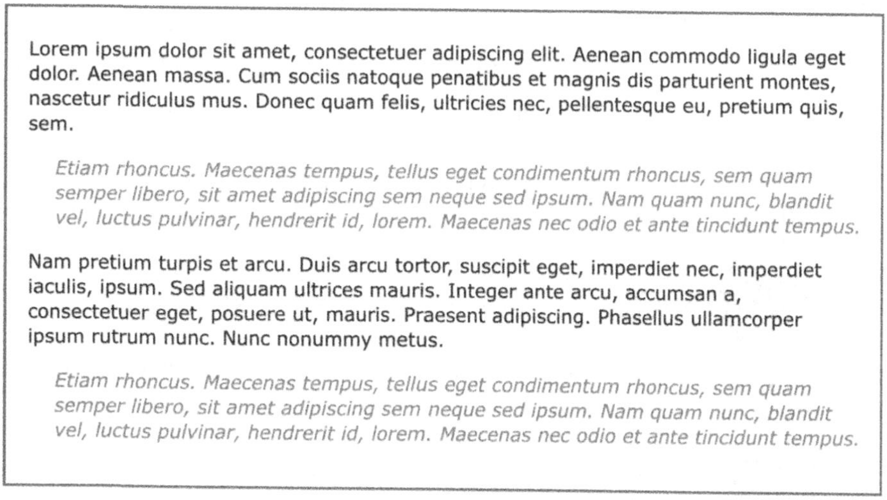

IMAGE

fig. 33

Lorem ipsum dolor sit amet, consectetuer adipiscing elit. Aenean commodo ligula eget dolor. Aenean massa. Cum sociis natoque penatibus et magnis dis parturient montes, nascetur ridiculus mus. Donec quam felis, ultricies nec, pellentesque eu, pretium quis, sem.

Etiam rhoncus. Maecenas tempus, tellus eget condimentum rhoncus, sem quam semper libero, sit amet adipiscing sem neque sed ipsum. Nam quam nunc, blandit vel, luctus pulvinar, hendrerit id, lorem. Maecenas nec odio et ante tincidunt tempus.

Nam pretium turpis et arcu. Duis arcu tortor, suscipit eget, imperdiet nec, imperdiet iaculis, ipsum. Sed aliquam ultrices mauris. Integer ante arcu, accumsan a, consectetuer eget, posuere ut, mauris. Praesent adipiscing. Phasellus ullamcorper ipsum rutrum nunc. Nunc nonummy metus.

Etiam rhoncus. Maecenas tempus, tellus eget condimentum rhoncus, sem quam semper libero, sit amet adipiscing sem neque sed ipsum. Nam quam nunc, blandit vel, luctus pulvinar, hendrerit id, lorem. Maecenas nec odio et ante tincidunt tempus.

NOTE

CSS uses strict hierarchies. Class selectors, for instance, rank higher than element selectors. If you apply a "p" element selector to a paragraph of text that's been assigned to a class, the class attributes will display and the element attributes will be ignored.

Id Selectors

Classes can be used by multiple and varied elements, but an id selector references a single element on the page. This functions similarly to a class where we add an HTML attribute to the element in question.

SNIPPET

03-07.html
and
03-08.css

```
<h1 id="pageTitle">...</h1>
```

When writing a rule with the id selector, begin with a "#" and then add the id of the specified element. For example,

```
#pageTitle {font-weight: bold;}
```

Rules using an id selector override any class selectors that may be assigned to the element or browser default styles.

Contrasting "class" with "id"

Classes are generally meant to apply to multiple elements, whereas ids reference only one element. Classes and ids are types of HTML element attributes that serve no direct function on their own. To further illustrate that point, let's examine common usage scenarios for each.

Let's say we have several paragraphs on a web page for a surf shop. We have already designated all our paragraphs with a `<p>` element in our HTML document. However, our website primarily has two types of paragraphs, one type for standard information about the surf shop and another more showy style for info on the shop's current sales. We want the ability to apply a certain set of rules to all the sales paragraphs. Therefore, we are going to establish a style in our CSS document called "bold-red":

03-09.css

```
.bold-red { font-weight: bold; color: red; }
```

In our HTML document, we can now call this class by modifying our opening tag as follows:

03-10.html

```
<p class="bold-red">
    40% off all surfboards and wetsuits this week. Don't
miss it!
</p>
```

Any element can be given this "bold-red" class, and in this particular instance, only this paragraph will be styled with the "bold-red" rule.

If this was the one and only bold-red paragraph we needed on the whole page (or throughout the whole site), then we could use an id instead of a class definition. Ids style one specific element, whereas classes, once defined, can be invoked again and again to style a multitude of elements. In general, CSS rules may apply to several types of elements, so keeping them flexible saves you time on more complex pages. We could easily use this "bold-red" class on an h1 tag or any other element we want to highlight on our page, and it's much easier to invoke a class than to recode all your descriptors and attributes.

You may wonder why we should use ids at all if classes are so flexible and powerful. It's an excellent question; at first glance, ids seem superfluous. But since ids allow us to specifically target a particular element, we can apply specific styles to just that element without resorting to inline styles.

Ids are often used to designate a singular exception to a prevailing class definition: recall our example of the house. As a rule our windows may all have white trim, but if we want the bathroom window to have gray trim, then we can assign an id to the bathroom window and style that id to specify gray trim. This would only affect that one window.

NOTE

Ids also allow JavaScript to target one specific element on a page.

Inline Styles

Inline styles are used less frequently than the aforementioned selectors. They are more tedious to apply, but they are still useful for robust customization and control. They are added to the opening tag of an element in the HTML. Inline styles will override id, class, and element selectors as well as browser default styles.

03-11.html

```
<h2 style="color: blue;">Matterhorn</h2>
```

Standard CSS syntax is used (`attribute type: attribute detail;`) just as it would be when writing a global CSS rule, even though inline styles are by definition not global and must be added to every individual element that the programmer/designer intends to stylize.

The application of inline styles should be constrained to one line of text.

Using the web page starter template (`starter.html`), included in your Digital Assets (clydebankmedia.com/htmlcss-assets), try adding various styles like bold, italics, and color to some sample text. For experience with all three methods, you can apply the styles inline, directly to the paragraph element, as a class, or as an id. Be as creative as you want and experiment with the various colors you can assign by name. The Visual Studio Code editor, as shown in figure 34, will show a preview of the color as you type it.

fig. 34

```
p {
    color: ■black;
}
```

The color preview feature of Visual Studio Code

Rendering Engines

When a web page is loaded, the code is processed (parsed) from the top down. The browser will go through the HTML file and each individual element is created and then styled according to any CSS rules. The part of the browser that handles this activity is called the ***rendering engine***. As of this writing, there are a few different rendering engines used in modern browsers. Apple's Safari browsers use WebKit. Chrome and Microsoft Edge use a WebKit variant called Blink, and Firefox uses an engine called Gecko. There are several others, but WebKit, Blink, and Gecko are the most widely used.

GRAPHIC

fig. 35

BROWSER	RENDERING ENGINE
Lunascape	Gecko, Trident, WebKit
Internet Explorer	Trident
Firefox	Gecko
Google Chrome	WebKit (Blink)
Safari	WebKit
Opera v.15+	WebKit (Blink)

As a beginner, you may be wondering why we are focusing on something as technical as the rendering engines used by different web browsers. Although HTML and CSS have been mostly standardized, there are still some variations in the way that different browsers handle the rendering of your code. This is particularly important when you are deciding which CSS features to use. In many cases, something that looks fantastic while you are testing it in Chrome might look strange (or not render at all) when you look at it in Internet Explorer or Edge.

Identifying and accounting for these inconsistencies is part of the cross-browser testing that needs to take place before a project is complete. There are almost always ways to navigate and work around browser inconsistencies, but it often requires writing multiple sets of rules in your CSS code.

As new features are added to browsers, they may display content in different ways. However, over time they tend to become uniform and standardized.

How Do I Know Which Browsers to Code For?

Many people will tell you to check the statistics for your site to determine which browsers the bulk of your users are running. This is always a good idea. Of course, if you haven't launched the site yet, how could you know? As a rule, it's a good idea to consider, at the very least, the big three or four: Chrome, Internet Explorer, Edge, and Firefox.

Many analytics tools, such as Google Analytics, are free. Google Analytics is very popular for this reason and because it provides a large amount of data about your site traffic, including which browsers your site visitors are using. Other excellent options for analytics include Matomo (previously known as Piwik) and AWStats.

How Do I Know How to Size the Elements on My Pages?

In the earlier days of the web, sites were designed to be as wide as possible. This was because developers simply wanted or needed to take advantage of every pixel. The more modern and mature response to the question of appropriate page width is for HTML coders to choose a width that is appropriate for the content and responsive to the site's users.

When specifying sizes in CSS (like margins and padding), using percentages and device-independent intervals allows the browser to scale the size in proportion to the available screen. For example:

03-12.css
and
03-13.css

```
p { width: 200px; }
```

This will render paragraphs no more than 200 pixels wide. But using percentages, like this . . .

```
p { width: 80%; }
```

. . . tells the browser to render a paragraph to be 80% of the available container, which allows for better scaling across devices.

You can use your analytics software to detect what resolutions your users are using. One important point to consider is that many users will access your site on a phone or other mobile device. For this reason, you may wish to consider using a responsive design that will change the layout of your site depending on the dimensions of the device being used. We will be discussing responsive design tips and techniques in chapters 13 and 14.

How Can I Tell Which Features Are Supported?

Browsers are constantly updated with new programming to support the latest and greatest features. Given this dynamic and ever-evolving environment, it's helpful to know which features are supported by which rendering engines at any given moment. A good reference tool is Can I Use: www.caniuse.com. This website provides a list of browsers and browser versions that support specific features and also explains the more subtle distinctions between rendering engines.

Beyond the Web

Along with HTML, CSS now has uses beyond creation of web pages. It is used to format e-books, maps, and more, in concert with other programming languages. CSS as a standard is quite active and is continually in the process of development, with new functionalities being added regularly. Like HTML, CSS revisions are now subject to a "living standard" and are adjusted incrementally based on developer usage and community feedback. CSS will likely remain with us until we reach a dramatic shift in the way online data is displayed.

Chapter Recap

» CSS is applied to elements via inline, internal, or external CSS rules.

» CSS rules can apply to all elements, a particular type of element, a user-defined class of elements, or a specific element marked with the id attribute.

» The use of inline CSS is discouraged except for troubleshooting purposes.

» Like HTML, CSS is a living standard.

PART II

DIGGING IN

| 4 |
HTML Structure

Chapter Overview
» HTML elements have tags and attributes.
» Comments do not render on the page.
» Elements are nested.

Before we begin creating an HTML document, let's look at the components that make up an HTML page. As previously mentioned, HTML documents are essentially text documents that contain content marked up to give instructions to the browser.

Hopefully, by now, you have chosen your preferred text editor and web browser. As we venture into part II of this book, be sure to have these tools handy. It is best to practice these skills as you learn them!

Elements
In our breakdown of HTML structure presented in chapter 1, we looked at the fundamental building block of HTML, the element (figure 36).

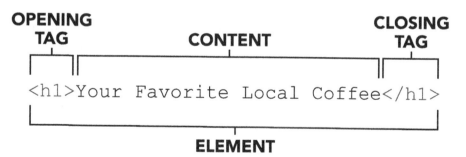

fig. 36

Elements can be easily added to fit the needs of our website. For example, if our page had a lot of text, we would have multiple elements for different sections, articles, headers, and footers. On more graphical sites, we would have image elements, embedded sound, and possibly video elements as well. Any content we have on the page will be placed within opening and closing tags that identify the content inside them.

NOTE

You may see some HTML elements you don't recognize in some of our examples. Don't worry—we'll address them. For now, they serve to illustrate the point in this section.

SNIPPET

04-01.html

```html
<!DOCTYPE html>
<html>
    <body>
    <h1>This is a Heading</h1>
    <p>And this is a paragraph of text.</p>
    <section>
        <h2>Here is a Section Heading</h2>
        <p>And here is a paragraph within a section.</p>
    </section>
    </body>
</html>
```

IMAGE

fig. 37

Tags

As we see in figure 37, every element is composed of opening and closing tags that define the beginning and end of the element. The content of an element depends on the type.

Regardless of the content, most elements will have an opening tag and a closing tag.

For example, let's look at the `<html>` element. All other HTML elements are listed inside the `<html>` element. It is therefore considered the "highest level" element on the HTML page. As with every other element, the `<html>` tag is enclosed between "<" and ">" brackets. The opening tag is `<html>`, and the closing tag is identical except for the use of a "/" to designate the end of a block, like this: `</html>`. All the content of the `<html>` element (including whole other elements) exists inside of these tags.

fig. 38

```
<!DOCTYPE html>
<html>
  <body>
  <h1>This is a Heading</h1>
  <p>And this is a paragraph of text.</p>
  <section>
    <h2>Here is a Section Heading</h2>
    <p>And here is a paragraph within a section.</p>
  </section>
</body>
</html>
```

As seen in figure 38, "html" tags, `<html>` and `</html>`, define the beginning and end of all content on an HTML page. In other words, everything on an HTML page falls between these two tags (except for the `DOCTYPE` tag, which we will cover later in this chapter).

NOTE

While HTML is not case-sensitive (browsers don't care whether a word is typed in upper or lowercase letters), it is good practice to use a consistent style. It is considered best practice for most element types to be written in lowercase. In general, most developers agree that lowercase is easier to read and easier to type. While the `DOCTYPE` tag is often found typed in all caps, there's no hard-and-fast rule underlying this trend. Sometimes you may see elements written in camel case (e.g., camelCase), but most of the time that is reserved for other programming elements on a page, such as JavaScript. It is highly recommended that you use lowercase element types.

Attributes

Many elements need additional information, which we call **attributes**. Attributes allow coders to assign additional options to a tag. We say *tag* and not *element* because attributes are applied to the opening tag of an element, not the ending tag. If we think of a sentence as being composed of a subject, a verb, and an object, we can think of attributes as adjectives or adverbs; they are descriptive of a tag. Even though we only insert attributes in the opening tag, those attributes apply to the entire element.

04-02.html

Let's use our `<html>` tag as an example and add a language attribute:

```
<html lang="en">
</html>
```

Here we state that the HTML document will be in English. This is not a required attribute, because English is defined by default, but this is how one would indicate that an HTML document is in a different language.

You can find abbreviations for other languages, and what to do when multiple languages are used, on the World Wide Web Consortium at www.w3.org.

Attribute tags can also set the class or id of an element. The HTML tag `<div></div>`, short for "division," is used to define and delineate special sections of HTML.

In this example…

04-03.html

```
<div class="callout">
</div>
```

…the class of the div is "callout."

All attribute tags take the following format: `name="value"`, where name is the name of the attribute (in this case, "class") and "value" is the value given to the element.

You can name classes whatever you wish, but for easy future reference it is a good idea to give them meaningful names that fit their intended purpose.

Comments

Often you will want to leave notes or comments for your own reference in your HTML text editor. These notes may relate to the handling of the project, coding strategies, or future follow-up tasks. You want the notes to be visible to you and your team members, but you obviously do not want them visible on the web page itself.

Comments can be entered by enclosing them in `<!-- -->`

04-05.html

```
<p>
  This text will show on the page inside a paragraph.
  <!-- This is a comment and will not show on the page -->
  This will appear.
</p>
```

Comments are particularly helpful when one is working with a team.

04-06.html

```
  <!-- Sarah will code this section on Friday, and Jason
will code the following section next week. Remember to
consult the HTML CSS QuickStart Guide while you work. It's a
great tool! -->
```

Comments can also help you distinguish between sections of the page.

```
<!-- We will feature our fall products in this section -->
```

04-07.html

HTML Document Format (Basic Structure)

HTML pages are generally built with a consistent structure with a few main sections. The first item you will encounter when looking at an HTML page is a declaration known as `<!DOCTYPE html>`. A "declaration" is a statement included at the beginning of a piece of code that tells the browser (or compiler in the case of other coding languages) useful information about the nature of the following code. In this case, the DOCTYPE declaration tells a browser to expect an HTML5 document. This is followed by the `<html>` designation, which contains all useful information about the page as well as any content.

Past versions of HTML had differently worded DOCTYPE declarations.

At its most rudimentary level, the content of a web page contains these elements:

04-08.html

```
<!DOCTYPE html>
<html>
  <head>
  </head>
  <body>
  </body>
</html>
```

You may notice there are two other elements, `<head></head>` and `<body></body>`, contained within `<html></html>`. Because the tags of these two elements open and close within the `<html></html>` element, these elements are said to be child elements of the `<html></html>` element. Child elements are usually indented in the text editor so that anyone viewing the code can easily see how they relate to the overall hierarchical structure.

Let's look at a more detailed and fleshed-out example of HTML code to better see all of these elements in action:

04-09.html

```
<!DOCTYPE html>
<html lang="en">
    <head>
        <meta charset="utf-8">
        <title>My First Lorem Ipsum Web Page</title>
        <meta description="This is my first web page!">
    </head>
    <body>
        <h1>Header Lorem</h1>
        <p>
        Lorem ipsum dolor sit amet, consectetuer adipiscing
elit. Aenean commodo ligula eget dolor. Aenean massa. Cum
sociis natoque penatibus et magnis dis parturient montes,
nascetur ridiculus mus. Donec quam felis, ultricies nec,
pellentesque eu, pretium quis, sem.
        </p>
        <p>
        Etiam rhoncus. Maecenas tempus, tellus eget
condimentum rhoncus, sem quam semper libero, sit amet
adipiscing sem neque sed ipsum. Nam quam nunc, blandit vel,
luctus pulvinar, hendrerit id, lorem. Maecenas nec odio et
ante tincidunt tempus.
        </p>
        <p>
        Nam pretium turpis et arcu. Duis arcu tortor, suscipit
eget, imperdiet nec, imperdiet iaculis, ipsum. Sed aliquam
ultrices mauris. Integer ante arcu, accumsan a, consectetuer
eget, posuere ut, mauris. Praesent adipiscing. Phasellus
ullamcorper ipsum rutrum nunc. Nunc nonummy metus.
        <p>
    </body>
</html>
```

<!doctype html>

As previously mentioned, the `DOCTYPE` declaration appears before anything else at the top of the document. You can think of a declaration as a message to the reader (in this case, the browser) that explains the code that follows. For example, if you were reading a book in Old English, there might be a statement at the beginning of the book saying, "This book is written in an archaic form of English. You may encounter odd spellings or word usage." That's all a declaration is: an alert to the browser.

In older versions of HTML, this tag was considerably longer, but it was greatly simplified in HTML5. You must use this if you plan to use HTML5-specific elements, or you may get strange results from some web browsers.

In this chapter, and in many long-form examples throughout this book, we'll display the `DOCTYPE` declaration in code samples, but in shorter samples it will be omitted. A wavy line like this ~ will denote the omission of this boilerplate code.

html

After the `DOCTYPE` declaration, all content on the page lies between a beginning `<html>` tag and a closing `</html>` tag. The HTML element serves as a container for the rest of the code on the page.

Head

The head tag contains the `<title>` tag and metadata for the web page. The title tag gives the document a name, and metadata provides the browser and search engines with additional information. The title is used in the name of a window, tab, or bookmark, but the metadata is not directly shown to the user (except, possibly, in search engine results). If the title isn't set, then the browser will use the name of the HTML file (for example, `index.html`).

The head element also contains information that helps the browser properly display the page, and it provides a first chance to include any CSS or JavaScript.

Let's take a closer look:

04-10.html

```
<head>
    <meta charset="utf-8">
    <title>My First Lorem Ipsum Web Page</title>
    <meta description="This is my first web page!">
</head>
```

In this example, there are a total of three tags within the head element: the title tag and two meta tags with different attributes. Meta tags are self-contained elements that only have the required information in an HTML attribute.

Let's examine the two meta tags we used in this example.

```
<meta charset="utf-8">
```

Here, we define the character set of the document. In our example, we select UTF-8, which includes characters you'll find in most European languages like English, Spanish, German, French, and Portuguese.

```
<meta description="This is my first web page!">
```

This meta tag gives search engines a description of the document. While not required, it helps with search engine rankings and should be defined when possible.

Body

The `<body></body>` element includes everything that will be visible in the browser window.

Nesting

It is important that HTML programmers avoid improper overlapping of tags. All child tags should be closed before you proceed to close the parent tags. For example, the following code will not work correctly:

```
<html lang="en">
<head>
</head>
<body>
</html>
</body>
```

In this example, the body tag is being closed after the last html tag. This is incorrect because elements must be closed in a last-in-first-out order. In other words, you cannot close a parent tag without making sure the child tags are closed.

While some browsers are more forgiving than others of mistakes in HTML code, your results will likely be unpredictable if you don't follow these structures.

In the examples, I have indented all nested content. This is not required for the browser to understand the code, but it makes the code a lot easier for a human to read and debug. Proper indentation is considered a best practice, but don't worry if your indentation isn't perfect. There are even some tools, such as DirtyMarkup, that will fix indents for you.

Putting It All Together

Returning to our main snippet of sample code from earlier in this chapter, "My First Lorem Ipsum Web Page," let's open it up in a browser and see how it looks.

fig. 39

You'll note there is no styling in figure 39. The only things we see are the title (in the browser tab), a header, and three paragraphs. The font is the browser's default font (typically Times New Roman). A font isn't the same as a character set and can be defined in CSS—we'll cover that in chapter 8.

You've just built your first web page and displayed it in your web browser!

ADDING A DESCRIPTION AND FIXING THE TITLE

It's time to resume your role as HTML/CSS programmer as we attempt to spruce up the website of a fictitious business—ClydeBank Coffee Shop.

If you haven't yet downloaded the ClydeBank Coffee Shop website, please do so from www.github.com/clydebankmedia/clydebank-coffee-shop. See appendix V for detailed instructions.

Our client states that their website doesn't rank well in search engines. Although a wide variety of techniques could address this, the most obvious thing we can fix is the lack of a meta description tag.

In the `index.html` file, we'll see these items nested within the `<head>` element:

04-11.html

```
<head>
    <meta charset="utf-8">
    <meta name="viewport" content="width=device-width,
initial-scale=1, shrink-to-fit=no">
    <title>Home</title>
    <link rel="stylesheet" type="text/css" href="css/style.
css">
</head>
```

Open your `index.html` file for the coffee shop site in your code editor. Replace "Home" with the page title "ClydeBank Coffee Shop," and then, using the appropriate code, add the meta description "ClydeBank Coffee Shop features premium coffee at an affordable price." Save your changes. If you aren't sure how to do this, you may need to spend some time reviewing this chapter, especially the "head" subsection. You can also reference appendix V for a walk-through, but I recommend you try it first on your own.

Once this change has been made, search engines will better understand our page and present it in the search results in a friendlier fashion. You can verify the change by reloading the page in your browser and noting the title of the tab. It should now say "ClydeBank Coffee Shop" instead of "Home." The meta description doesn't show on the web page itself, but you can verify this change was made by viewing the source in the browser (usually CTRL+U) and examining the head element.

Chapter Recap

» HTML is composed of elements and content within the elements, delineated between tags.

» Comments in HTML aren't shown to the end user but are helpful for notetaking and team projects.

» An HTML document contains a DOCTYPE declaration, an html element, a head element, and the body element, which contains all visible content on the page.

» HTML elements are nested together to form logical structures.

| 5 |
Basic HTML Elements

Chapter Overview
» HTML uses elements for structure.
» A wide assortment of HTML elements is available.
» Div and span tags allow for logical content grouping.

In the last chapter, we addressed the basic structure of an HTML page. To reiterate, HTML pages consist of a DOCTYPE declaration and "head" and "body" sections. In this chapter, we will pursue a more precise understanding of how some of the most common HTML tags work.

Let's look at some basic HTML. I encourage you to fire up your Visual Studio Code editor and experiment with the various HTML elements we discuss in this chapter.

SNIPPET

05-01.html

```
<!DOCTYPE html>
<html lang="en">
    <head>
        <meta charset="UTF-8">
        <title>Carter Dome</title>
    </head>
    <body>
Carter Dome
Carter Dome, or simply The Dome, is a mountain located in
Coos County, New Hampshire. The mountain is part of the
Carter-Moriah Range of the White Mountains, which runs along
the northern east side of Pinkham Notch. Carter Dome is
flanked to the northeast by Mount Hight and to the southwest
by Wildcat Mountain (across Carter Notch).

The origins of Carter Dome's name is unknown. Local folklore
suggests that it was named after a hunter named Carter,
while a neighboring peak is named after his hunting partner,
```

```
Hight.

The mountain is ascended from the west by the Carter Dome
Trail and Nineteen Mile Brook Trail, and from the east by
the Black Angel Trail.

Statistics

Elevation: 4,832 ft (1,473 m)
Prominence: 2,821 ft (860 m)
Coordinates: 44°16'02"N 71°10'44"W


    </body>
</html>
```

If we look at the raw HTML code, we can see that the information presented is relatively straightforward. The content is grouped in an organized fashion. We can see headers and clear paragraph breaks, and some list items. We would expect this code, when rendered, to be readable and understandable, right? Let's load the code into a web browser and see what it looks like.

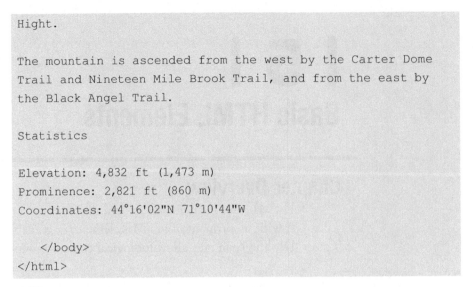

fig. 40

Right away we can see that the browser has ignored our careful formatting. Everything is displayed as a solid block of text. Though our markup was sufficient to tell the browser to (a) use HTML, (b) use the UTF-8 character set, (c) title the page "Carter Dome" (which can be seen on the browser tab), and (d) add a bunch of text to the body, we did not tell the browser how to organize and display the text.

As shown in figure 40, paragraph breaks are ignored by the web browser. Browsers are not intuitive, so we need to provide a set of instructions via HTML markup to tell the browser how to organize the text.

NOTE

When formatting text, the browser will ignore extra spaces (any beyond one), tabs, and line breaks as well as HTML comments. The only exception is the `<pre></pre>` element, which is used to format source code that should be displayed exactly as written.

Paragraphs

To break text into paragraphs, we need to define where a paragraph begins and ends. Paragraphs in HTML are defined using the `<p>` tag. To mark a paragraph, we place a `<p>` at the beginning and a `</p>` at the end, like this:

SNIPPET

05-02.html

```
<p>Carter Dome</p>

<p>Carter Dome, or simply The Dome, is a mountain located
in Coos County, New Hampshire. The mountain is part of the
Carter-Moriah Range of the White Mountains, which runs along
the northern east side of Pinkham Notch. Carter Dome is
flanked to the northeast by Mount Hight and to the southwest
by Wildcat Mountain (across Carter Notch).</p>

<p>The origins of Carter Dome's name is unknown. Local
folklore suggests that it was named after a hunter named
Carter, while a neighboring peak is named after his hunting
partner, Hight.</p>

<p>The mountain is ascended from the west by the Carter
Dome Trail and Nineteen Mile Brook Trail, and from the east
by the Black Angel Trail.</p>

<p>Statistics</p>

<p>Elevation: 4,832 ft (1,473 m)</p>
<p>Prominence: 2,821 ft (860 m)</p>
<p>Coordinates: 44°16'02"N 71°10'44"W</p>
```

After adding these `<p>` elements, if we save and refresh our page, we will get a result like the following (figure 41):

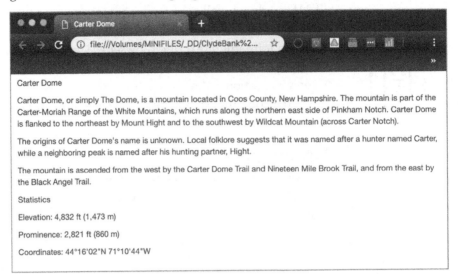

fig. 41

As you can see, the page is beginning to take shape. The paragraphs are clearly shown with line breaks in the page, not just in our code.

Headings

Headings are commonly used to visually delineate sections of text in a site. Headings in HTML take the format of "h" followed by a number to identify the level of heading.

In our HTML code for the "Carter Dome" web page, we currently have our heading inside `<p>` tags. Let's swap the `<p>` tags for `<h1>` tags. The "1" portion of the heading tag tells the browser we want it to show as the highest-level heading (with the largest font size).

```
<h1>Carter Dome</h1>
```

When we refresh the page, we will instantly notice the change. The `<h1>` tag is not unlike the `<p>` tag in that, when applied, it creates a paragraph break. However, the heading tag will, by default, bold the text and increase the font size (as in figure 42). Additionally, `<h1>` headings have more space above and below them than do normal lines of text.

Size and spacing around elements in HTML are often overridden in CSS.

fig. 42

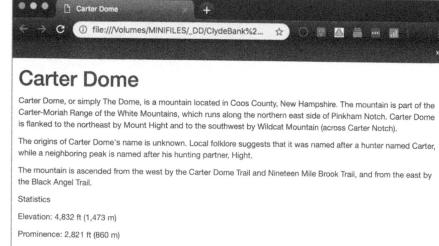

Now let's wrap the "Statistics" heading inside h2 tags, like so:

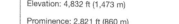

```
<h2>Statistics</h2>
```

If you reload the page, you will see that the h2 tag has an effect similar to the h1, except that, by default, it's a little smaller (figure 43).

fig. 43

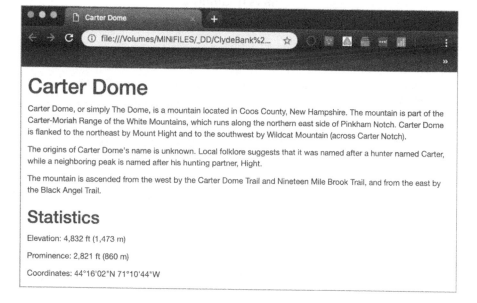

HTML has six default headings of different sizes:

```
<h1>This is heading 1</h1>
<h2>This is heading 2</h2>
<h3>This is heading 3</h3>
<h4>This is heading 4</h4>
<h5>This is heading 5</h5>
<h6>This is heading 6</h6>
```

This HTML will, by default, display as follows (figure 44):

fig. 44

This is heading 1

This is heading 2

This is heading 3

This is heading 4

This is heading 5

This is heading 6

NOTE

There are no firm limits on the use of h1 tags, but you'll rarely find more than one h1 tag on a page, since they are main headings. Sections of text are generally titled with h2, then subsections within each of those are titled with h3, and so on.

Headings are primarily used for document structuring purposes. CSS gives us the ability to style these in any way, but they should remain hierarchical (that is, h2 should delineate sections of text on a page, and h3 should be used for subsections, etc.). This may seem overly rigid—especially since HTML allows you the flexibility to structure headings however you choose—but there are advantages in adhering to a sequential and hierarchical approach with headings.

For web users with visual disabilities, text readers use headings to navigate a page. If a page is poorly structured, it will create a bad experience for those users.

Also, search engines tend to attribute greater importance to higher-level headings. When a search engine indexes a site, lower-level elements (h2, h3, etc.) are logically grouped with the content they decorate, thereby assigning more precise meaning to that text for the ranking algorithm. Using good heading structure will help your site rank more favorably in search engine results.

Lists

You may wish to break up points of data or key ideas into lists. In HTML, we designate lists in two ways. For numbered, or "ordered," lists we use the `<ol></ol>` tags to specify the beginning and ending of the list. For simple "unordered" lists (such as those with bullet points), we use `<ul></ul>`. For both types of lists, each element is identified as a "list item" and is marked with `<li></li>` tags.

Let's try this with the "Statistics" section of our page using this code:

05-03.html

```
<h2>Statistics</h2>
<ul>
    <li>Elevation: 4,832 ft (1,473 m)</li>
    <li>Prominence: 2,821 ft (860 m)</li>
    <li>Coordinates: 44°16'02"N 71°10'44"W</li>
</ul>
```

The code will display as shown in figure 45.

fig. 45

Carter Dome

Carter Dome, or simply The Dome, is a mountain located in Coos County, New Hampshire. The mountain is part of the Carter-Moriah Range of the White Mountains, which runs along the northern east side of Pinkham Notch. Carter Dome is flanked to the northeast by Mount Hight and to the southwest by Wildcat Mountain (across Carter Notch).

The origins of Carter Dome's name is unknown. Local folklore suggests that it was named after a hunter named Carter, while a neighboring peak is named after his hunting partner, Hight.

The mountain is ascended from the west by the Carter Dome Trail and Nineteen Mile Brook Trail, and from the east by the Black Angel Trail.

Statistics

- Elevation: 4,832 ft (1,473 m)
- Prominence: 2,821 ft (860 m)
- Coordinates: 44°16'02"N 71°10'44"W

If we chose to make this an ordered list (though it does not really make sense in this situation), we could do it like this:

05-04.html

```
<h2>Statistics</h2>
<ol>
    <li>Elevation: 4,832 ft (1,473 m)</li>
    <li>Prominence: 2,821 ft (860 m)</li>
    <li>Coordinates: 44°16'02"N 71°10'44"W</li>
</ol>
```

. . . which would display as follows (figure 46):

fig. 46

Statistics

1. Elevation: 4,832 ft (1,473 m)
2. Prominence: 2,821 ft (860 m)
3. Coordinates: 44°16′02″N 71°10′44″W

By default, all list items will be left-indented. Each `<li>` element will appear on its own line. Lists can be styled in many ways to make them extremely useful for several purposes, such as navigation bars. We will discuss alternate uses for lists in chapters 9 and 14.

EDITING THE COFFEE SHOP MENU

Add "Americano" to Your Coffee Shop Menu
Let's return to our great work in progress, the ClydeBank Coffee Shop website. It was just brought to your attention that the coffee shop is going to offer Americanos for $2.25. Update the website to reflect this change. You can find a walk-through of how to do this in appendix V.

Edit, Save, Refresh, and Repeat
For the most satisfying work experience, remember to keep your web page (.html file) open in a browser as you make edits in the code editor.

After you make and save your edits, you can simply refresh the web page in your browser window and your changes will instantly render. This *edit*, *save*, *refresh*, and *repeat* workflow will become a common habit in your web design career and will allow you to experiment quickly with new ideas as you continue to learn the ropes of HTML and CSS.

Links

Now is the moment you've been waiting for. The feature that makes HTML unique from other markup languages is *hypertext*. HTML uses "hyperlinks," commonly known as **links**, to connect sites with other sites or with web pages within the existing site.

Links are designated by "anchor" elements. The anchor tags, `<a></a>`, are responsible for creating that ubiquitous blue "link" text seen on many websites.

The `<a>` element can be used for many purposes, but for now let's focus on its most popular usage: creating links. Wrapping the `<a></a>` tags around content—typically text or an image—makes the content clickable.

To demonstrate, let's show a simple text-based link:

```
<a href="newpage.html">click me!</a>
```

05-05.html

The `<a>` tag denotes that a piece of text, in this case *click me*, is to be an anchor, meaning the user can click on it. Wrapping content between the `<a>` and `</a>` tags tells the browser that the content is intended to serve as a link. The `href` attribute (which stands for *hypertext reference*) tells the browser where to send the user upon clicking.

Any file or page pointed to with the `href` attribute needs complete information or the link will not work.

In our preceding example, clicking on the link will send the user to a local page (that is, on the same website) named newpage.html. This type of link is called a "relative" link, meaning the file newpage.html is assumed to be in the same directory as the current HTML document.

If we attempt to direct a hyperlink to a location that does not exist, the web browser will return a "404 Not Found" error message.

Q: What is a 404 error, anyway?

Answer: All web browsers use what we refer to as HTTP (hypertext transfer protocol) access codes to identify whether a file has been retrieved or delivered, as well as to provide a whole host of other information. You have likely seen these messages many times (sometimes customized to say something like "Oops! The page you are looking for isn't here."). When clicking on a link, you are providing instructions to the web browser to look for the item specified by the `href` attribute. The browser will perform an `HTTP GET` command to call the location specified. If the command succeeds, then the browser will return a 200, which means "OK." There are several reasons why a request can fail, but the 404 Not Found error is by far the most common.

MOST COMMON HTTP STATUS CODES		
CODE	**STATUS**	**MEANING**
200	OK	The request was successful.
301	Moved Permanently	The requested URL has changed. The new URL is provided in the response and the browser is directed to the new page.
302	Found	The requested URL has been temporarily changed. The browser is redirected to the new page.
304	Not Modified	This status informs the browser that the page hasn't been modified, so requesting a new copy of it isn't necessary. This saves time and bandwidth.
403	Forbidden	The visitor doesn't have the permissions necessary to access this content.
404	Not Found	The requested page couldn't be found on the server.
500	Internal Server Error	A problem in the website's backend code is preventing the page from being served to the browser.
503	Service Unavailable	This indicates that the server is overloaded or the backend functionality is offline.

GRAPHIC

fig. 47

We mentioned that our link to newpage.html is a relative link. Relative links can be used to link to content within the same site, but linking to other websites requires an "absolute" link. In an absolute link, the entire ***URL*** (universal resource locator) must be specified. For example:

```
<a href="https://www.google.com/search/howsearchworks/">Google</a>
```

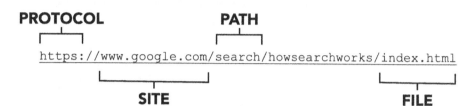

fig. 48

Relative links only use the file (and sometimes path) part of the URL structure, but absolute links use the entire URL, including protocol, site, and, optionally, path and file. Since each website handles its file structure differently, files and paths may not be needed in the destination absolute URL, but the protocol and site name will always be included (figure 48).

Though we're discussing HTTP, most links these days use HTTPS, which stands for hypertext transfer protocol secure. The "secure" portion indicates that encryption is provided over the HTTP connection, protecting requests and responses between web server and web browser from prying eyes. This encryption uses a technology commonly called SSL, though this is an older term and TLS (transport layer security) is now used.

Relative paths are usually used for local pages within a site, but you are free to use absolute paths. If you do use absolute paths, changing your domain name (the "site" portion of the URL) becomes a lot more cumbersome, because you will have to manually change all your absolute links.

The "target" attribute tells the browser in which frame to open the link. Since frames are rarely used nowadays, the most common use of the target attribute is to tell the browser to open the link in a new tab. To do this, set the target attribute to "_blank," like so:

```
<a href="https://www.google.com/" target="_blank">Google</a>
```

In HTML5, the "download" attribute was introduced to the `<a>` tag. This allows you to specify that the file should be downloaded rather than viewed. Consider the following example:

```
<a href="files/file.txt" download>Download this file</a>
```

If you hadn't used the download attribute, the text file (files/file.txt) would have been displayed directly in the browser. But in this case, due to the download attribute, the file will be downloaded.

Another type of link that uses the `<a>` tag is the "anchored" link, which can be used to link to a different section of the current page. Also known as placeholders, jump links, and in-page links, anchor links are often used on large pages (think of sites with a multitude of different content sections, such as Wikipedia).

To use an anchored link, you must first add an id attribute to your destination heading. In the following example, we will identify an h2 heading with the name "stats":

```
<h2 id="stats">Statistics</h2>
```

Now that the heading has a named id, we can set up a link to that heading anywhere on the page using "#stats":

```
<a href="#stats">View the statistics</a>
```

In HTML and in CSS, "#" always refers to an id attribute.

Images

In many cases, we will want to add images to our web pages. HTML uses the `<img>` element to tell the browser to load an image. Image elements do not require closing tags, because all the needed information is provided via their attributes.

The primary attribute of the `<img>` element is the `src` attribute. This attribute acts much like the `href` attribute of the `<a>` tag in that it requires a file name or URL. In this case, however, rather than following a link to another page, the `src` attribute tells the browser where to find the image file.

```
<img src="images/Carter-Dome.jpg">
```

Just like with a link, you can use either a relative or an absolute path to the image file:

```
<!-- This path starts from the same folder of the HTML file -->
<img src="images/Carter-Dome.jpg">
<!-- This path starts from the site's root directory -->
<img src="/images/Carter-Dome.jpg">
```

In the first example, we are using a relative path to reference the file Carter-Dome.jpg in the images folder. In the second line, we use the absolute path.

Be careful when using absolute paths with the `<img>` element! If you are loading an image from another site, you should seek permission from the website owner, as you are using their server resources to serve the image to your viewers.

Copyrights are important. You should only use images on your site that are yours or that you have permission from the copyright holder to use. To do otherwise puts you in serious legal jeopardy. I recommend using the search engine at Creative Commons to search for free-to-use images: https://search.creativecommons.org/

If you need to refer to an image or file that's in a directory above the current folder, you can use the `..` shortcut to refer to that path.

```
<img src="../images/Carter-Dome.jpg">
```

This is especially useful when referring to files in CSS because the CSS file will likely be in a folder called CSS, so the two-dot shortcut will tell the browser to go up one directory (from the CSS file itself). At that point, the relative path takes over, in this case, "images/Carter-Dome.jpg," telling the browser where to find the image.

In any of these cases, it is best to avoid using spaces or special characters in file names, as some servers and browsers may not process these names correctly. If you need a space, use an underscore or dash instead, as we have done in "Carter-Dome.jpg."

As mentioned in the introduction, it is best to keep your images in a designated directory—one that is separate from your HTML files. In the case of our Carter-Dome.jpg image, we are pointing to our image in a local directory called "images."

05-12.html

```
<img src="https://www.yoursite.com/images/Carter-Dome.jpg">
```

The image will be displayed in the browser in its native (actual) size if the `width` and/or `height` attributes are not specified in the `<img>` element, so it is important to resize the image file to meet the design requirements of your page. You can use the `width` or `height` attributes to resize the image during page rendering, or use CSS to set sizing specifications (we will discuss this in chapter 7). Using the correct size saves bandwidth and provides a better experience for users (especially those with slower connections).

05-13.html

```
<img src="images/Carter-Dome.jpg" height="600" width="800">
```

The numbers for each of these dimensions, height and width, are specified in units called pixels. Pixels are small points that together make up an image. An image that is 600 pixels wide and 800 pixels tall contains 480,000 pixels. Pixels are not the same size on every screen, because different devices render pixels with different densities. We'll address this further when we discuss CSS in chapter 7 and in appendix III.

Even if the image file is sized correctly, it's still a good idea to specify the width and height, so the browser knows how much space to reserve while the page is rendering.

As a best practice, "alternate text" should be added to all images. Alternate text describes the image and serves several important functions:

» It helps search engines identify the image (search engines cannot "see"—not yet, anyway).

» It provides an important service to visually impaired people who may rely on alternate text audio transcriptions in their web browsing.

» It provides displayable placeholder data in the event the image does not load properly.

Alternate text is added using an "alt" attribute in the `<img>` element:

```
<img src="images/Carter-Dome.jpg" height="600" width="800"
alt="A picture of Carter Dome">
```

05-14.html

Other Tags

There are a few other commonly used tags that warrant discussion in this chapter. The following tags have very simple effects and do not require closing tags.

» `<hr>` Use this tag to produce a "horizontal rule," or a line across the page. This helps to divide content; for example, to separate sections of a page. A typical use is to divide the footer from the rest of the page.

» `<br>` Use this tag to produce a manual line break. This is especially helpful when you want to place line breaks inside of paragraphs.

Q: A break is a break, right? How does a coder decide whether to begin a new `<p>` element or use the `<br>` tag?

Answer: Paragraphs separate groups of sentences into meaningful chunks of text. They usually start with a thesis or proposal and end with a conclusion. A new paragraph starts a new thought and, by keeping your text organized as in a regular document, provides benefits in both visual style and logical format and flow. The `<br>` tag does not start a new paragraph, and this gives you the freedom to control the display of text within a `<p>` element without disrupting the logical organization of the page.

Divs and Spans

So far, every HTML element discussed has had a specific and singular purpose that is immediately observable when using that element in a web page. Divs and spans are a bit different. By default, if you designate text, images, or any other elements contained in a div or a span, it will make no visual changes to your document. These two elements are designed to work with CSS to allow you to style parts (span) or full sections of content (div) in a unique way.

By default, `<div>` does nothing visually but provides a way to identify a block of content, usually via CSS or JavaScript. It is like the `<p>` tag in that it is often used to logically group blocks of content.

`<span>`, like div, has no effect on the layout of text itself. Instead, it provides a way to logically group smaller blocks of content, usually within `<div></div>`. While `<div>` refers to larger segments of elements, `<span>` designates single lines of text.

Let's demonstrate how `<span>` and `<div>` work together:

SNIPPET

05-15.html

```html
<!DOCTYPE html>
<html lang="en">
<head>
    <title>Div vs. Span</title>
    <style>
        span {
            color: white;
            background-color: darkgrey;
        }
        div {
            color: lightgrey;
            background-color: black;
        }
    </style>
</head>
<body>
    <header>
        <h1>DIVs vs SPANs</h1>
    </header>
    <main>
        <div>The div element provides a way to identify a
block of content that can be styled by CSS specified in the
style element.</div>

        <p>Without the style element, a div would be
indistinguishable from a paragraph within the body of
an HTML document. However, paragraphs like this aren't
automatically styled unless specified in the style element.</p>
        <span>Spans</span>
        <span>are not blocks</span>
        <span>of text,</span>
        <span>so they remain</span>
        <span>inline without wrapping like divs</span>
        <div><p>You can even put a <span>span</span> inside of
a div if there is something inside requiring <span>special
styling</span></p></div>
    </main>
</body>
</html>
```

If we set our div formatting to light grey text on a black background, and our span formatting to white text on a dark grey background, we should get a web page that is displayed like this (figure 49):

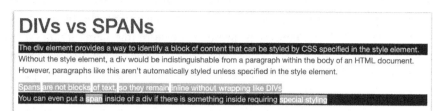

fig. 49

05-16.html

```
<div class="div-example">
    <p>This is a large block of text. We are using multiple
lines.</p>
    <p>As we can see, we can use paragraphs inside div
elements. This serves to break up the layout.</p>
    <p>We can have multiple paragraphs inside a div, but they
are all still seen as part of the div, decorated with the
"div-example" class.</p>
    <p>On occasion, we may want to<span class="span-
example">style a single line of text without any breaks</
span>, so we enclose it within a span element.</p>
</div>
```

If you try this on a page, you'll see very little display formatting other than the line breaks provided by `<p>` tags. However, the `<div>` and `<span>` tags will prove useful when formatting with CSS.

Visual Studio Code has a nifty shortcut for designing multiple elements that is most useful for creating divs and spans. Type `div*3`, then hit ENTER, and three div elements will appear. Replace `div` with `span` or any other element, and `3` with the number of elements you want to create.

Semantic Elements

A semantic element is an HTML element named after its intended purpose. The name of a semantic element, like `<header>`, precisely defines its content type, position, and purpose. Non-semantic elements, such as `<div>`, are important for page structure, but the tags do not describe the element's function.

The benefits of semantic elements extend far beyond providing a friendly naming scheme. Semantic elements make it easier to read, understand, and maintain HTML code. Browsers can display semantic elements in a way that makes sense for the user's device. For example, when you print something from your browser, semantic elements allow the browser to easily recognize text intended for printing while skipping elements like headers and footers that might print awkwardly or consume excess ink and paper. Additionally, screen readers and accessibility extensions can better interpret the organization and context of important parts of a document.

Even though semantic elements serve a defined purpose within the overall logical flow of the HTML document, CSS can style and position them in ways that might deviate from their intended purpose or display (as is the case with any HTML element).

Header

The `<header>` element denotes content that is intended for the top, or head, of the page. Here's an example:

05-17.html

```
<header>
    <img src="images/logo.jpg" alt="Our Magnificent Logo">
    <h1>Welcome to Our Site</h1>
    <p>Come for the information. Stay for the cookies.</p>
</header>
```

When used inside another semantic element like `<article></article>`, the header element can be used to mark content that serves as an introduction to the rest of the content within the containing element. An example of this can be found under the "Article" heading of this chapter.

Footer

The `<footer>` element specifies content intended for the bottom of the page. Consider this example:

05-18.html

```
<footer>
    <p>Copyright &copy; 2020, Our Magnificent Company, All
Rights Reserved.</p>
    <p>Please read our <a href="terms.html">Terms of Use</
a> and <a href="privacy.html">Privacy Policy</a>.</p>
</footer>
```

As with the `<header>` element, a `<footer>` can exist within another element and serve to mark content intended to be at the bottom of the containing element.

Aside

The `<aside>` element allows you to mark a section of content to be separate from the rest of the article. This is commonly used for quotes, definitions, and callouts.

05-19.html

```
<aside>
    <p><strong>IMPORTANT:</strong> Content in this article
may be completely fictitious.
    </aside>
```

Article

The `<article>` element provides a logical way to delineate a piece of content separate from the rest of the site. An article element may contain (but is certainly not limited to) a blog article, a social media post, or even a comment. Any content that is independent from the rest of the page can be wrapped inside an article element.

An article is not limited to text. It may have images, tables, or even other semantic elements within it. Consider this example:

05-20.html

```
<article>
    <header>
    <h2>A Tale of Two Articles</h2>
        <p>By Charlie Kitchens, Feb 20, 2020</p>
    </header>
        <p>It was the best of articles and the worst of
articles. Some article written long ago, never mind precisely
how long, was phenomenal. Others? Not so much.</p>
    </article>
```

Here we wrap introductory content, such as the title, author, and date, inside a header element within the article element. In this case, the article element is serving as a container for other elements while still maintaining its stated purpose of being an article.

Section

The `<section>` element serves as a logical collection of other parts or, as the name implies, sections of a page.

Consider a blog page with a header, footer, menu, sidebar, and list of articles. Each of those elements has a stated purpose obvious in the name, but the section element provides a more generic way to group elements. For example, if a page has multiple articles, a section element can contain those articles to keep them separate from the other structural parts of the page.

You can see an example of the section element in use in code snippet 05-21.

Main

The `<main>` element contains the primary content on your page, providing a canvas where all other semantic elements can logically organize within a master containing element. Now we can use all the elements we've learned about to form a logical, self-explanatory structure for our page.

SNIPPET

05-21.html

```
<!DOCTYPE html>
<html lang="en">
<head>
    <meta charset="utf-8">
    <title>An Outstanding Blog</title>
</head>
<body>
<header>
    <img src="images/logo.jpg" alt="Our Magnificent Logo">
    <h1>Welcome to Our Site</h1>
    <p>Come for the information. Stay for the cookies.</p>
</header>
<main>
    <section>
        <article>
            <header>
                <h2>A Tale of Two Articles</h2>
                <p>By Charlie Kitchens, Feb 20, 2020</p>
            </header>
            <p>It was the best of articles and the worst of
```

```
articles. Some article written long ago, never mind precisely
how long, was phenomenal. Others? Not so much.</p>
        <aside>
            <p><strong>IMPORTANT:</strong> Content in this
article may be completely fictitious.
        </aside>
            <p>You may be surprised to learn that the
internet contains a wide assortment of articles of varying
quality. Finding good articles can be difficult, so consider
the source of everything you read.</p>
    </article>
    <article>
        <header>
            <h2>Another Great Article</h2>
            <p>By Mark Samuel Clemons, Feb 17, 2020</p>
        </header>
        <p>One of the crowning achievements of my
childhood was convincing my friends to write an article
for me. It wasn't as easy a crime as my infamous fence
whitewashing scheme, but it was nevertheless effective.</p>
    </article>
  </section>
</main>
<footer>
  <p>Copyright &copy; 2020, Our Magnificent Company, All
Rights Reserved.</p>
  <p>Please read our <a href="terms.html">Terms of Use</a>
and <a href="privacy.html">Privacy Policy</a>.</p>
</footer>
</body>
</html>
```

Putting It All Together

SNIPPET

05-22.html

```
<!DOCTYPE html>
<html lang="en">
    <head>
        <meta charset="UTF-8">
        <title>Carter Dome</title>
```

```
        <meta description="Carter Dome is a mountain located
in New Hampshire.">
    </head>
    <body>
        <h1>Carter Dome</h1>
        <img src="images/Carter-Dome.jpg" height="600"
width="800" alt="A picture of Carter Dome">
        <p>See <a href="#stats">statistics</a> or find <a
href="#additional">additional reading</a> on Carter Dome.</p>
        <p>Carter Dome, or simply The Dome, is a mountain
located in Coos County, New Hampshire. The mountain is part
of the Carter-Moriah Range of the White Mountains, which
runs along the northern east side of Pinkham Notch. Carter
Dome is flanked to the northeast by Mount Hight and to the
southwest by Wildcat Mountain (across Carter Notch).</p>
        <p>The origins of Carter Dome's name are unknown.
Local folklore suggests that it was named after a hunter
named Carter, while a neighboring peak is named after his
hunting partner, Hight.</p>
        <p>The mountain is ascended from the west by the
Carter Dome Trail and Nineteen Mile Brook Trail, and from
the east by the Black Angel Trail.</p>
        <hr>
        <div id="stats">
            <h2>Statistics</h2>
            <ul>
                <li><span class="cat">Elevation:</span> 4,832 ft
(1,473 m)</li>
                <li><span class="cat">Prominence:</span> 2,821
ft (860 m)</li>
                <li><span class="cat">Coordinates:</span>
44°16'02"N 71°10'44"W</li>
            </ul>
        </div>
        <hr>
        <div id="additional">
            <h2>Additional Reading</h2>
            <p>For more information, please see the <a href="
https://en.wikipedia.org/wiki/Carter_Dome"> Wikipedia
article on Carter Dome</a>
```

```
      </div>
    </body>
</html>
```

You may have noticed that the example uses the id and class attributes on some of its div and span elements. The id attributes provide a way to link to those sections on the page, but the class attributes are, as of yet in our studies, unused. We'll get into that in the next chapter.

EDITING THE "ABOUT" PAGE AND NAVIGATION

"About" Page

The ClydeBank Coffee Shop needs an About page. We made the `about.html` file back in the introduction, but we didn't add content. It is merely a copy of `template.html`. Open the `about.html` file in your text editor and a paragraph tag in the main content area. The main content area can be identified as the div element with the following comment:

```
<!-- CONTENT GOES HERE -->
```

Remove that comment and place the following text in a paragraph tag:

ClydeBank Coffee Shop welcomes you to our website. If you're in the area, we kindly ask you to stop by and have a cup with us.

To complete the About page, change the title tag to "About ClydeBank Coffee Shop." Don't forget to close the paragraph tag, then refresh the `about.html` file in your browser to see your changes. Feel free to add additional text if you wish.

I recommend trying this change on your own. If you get stuck, you can refer to appendix V, "ClydeBank Coffee Shop Solutions" under "Chapter 5: About Page."

Navigation

Our client called for our help to address another issue—some of the links in the navigation menu don't work correctly. We can certainly fix that with our newly gained knowledge of links.

In the `index.html` file, you'll see these items nested within the navigation:

05-23.html

```html
<div class="container">
    <ul>
        <li class="active"><a href="index.html">Menu</a></li>
        <li><a href="#">About</a></li>
        <li><a href="events.html">Events</a></li>
        <li><a href="contact.html">Contact</a></li>
    </ul>
</div>
```

The pound sign # normally denotes an in-page link, but in this case, it's used as a placeholder. The browser will display the link, but clicking on it will perform no action. The links should point to the appropriately named pages.

» Home – `index.html`
» About – `about.html`
» Events – `events.html`
» Contact – `contact.html`

If you did not complete the coffee shop exercise at the beginning of the book where you create an `about.html` file, then you obviously can't link to your About page. Take a moment to go back to the Introduction chapter and find the section called "Accessing the Horrible Coffee Shop Website." Complete the exercise found at the bottom of that section.

Open your text editor and change these links to the pages above as needed (you only need to do it for the `about.html` page, but you'll need to make this change in all of the `.html` files in the site). If you are unclear on why or how this is done, you may need to spend some time reviewing this chapter, specifically the "Links" section. The answer is in appendix V, but try it on your own first.

Here's a quick tip. Since you're going to be updating your navigation links in several HTML files, use the "Open Folder" option in your text editor. Go to File >> Open Folder, then select the folder containing your locally hosted coffee shop site (the one you downloaded from GitHub and saved onto your computer). All HTML and CSS files from that folder will open in your text editor. You will be able to quickly move from file to file using your text editor's navigation menu or tabs (figure 50).

IMAGE

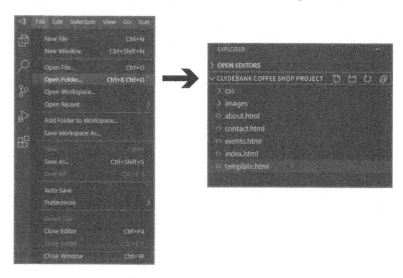

fig. 50

Be sure to add the `about.html` link to the `template.html` file as well, and save all your changes after you make them in the text editor. And remember, don't be shy with your text editor. Click on some new buttons; explore some of the various functionalities that you don't currently understand. If you feel you've messed something up with your website, just use Ctrl+z to undo it. You're going to learn a lot through play and experimentation. Enjoy it. And if you get stuck, you can reference appendix V, but please try this task on your own. When you're done, you'll have fixed the navigation on the website and let visitors know those pages will be coming soon. Great job!

Chapter Recap

» HTML requires elements to provide structure and organization.

» Headings and paragraphs organize text.

» Links can be relative, where they assume the content is in the same directory, or absolute, where the full location, including site name, is specified.

» `<div>` and `<span>` tags provide organizational structure but generally serve as a way to style content via CSS and provide functionality with JavaScript code.

» Semantic elements are named after their intended use on a page and provide well-formatted, easy-to-maintain, and easy-to-read structure.

| 6 |
CSS Structure

Chapter Overview
» Content is defined by HTML and styled by CSS.
» CSS rules are made up of selectors and properties.
» CSS has a cascading hierarchy.

Until now we have been dealing with textual content in HTML. We have used tags for logically grouping text into paragraphs and sections (via `<div>`), adding images, and even linking to other pages and sites. Since organization has largely been our focus, we have been at the browser's mercy regarding how our code is visually presented to the user.

That's where CSS comes into play. HTML defines the content, and CSS styles it. With CSS, we can override the visual defaults of the browser and adjust how it displays our content in a wide variety of ways. CSS allows us to define attributes and appearance for all our tags and gives us the power to create styles that can apply to multiple tags and div segments on our page.

Beyond appearances, though, CSS liberates our HTML from having to define appearance and lets our HTML code focus on content. By separating content and style, we gain tremendous advantages in code readability and maintainability.

Where CSS "Lives"

CSS rules can be placed in many locations (in descending order with the preferred, best-practice usage on top). We covered this in chapter 3, but since the file structure and interaction of HTML and CSS files can be confusing, let's do a quick review before diving further into this topic. CSS rules can be designated in the following ways:

» Defined via a separate .css file (called a style sheet)
» Included within `<style></style>` tags within `<head></head>`
» Included within `<style></style>` tags anywhere in the HTML
» Placed "inline" within individual tags

.css Files

Generally the best and most common approach to using CSS is to store CSS rules in a separate file that can be referenced repeatedly by multiple pages on a site.

06-01.html

This is handled by calling it within `<head>` using a special `<link>` element.

```
<link rel="stylesheet" type="text/css" href="style.css">
```

You can see that the `<link>` element uses an "href" attribute much like the `<a>` element. We specify in the "rel" (relation) attribute that we are referencing a style sheet and that the type is `text/css`. Like `<img>` elements, `<link>` elements do not need closing tags.

You can include multiple style sheets in the `<head>` element in the same way, like this:

06-02.html

```
<head>
    <link rel="stylesheet" type="text/css" href="style.css">
    <link rel="stylesheet" type="text/css" href="style2.css">
</head>
```

The second style sheet, `style2.css`, will be appended to the previous sheet. If any selectors have new rules, they will override any existing rules in `style.css`.

You may also use multiple `<style>` elements inside the `<head>` or `<body>`, though combining them into one, or, ideally, using a .css file, is preferred.

The use of .css files follows the DRY (Don't Repeat Yourself) principle in allowing you to specify CSS rules once and use them on as many pages as you like. Changing the CSS file allows you to quickly alter the look of the entire site.

Style Tags

Style tags allow for the inclusion of CSS rules directly on the HTML page. Unlike CSS files, `<style>` tags apply only to the page on which they are used. The most common way to use the `<style>` tag is to place it in the `<head>` element, like this:

06-03.html

```
<head>
    <style>
        p {
            font-weight: bold;
            color: red;
        }
        h1 { font-size: 12x; }
    </style>
</head>
```

You can also place the `<style>` element anywhere in the `<body>` element, but this isn't the preferred method because CSS rules applied in the body will override any .css files or `<style>` elements in the head.

Inline Styling

To include any CSS styling on an individual element, you create a named "style" attribute and set it to match the styling you would like for that specific instance of that element. For example:

```
<p style="font-weight: bold; color: red;">This will be
bold-red.</p>
```

06-04.html

This inline style applies only to this paragraph element on this HTML page.

3 APPROACHES TO APPLYING CSS

fig. 51

❶ .CSS Files
Style an entire page

```
<head>
<link
rel="stylesheet"
href="style.css">
</head>
```
.CSS

❷ Inline Styling
Style a specific element

```
<p
style="font-weight:
bold; color:
red;">This will be
bold-red.</p>
```

❸ Style Tags
Style an entire page

```
<head>
<style>
p { font-weight:
bold;
color: red; }
h1 { font-size: 12x; }
</style>
</head>
```

The web browser will interpret CSS rules in the order in which they are received. Each subsequent rule overrides any previous rule. Any rules you place in the `<head>` element with `<style>` tags will be interpreted in the order specified and not given precedence over any referenced .css files. Rules placed in a `<style>` element in the `<body>` will always be processed last, in the order listed in the code. Inline styles will override any CSS rule, no matter its source or location in HTML (figure 51).

An Example CSS File

A CSS file is essentially a series of rules made up of selectors and properties. Here is a typical CSS file:

06-05.css

```css
/* Set a default font and size for the entire document */
body {
    font-family: Arial, Helvetica, sans-serif;
    font-size: 12px;
}


h1 { font-size: 22px; }
h2 { font-size: 18px; }
h3 { font-size: 16px; }


.bold-text { font-weight: bold; }
.red-text { color: red; }
```

What makes this a CSS file is simply a .css extension at the end of the file name. For example, "style.css" is recognized as a CSS file, but the "style" part of the file name can be anything you like. You could use the rules featured here in a `<style>` element as well.

In this file, the body, h1, h2, and h3 tags are redefined with specific attributes, and two CSS classes are created: .bold-text and .red-text. There is also a comment at the top of the file set apart with `/*` and `*/`. Any text between these two markers is ignored by the browser.

While there is no strict organizational requirement for the file, it is generally best practice to define overrides in a logical, hierarchical manner. For example, since `<body>` is the containing element of the document content, override it first. Then drill down into other elements. This organization will keep the file easy to read and maintain.

There is one other item about the format that is worth noting. The { } characters contain the properties we define. If there are several properties in a rule, specifying them one per line is visually appealing and easy to read:

```css
body {
    font-family: Arial, Helvetica, sans-serif;
    font-size: 12px;
}
```

In contrast, the heading tags in this example have only one property assigned, so listing the property on the same line maintains that readability:

```css
h1 { font-size: 22px; }
h2 { font-size: 18px; }
h3 { font-size: 16px; }
```

Of course, you do not have to stick to this arrangement, but it is a common method of CSS file organization. Whichever styling you choose, consistency and readability are the keys to clean, maintainable code.

Selectors

As we've previously discussed, CSS rules are made up of selectors and properties. The selector is the element or type of element that we wish to modify, and the properties are the rules that we wish to apply to it.

Since this is crucial to the forthcoming content, let's review the different types of selectors that are available to us.

Element

Element selectors simply refer to HTML elements, such as p, h1, div, span, etc. Element selectors can be applied to any element that has a closing tag. For example, if we want all content that lives within `<p>` elements to be bold and in a purple font, then we would describe our p selector using the "font weight" and "color" properties:

06-06.css

```css
p {
    font-weight: bold;
    color: purple;
}
```

Class

A class is a type of CSS rule that matches no HTML element by name but can be used to style any number of HTML elements. In our previous example, we defined two classes—bold text and red text. If we want to bold just one paragraph, we assign the bold-text class to that specific paragraph, like so:

06-07.html

HTML:

```
<p>This is a standard paragraph.</p>
<p class="bold-text">This paragraph is bold. It stands
out!</p>
<p>This is a standard paragraph, too.</p>
```

We can use our red-text class in a similar manner:

```
<p>This is a standard paragraph.</p>
<p class="red-text">This paragraph is red. It stands out
more!</p>
<p>This is a standard paragraph, too.</p>
```

These paragraphs with class definitions are given the attributes assigned in the CSS file. Since the font color is set to red in the red-text class, that paragraph will be given red text.

Now let's say we want to change all the special paragraphs with red text to purple. All we have to do is change the applicable CSS rule:

06-09.css

CSS:

```
.red-text { color: purple; }
```

Now the text inside the paragraph will be purple, even though the class name is still red-text:

06-10.html

HTML

```
<p>This is a standard paragraph.</p>
<p class="red-text">This paragraph is red. It stands out
more!</p>
<p>This is a standard paragraph, too.</p>
```

The properties of a CSS class define its appearance and behavior, not the class name you give it. In this case, you have two choices: rename the class (which could be difficult if it is used many times throughout your site) or create a new rule. Given that you want to color the text purple, creating a new rule would be best.

Let's look at our updated style sheet:

CSS

06-11.css

```css
/* Set a default font and size for the entire document */
body {
    font-family: Arial, Helvetica, sans-serif;
    font-size: 12px;
}


h1 { font-size: 22px; }
h2 { font-size: 18px; }
h3 { font-size: 16px; }


.bold-text { font-weight: bold; }
.red-text { color: red; }
.purple-text { color: purple; }
```

One final note about CSS classes—you can use *multiple* classes on an element, like this:

HTML

06-12.html

```html
<p class="bold-text red-text">
    This paragraph shines so much you need shades just to
look at it!
</p>
```

By combining the bold text and red text classes, we created an easy and consistent way to give a paragraph special attention.

When creating your CSS classes, try to focus on as few properties as possible, and consider combining classes in some elements for easier readability and fewer lines of code.

Id

Ids allow you to reference specific instances of elements in your HTML. While class element rules reference every instance of that element, ids reference only a specific use of an element.

Going back to our previous CSS example, let's add an id definition:

```css
/* Set a default font and size for the entire document */
body {
    font-family: Arial, Helvetica, sans-serif;
    font-size: 12px;
}

h1 { font-size: 22px; }
h2 { font-size: 18px; }
h3 { font-size: 16px; }

.bold-text { font-weight: bold; }
.red-text { color: red; }
.purple-text { color: purple; }

#top-ad {
    background-color: yellow;
    color: red;
}
```

Now we've added an id called "top-ad." It will only be used once per page and will feature red text on a yellow background. Not a chance a reader's eyes will miss it! Let's use it on a page:

```html
<body>
<p id="top-ad">SUMMER SALE ON NOW!</p>
<p>You'll love our prices. 50% off? That's so yesterday.
Try 70% off!</p>
<p>We have the <span class="bold-text">best</span> widgets
money can buy.</p>
</body>
```

Here, the first paragraph will be given our lovely yellow/red hot-dog-stand color combination. And in the middle of the third paragraph, we invoked a class style to bold a word inside the paragraph.

You cannot have more than one instance of the "top-ad" id on a single page, but you *can* use classes as many times as you like, and even combine them.

Selectors are first applied to elements, then to classes, and finally to ids. If we set both an id and a class on an element in the HTML, and the rules conflict with one another, the browser will choose the properties associated with the id over those of the class.

Pseudo-Classes

Pseudo-classes are identifiers added to a CSS selector that let you style an element in a specific state or apply a style to a specific subset of that element. If you read that sentence three times and are scratching your head, don't worry—this is a complex topic that is best explained with an example.

A common use of a pseudo-class is to decorate the various states of the anchor (link) element. Let's consider these two examples:

06-15.css
and
06-16.html

CSS

```
a { color: red; }
```

HTML

```
<a href="https://www.ClydeBankMedia.com/">ClydeBank Media</a>
```

In this example, the links will be colored red instead of the browser default, which is usually blue. However, links have various states, including visited, active, and hover. Let's expand our example:

06-17.css

CSS

```
a:link { color: red; }
a:visited { color: purple; }
a:active { color: black; }
a:hover { color: green; }
```

06-18.html

HTML

```
<a href="https://www.ClydeBankMedia.com/">ClydeBank Media</a>
<a href="https://www.google.com/">Google</a>
<a href="https://www.yahoo.com/">Yahoo</a>
```

In the three-link example, any unvisited link will be colored red, a visited link will be purple, the active (current) link will be black, and when you hover over the link it will turn green. Save this HTML and CSS in your browser and observe this behavior for yourself.

Link, visited, active, and hover are pseudo-classes. They define states of the anchor element. Most elements have a "hover" state, so you can create interesting effects with any element.

Nested Elements

Pseudo-classes can also be used to define the style of elements within other elements. Consider this example:

CSS

06-19.css

```css
article h2 {
    font-size: 16px;
    font-weight: bold;
}
```

HTML

06-20.html

```html
<article>
    <h2>A Super Interesting Article</h2>
    <p>You have to read this!</p>
</article>
```

In this case, *only* the h2 elements within article elements will be set to have 16-pixel bold fonts. H2 elements outside article elements will continue to be styled as usual.

:first-child / :last-child / :nth-child(n)

You can also use `:first-child` and `:last-child` to style only the first and last child occurrences of an element. For example, if you wanted the first paragraph of any article to be bold, you'd use this:

```css
article p:first-child { font-weight: bold; }
```

If you wanted to apply a style to the second paragraph, you would use the `:nth-child(n)` pseudo-class.

06-21.css
and
06-22.css

```css
article p:nth-child(2) { font-weight: bold; }
```

Adjust the value of n (in the previous example, 2) to match your desired position.

Pseudo-Elements

Pseudo-elements allow you to apply CSS styles to specific parts of an element, or to add content before, after, or within an element. Pseudo-elements use a syntax similar to pseudo-classes except they use two colons between the element and the pseudo-element name.

Let's look at a very practical example using the `::first-line` pseudo-element.

06-23.css

CSS

```
article::first-line { font-style: italic; }
```

HTML

```
<article>
    <p>Those interested in learning more about HTML
and CSS should consult the ClydeBank Media HTML and CSS
QuickStart Guide. It is a fantastic resource.</p>
    </article>
```

06-24.html

In this example, the first line of the article will be rendered in an italic font. The extent of the "first line" is based on the width of the browser window. On a phone, it may represent just a few words, but on a wide-screen device it may encompass the entire first paragraph, if the font is small.

In the same vein as first-line, you can use ::first-letter to style the first letter of a text-based element. You can also use the ::selection pseudo-element to alter the style applied by the browser when a user clicks that element on your web page.

::before and ::after

The `::before` and `::after` pseudo-elements allow you to add text before and after elements on a page.

If we want to add NOTE: before each paragraph, we use `::before`, like this:

```
p::before { content: "NOTE: "; }
```

If we want to style this inserted content, we can do that, too.

```
p::before {
    content: "NOTE: ";
    font-weight: bold;
    color: red;
}
```

Construct an HTML page with at least a paragraph of text. Use `::first-letter` to increase the font size, bold, and italicize it. This technique is sometimes used in books for additional style and interest (figure 52).

Lorem ipsum dolor sit amet, consectetur adipiscing elit, sed do eiusmod tempor incididunt ut labore et dolore magna aliqua. Ut enim ad minim veniam, quis nostrud exercitation ullamco laboris nisi ut aliquip ex ea commodo consequat.

Decorative styling of the first letter of a paragraph

CSS Cascade Hierarchy

CSS, by definition, "cascades" between styles. Rules follow, or cascade over, the HTML elements they decorate.

We have discussed the cascading order of CSS rules (from external files to `<style>` elements to inline styles) and the selector hierarchy. But properties have a hierarchy, too.

One situation where this is most evident is when we use third-party CSS files and frameworks. Some of them are quite large, and it's impossible to know every element and class definition. Because of this, we are sometimes forced to use the `!important` declaration on properties to ensure that our overrides percolate to the top of the priority chain. Here's an example:

```
.very-important { font-weight: bold: !important; }
```

In this case, the bolding of text in an element with this class name will override *most* other rules, even if the font-weight is set to a different value by a competing CSS rule. This is extremely helpful for troubleshooting confusing rule cascade issues and for quick, one-off fixes.

However, if you find yourself using `!important` more than occasionally, then you have an issue with the structure of your CSS rules. This power, when used sparingly, is helpful, but it can quickly turn into a mess if you aren't careful.

Continuing with Carter Dome

Remember our Carter Dome page from chapter 5? In the "Putting It All Together" section, we built a complete HTML page. Not a great page, but complete (sort of). Unfortunately, it had no styling beyond the browser defaults. Let's try using what we learned in this chapter to spruce up the Carter Dome page. Go to our GitHub repository for this title at www.github.com/clydebankmedia/htmlcss-quickstartguide. Locate the complete Carter Dome web page code found near the end of chapter 5 (Snippet_05-22.html).

Open your text editor and create a new file: File >> New. Then copy all the Carter Dome code into the text editor.

Create a `<style></style>` section in the `<head></head>` and add CSS code to designate interesting modifications for the heading and paragraph text.

Save this file somewhere on your computer. Be sure to save it as file type ".html," as it may save as a text file by default. Next, open the newly created .html file with your browser and behold your masterpiece. If you don't see anything new, try refreshing the page.

Keep your text editor and browser open. Make changes to the code and save them in your text editor. Then refresh your browser to see those changes rendered instantly.

If you're feeling extra adventurous, don't use `<style>` tags, but create a whole new style.css file and link to your style sheet in the `<head>` element of the Carter Dome page.

Press the gas pedal on your newfound CSS knowledge, and feel free to experiment with ideas you don't quite understand yet (or ideas suggested by your text editor). Remember, you're not yet on the clock, clearing lucrative billings from clients. You're just trying to learn how things work. Try to create the coolest looking web page you can. What do you come up with?

Carter Dome

See statistics or find additional reading on Carter Dome.

Carter Dome, or simply The Dome, is a mountain located in Coos County, New Hampshire. The mountain is part of the Carter-Moriah Range of the White Mountains, which runs along the northern east side of Pinkham Notch. Carter Dome is flanked to the northeast by Mount Hight and to the southwest by Wildcat Mountain (across Carter Notch).

The origins of Carter Dome's name are unknown. Local folklore suggests that it was named after a hunter named Carter, while a neighboring peak is named after his hunting partner, Hight.

The mountain is ascended from the west by the Carter Dome Trail and Nineteen Mile Brook Trail, and from the east by the Black Angel Trail.

Statistics

- Elevation: 4,832 ft (1,473 m)
- Prominence: 2,821 ft (860 m)
- Coordinates: 44°16'02"N 71°10'44"W

Additional Reading

For more information, please see the Wikipedia article on Carter Dome

fig. 53

Can you beat this?

Chapter Recap

» HTML code defines content and structure, and CSS applies style to those structures.

» CSS rules contain selectors that reference HTML elements, classes, and ids. Those selectors are assigned properties that modify the appearance and behavior of those elements.

» CSS can be placed in a .css file, in a style element in the head element, in a style element within the body element, or inline via the "style" attribute on the opening tag of an HTML element.

» Pseudo-classes allow you to style specific states and variations of elements, while pseudo-elements let you style specific parts of elements and add content before and/or after an element.

| 7 |

Using CSS to Size and Space Elements

Chapter Overview
» CSS uses a box model for formatting.
» Elements have size, border, padding, and margins.
» Border boxing makes spacing easier.

Much of the power of CSS's formatting abilities lies in the CSS "box model." The box model is a specific set of properties that are commonly used to delineate various elements of a web page layout. Properties that control the margin, border, and padding define the spacing around elements on the page.

If we think of HTML elements as a set of discrete blocks, the box model helps us specify how those blocks should be arranged, both in relation to other elements and on the page itself.

Imagine cars on a road. If we think of each element as a car, then we can specify the width of a lane and the amount of space between cars. We can also specify elements specific to each individual car, such as how the seats are placed in relationship to the body of the car.

fig. 54

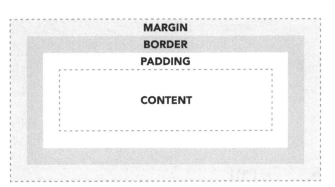

Using the box model, we can specify the dimensions of the element's *content*, the *padding* that specifies space around the content, and a *border* of the content (the outer body of the car), which specifies thickness, style, and more. We can use *margins* to create an invisible force field around the vehicle, so that nothing can bump up too close (figure 54).

Content

The "content" part of the box model is simply the portion that is to be displayed. It can be text, images, or any other HTML element (usually) wrapped within a `<div>` element. Divs are quite helpful in delineating content sections on a page because they don't do anything themselves—they simply serve as containers for content.

We can control the dimensions of a block of content by changing its width and height properties. We can make it a fixed size or specify dimensions in percentages so that it is relative to the size of the page (or containing element).

Let's go back to our example style sheet from chapter 6.

CSS

07-01.css

```css
/* Set a default font and size for the entire document */
body {
    font-family: Arial, Helvetica, sans-serif;
    font-size: 12px;
}

h1 { font-size: 22px; }
h2 { font-size: 18px; }
h3 { font-size: 16px; }

.bold-text { font-weight: bold; }
.red-text { color: red; }
.purple-text { color: purple; }

#top-ad {
    background-color: yellow;
    color: red;
}
```

To demonstrate content sizing, we can start with an image. On our fictitious sales page, we would like to add a picture of a car.

07-02.html

HTML

```html
<img alt="A nice car for sale." src="images/car.jpg">
```

If we want to alter the image's dimensions, we have three options in CSS: define the properties in an inline style, use a custom class, or use an id. It's generally best to avoid inline styles, so we should create a class or id. Recall that ids are used only once on a page, but classes can be used as many times as we like. Since this would be the only picture of a car on this page, it is best to give it an id, like this:

07-02.html

HTML

```
<img id="car" alt="A nice car for sale." src="images/car.jpg">
```

Now let's define the image's size.

07-04.css

CSS

```
#car {
    width: 640px;
    height: 480px;
}
```

With this CSS rule, we assign the properties *width* and *height*, in pixels (px), to the element with the id of "car." (See figure 55.)

fig. 55

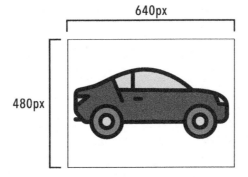

fig. 56

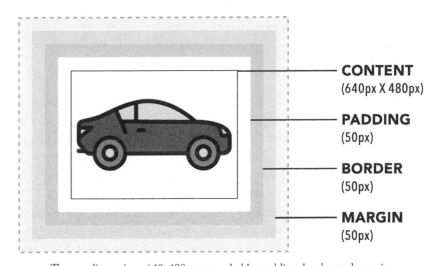

CONTENT
(640px X 480px)

PADDING
(50px)

BORDER
(50px)

MARGIN
(50px)

The car, dimensions 640x480, surrounded by padding, border, and margin

If we want the car image to be resized according to the size of the containing element (in our case, the screen), we can use a percentage indicator:

07-05.css

```css
#car {
    width: 25%;
    height: 25%;
}
```

Now the image will be resized to 25% of the width and height. You can set one of these attributes to "auto" and have the browser calculate the other dimension for you in proportion to the first one.

When considering dimensions of content like images, it is important to remember that your page will be viewed on a variety of devices. You might be fine with a car image expanding to 1000 pixels or more on a large monitor, but that size yields poor results on mobile devices.

To help alleviate this issue, CSS provides a max-width and a max-height property. Specifying one or both of these ensures that an image can never be resized past a certain point. And, as you might have suspected, we can also use min-width and min-height to specify minimum sizes. Let's put this into practice.

CSS

07-06.css

```css
#car {
    width: auto;
    height: auto;
    min-width: 320px;
    min-height: 240px;
    max-width: 1280px;
    max-height: 960px;
}
```

HTML

```html
<img id="car" alt="A nice car for sale." src="images/car.jpg">
```

07-07.html

Under these settings the image cannot be reduced to more than 320 by 240 pixels, nor be enlarged to more than 1280 by 960 pixels (figure 57).

You may have noticed that these minimum and maximum numbers are relative to each other. The minimum width size is 320 pixels, which is half of the default 640 pixels we defined earlier. The maximum width size is 1280 pixels, which is double the original width and four times the minimum. You are not required to use this technique, but doing so helps ensure your images are not awkwardly scaled by the browser.

MIN-WIDTH VS. MAX-WIDTH

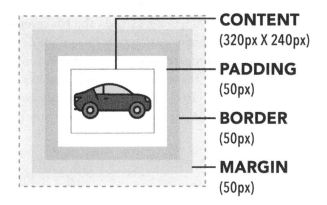

CONTENT
(320px X 240px)

PADDING
(50px)

BORDER
(50px)

MARGIN
(50px)

GRAPHIC

fig. 57

CONTENT
(1280px X 960px)

PADDING
(50px)

BORDER
(50px)

MARGIN
(50px)

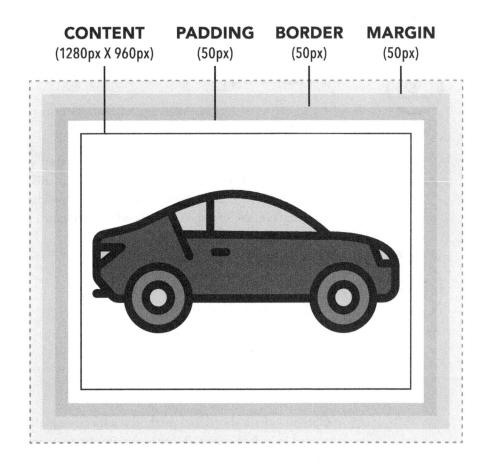

Padding

The padding property creates space between the content of an element and its outer edge. This is used to make room between elements so they aren't crowded on the page.

Padding extends the background properties (image, color, etc.) of the content area. Text or images inside an element of padding will appear to have "bumpers" around them that retain the background style. Padding can be set for the top, right, bottom, and left of an element. Let's put this into practice.

Remember our atrociously colored yellow and red ad (Snippet_07-01. css)? Let's add some padding around it (figure 58):

07-08.css

```
#top-ad {
    background-color: yellow;
    color: red;
    padding: 10px;
}
```

fig. 58

10px padding SUMMER SALE ON NOW!

You'll love our prices. 50% off? That's so yesterday. Try 70% off!

The padding space will still have the background color of the element, but the ad text will now have space around it. In this case, by specifying `padding: 10px;`, we are assigning ten pixels of padding to the top, right, bottom, and left. We can specify each side individually, too:

07-09.css

```
#top-ad {
    background-color: yellow;
    color: red;
    padding-top: 10px;
    padding-right: 12px;
    padding-bottom: 10px;
    padding-left: 12px;
}
```

CSS provides a shorthand method for specifying all sides of an element, designated in a clockwise fashion: top, right, bottom, and left. Each value is separated by a space:

```
#top-ad {
    background-color: yellow;
    color: red;
    padding: 10px 12px 10px 12px;
}
```

This produces results identical to those specified individually.

If the top and bottom or left and right dimensions match, we can condense this code even further. The browser will assume that if only two padding dimensions are specified, the first is the top and bottom and the second is the left and right:

```
#top-ad {
    background-color: yellow;
    color: red;
    padding: 10px 12px;
}
```

Borders

To create a border around an element, we specify the border's width, style, and color. Let's return to the example of our vibrant ad. Say we want to give it a purple border. It is doubtful anyone would ever use such an awful color combination, but it would certainly draw the visitor's attention (figure 59).

```
#top-ad {
    background-color: yellow;
    color: red;
    padding: 10px 12px;
    border: 1px solid purple;
}
```

1px border —

SUMMER SALE ON NOW!

You'll love our prices. 50% off? That's so yesterday. Try 70% off!

In this case, the border will be one pixel thick, solid in style, and colored purple. This border will be applied to all sides of the div, but we can specify different borders if we like. For example, the following border specification creates a somewhat three-dimensional effect (figure 60):

07-13.css

```
#top-ad {
    background-color: yellow;
    color: red;
    padding: 10px 12px;
    border-top: 3px solid gray;
    border-right: 3px solid black;
    border-bottom: 3px solid black;
    border-left: 3px solid gray;
}
```

Making the bottom and right borders darker than the top and left ones gives the "box" of the ad a drop-shadow effect. In chapter 8 we will explore adding such effects via CSS, but this simple demonstration shows how each border can be different if we so desire.

fig. 60

3px border — | SUMMER SALE ON NOW!

You'll love our prices. 50% off? That's so yesterday. Try 70% off!

Additionally, we can specify individual properties of the entire border. This is useful if we want to specify, for instance, a border size and a color but are otherwise content to accept the default style.

07-14.css

```
#top-ad {
    background-color: yellow;
    color: red;
    padding: 10px 12px;
    border-width: 1px;
    border-color: purple;
}
```

Margins

We use margins to create spacing between elements on the page. While padding gives us room *within* elements (like the distance between seats in a car), the margins serve as a buffer zone *between* elements (other cars on the road). If we want *all* images on the page to have a five-pixel margin around them, then we will specify it like this (figure 61):

07-15.css

```css
img { margin: 5px; }
```

fig. 61

Like padding and borders, margins can be set individually for top, right, bottom, and left:

07-16.css

```css
img {
    margin-top: 5px;
    margin-right: 10px;
    margin-bottom: 5px;
    margin-left: 10px;
}
```

Just like padding and borders, you can specify them in one line:

```
img { margin: 5px 10px 5px 10px; }
```

or

```
img { margin: 5px 10px; }
```

Negative Margins

You can assign negative numbers to margins. This allows an element to break the margin boundaries of the element next to it. It's helpful when you want to overlap a series of elements (figure 62).

CSS

```
#red-car { margin-left: -20px; }
```

HTML

```
<img id="car" alt="Another car" src="images/car.jpg">
<img id="red-car" alt="A red car" src="images/red-car.jpg">
```

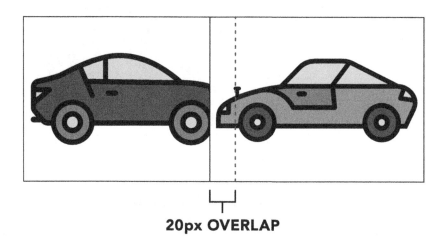

20px OVERLAP

In this example, the right side of the red car image is overlapped by the other car image by 20 pixels.

Box Sizing

The box-sizing property specifies the method we use to determine the overall size of an element. Let's go back to our car analogy—we can look at box sizing as a way to define the amount of space we need for our car on the road. There are several ways to do this. By default, if we don't define box size, our element is measured exactly as we say it is; if our content is forty pixels wide, that's how much space is used. However, we need to consider the other cars on the road. If a roadway was fifteen feet wide and there were two cars on it that were each seven-and-a-half feet wide, they would technically fit, but they'd be jammed up against each other and neither could move.

Space on a web page is similar. We usually want space between our elements so that the layout isn't claustrophobic. That's where the box-sizing property "border-box" comes into play.

However, if we use the border-box property, this will define the borders as *part* of the content. While this decreases the amount of space available for content, it is more realistic, so we don't try to jam things into the box that won't fit. This can provide us with better control over the overall size. Using border-box is particularly useful for sites that need to be flexible or responsive.

This is a personal preference—you could handle box sizing in other ways. But many web designers use border-box as the default box-sizing property when laying out commonly used elements at the beginning of a project, as it makes spacing calculations easier.

The following code can be used to set all the elements on a page to use border-box.

NOTE

*:before, and *:after are types of pseudo-elements. We'll address these in a later chapter, but for now, just know that they direct all elements contained in the HTML element to use border-box.

SNIPPET

CSS

```css
html { box-sizing: border-box; }
*, *:before, *:after { box-sizing: inherit; }
```

07-21.css

Chapter Recap

» The CSS box model is a representation of the space and borders around elements.

» Padding describes the space around the content but within the content's boundary.

» Border describes the style, color, and size of a line around the content.

» Margins describe the space between elements.

18

Text Formatting

Chapter Overview
» Fonts are arranged in families.
» CSS can adjust font face, color, shadow, and more.
» Fonts can be loaded from the Web.

In the last chapter we covered element sizing, padding, and borders with CSS. In this chapter, we will deal with the formatting of text inside those boxes.

Font

Before we discuss the individual properties of fonts, let's go over the broad aspects of fonts and the selection and use of font on a web page.

Fonts are arranged in *families*. Serif and sans-serif are the two primary families. The little lines at the end of a letter are called serifs, and thus fonts that feature these attributes are called serif family fonts. If a font doesn't have these lines, it is called sans-serif (meaning without serif).

fig. 63

SERIF FONT Aa Bb Cc

SANS-SERIF FONT Aa Bb Cc

In general, serif fonts are older and are commonly used in printing, whereas sans-serif fonts are more modern and more often used on screens. Choosing a font is largely an aesthetic decision, though readability and user experience are important considerations.

Font-family

The font-family attribute allows us to assign a list of fonts, in order of preference, to an element. If the first font listed isn't available, the browser will fall back to the next, and so on until it reaches the end of the list, so it is best to specify the fonts in order of priority.

In the example from chapter 7, we specified a font-family for the body element:

08-01.css

```css
/* Set a default font and size for the entire document */
body {
    font-family: Arial, Helvetica, sans-serif;
    font-size: 12px;
}

h1 { font-size: 22px; }
h2 { font-size: 18px; }
h3 { font-size: 16px; }

.bold-text { font-weight: bold; }
.red-text { color: red; }
.purple-text { color: purple; }

#top-ad {
      background-color: yellow;
      color: red;
}
```

First, the browser will try to use Arial. If Arial can't be found, it will use Helvetica. If neither of those is present on the system, the default sans-serif font will be used.

Note that assigning the font-family attribute to the body element will result in the chosen fonts being applied to all text on the page, unless the rule is overridden with a style or via an inline style.

Font-size

The font-size property specifies how large we would like the text to appear. Length units are usually set in pixels (px) but can also be set in other units, including the following (figure 64):

px	Pixels (devices have different pixel density, so sizes will vary)	
em	Value is relative to default size of element (1.5 em = 1.5 times current size)	
rem	Value is relative to root element (html)	
mm	Millimeters	
in	Inches	
cm	Centimeters	

GRAPHIC

fig. 64

Let's say we want our exciting ad copy to be twice as big as the default. In that case, we'll set it like this:

SNIPPET

08-02.css

```css
#top-ad {
    background-color: yellow;
    color: red;
    font-size: 2em;
}
```

How do we know the default size? In our example CSS, we set the font-size of the body element to 12 pixels. So, the element with the top-ad id will be 24 pixels.

It's worth noting that the em size is relative to the containing element. In most cases, this is the body, but if the top-ad element is inside another element, like this . . .

SNIPPET

08-03.css

HTML

```html
<div id="our-header">
    <div id="top-ad">
        Don't miss this sale!
    </div>
</div>
```

. . . and #our-header has another font size set:

SNIPPET

08-04.css

CSS

```css
#our-header { font-size: 14px; }
```

Then the 2 em font size on the top-ad element will double the `#our-header` font size and not the body size. This will yield a 28-pixel font. When using em, it's important to take note of any containing elements that might be present. We can bypass this potential ambiguity by using rem, because the rem unit uses the root (html) size, not the size of any containing elements.

Font-weight

The font-weight property is used to increase or decrease the "boldness" of the text. Font weight can be defined with either predefined names or numeric value.

Our four predefined (and preferred) named settings are "normal," "bold," "bolder," and "lighter." If we decide to use numeric values instead of a predefined name, then we will be working in increments of 100, from 100 to 900. The higher the number, the greater the boldness value; 400 corresponds to "normal" and 700 corresponds to "bold."

Not every font has a specified bold value, so specifying anything other than "normal" in the font-weight attribute could have little to no effect. If you will be using bold text, it is important that you test it with the font(s) you wish to use.

As if our top-ad wasn't eye-catching enough, we're now going to bold the text:

08-05.css

```
#top-ad {
    background-color: yellow;
    color: red;
    font-size: 2em;
    font-weight: bold;
}
```

Line-height

In some cases, the default line spacing in a browser is not adequate for our design needs, so we can specify the height of a line. The line-height property defines how much space is used for each line of text. The default height rendered by most browsers is 120% of the font-size setting (figure 65).

LINE HEIGHT 100%

Lorem ipsum dolor sit amet, consectetuer adipiscing elit, sed diam nonummy nibh ut euismod tincidunt. ↕1

LINE HEIGHT 120%

Lorem ipsum dolor sit amet, consectetuer adipiscing elit, sed diam nonummy nibh ut euismod tincidunt. ↕1.2

GRAPHIC

fig. 65

We can specify line height using a name, a percentage, or a ratio, and the default values are as follows: normal, 120%, and 1.2, respectively. In this example, we set the line height for all paragraphs to 1.4:

SNIPPET

08-06.css

```
#special-paragraph { line-height: 1.4; }
```

In the previous example, we are using a proportional line height with a ratio of 1.4. You can use a pixel value, but when setting line heights for multiple elements, it is best to specify a proportional line height. This helps avoid issues with the built-in differences in default line heights for headings and other non-text elements.

Letter-spacing

The letter-spacing property allows us to alter the space between letters in text. Any values we use are treated as relative offsets to the default spacing. If we set the letter spacing to one pixel, one pixel will be added between each letter in the element. Specifying a negative value will cause letters to overlap each other.

SNIPPET

08-07.css
and
08-08.html

CSS

```
.larger-spacing { letter-spacing: 2px; }
```

HTML

```
<h2 class="larger-spacing">This header has an extra 2px
between its letters</h2>
```

IMAGE

This header has an extra 2px between its letters

fig. 66

Color

To change the color of text within a block of text, we define the "color" property. Colors can be defined in three ways: by name, hexadecimal code, or RGB code.

Named Colors

The easiest yet most limited way of adding color to text is to use the named color. For instance, our red-text class changes all text in that class to red:

```css
.red-text { color: red; }
```

08-09.css

Hexadecimal Code

Hex code allows us greater flexibility in color choice. Colors in HTML and CSS can be represented in a simple format known as "hexadecimal," or "Base 16." Hexadecimal color codes are represented using a string of six characters composed of numbers and letters from A to F. A "#" character is placed in front of our character string to indicate that it is a hex number. For example, #000000 represents black, or the complete absence of color. White is represented by #FFFFFF.

If we want to display red in hexadecimal, we can convert the preceding code to this:

```css
.red-text { color: #FF0000; }
```

08-10.css

The hex number for most colors is quite a bit more jumbled than the basic black (#000000), white (#FFFFFF), and red (#FF0000). For example, we get a nice shade of blue using the following code:

```css
.royal-blue-text { color: #4169E1; }
```

08-11.css

RGB

The third way of specifying colors is with RGB (red, green, blue) notation. Colors on a screen are composed of different levels of red, green, and blue light, and specifying these levels in values from 0 to 255 allows us to create the full spectrum of visible display colors.

08-12.css

To display our previous example in RGB, we would use:

```css
.red-text { color: rgb(255, 0, 0); }
```

Red is the result of this RGB configuration because there are 255 units of red light intensity (the maximum intensity), and there are zero units of green and blue intensity. In our royal blue example, red has an intensity of 65, green 205, and blue 225:

08-13.css

```css
.royal-blue-text { color: rgb(65, 205, 225); }
```

Text Shadow

Beyond these basic settings, there are interesting effects that we can apply to text to make content pop out on a page. A property called "text-shadow" can be used to create a handful of unique special effects, such as 3D lettering, blurring, and glow.

The text-shadow property requires the following values:

08-14.css

```css
text-shadow: horizontal-shadow vertical-shadow;
```

The horizontal shadow value tells the browser in pixels (or another unit such as em) how large the horizontal shadow should be, while the vertical shadow, as its name suggests, defines the length of the vertical shadow. You can optionally specify a color and a blur radius (the strength of a blur effect on the shadow).

Let's add an effect to the text of our #top-ad element:

CSS

```css
#top-ad {
    background-color: yellow;
    color: red;
    font-size: 2em;
    font-weight: bold;
    text-shadow: 2px 2px #C0C0C0;
}
```

In the previous example, we added a 2-pixel by 2-pixel shadow colored #C0C0C0 (a light silver). If we want to soften the shadow, then we can add a blur radius. This is a very small and subtle change but will make the shadow appear more natural.

CSS

```css
#top-ad {
    background-color: yellow;
    color: red;
    font-size: 2em;
    font-weight: bold;
    text-shadow: 2px 2px 1px #C0C0C0;
}
```

This will add a slight blur to the shadow. If this is our top-ad element...

HTML

```html
<div id="top-ad">ON SALE NOW!</div>
```

...then it will look like this (figure 67):

Text shadow is not supported in some older web browsers.

Custom Web Fonts / Google Fonts

Historically, web developers were restricted to a very limited list of web-safe fonts. Using a font that most computers did not have meant that the font was rendered on a user's screen with a default substitute. The font-family attribute helped browsers pick alternative fonts if a special font was unavailable.

This limitation affected graphic design choices. Those wishing to use special fonts often resorted to creating images of their decorative text and loading them onto the page with the `img` tag. Because of this historical limitation, many sites continue to use a set of default fonts that are available on most browsers. Times New Roman, Arial, Helvetica, and Verdana are still popular, as these fonts (or namesake equivalents) are installed on most devices.

Thankfully, we now have a way to load any font we want. Unfortunately, not all browsers agree on the method web designers can use to load them. But there are tools like Font Squirrel's Webfont Generator that allow us to generate the variations of code required to display a custom font.

Nearly all fonts have license agreements, so unless a font is known to be in the public domain, be sure you have permission to use it on your website.

Google Fonts allows developers to select from a wide variety of fonts, identify the different font weights and font styles that can be used (italic, etc.), and even see the language support for each selection. The CSS is also presented and can be easily copied and pasted into your code.

Visit go.quickstartguides.com/htmlcss to access your Digital Assets containing updated URLs that will direct you to Font Squirrel's Webfont Generator and Google Fonts.

Regardless of how you implement your custom web fonts, the technique for using them is the same. Just add them to the font-family declaration with appropriate fallback fonts. The following example uses a Google font called Open Sans:

08-18.css

```css
h2 {
    font-family: 'Open Sans', Arial, Helvetica, sans-serif;
    font-size: 28px;
    line-height: 1.4;
    letter-spacing: 4px;
}
```

Custom web fonts behave in the same way as any other font; all the CSS properties we discussed can be applied to them. However, custom fonts have a slight drawback. To work properly on a site, they must be downloaded to the user's machine at the time the page loads, which adds a small amount of additional load time. Site speed is an important consideration for both user experience and search engine optimization, so you should only load fonts via CSS that you intend to use. Large, decorative fonts will take more time to load, so consult the file size (and Google Font's load statistics) for more information.

Practice Exercise

Remember our Carter Dome example? Here's a new and improved version. But if you save this and view it in a browser, it will appear unchanged.

HTML

08-19.html

```html
<!DOCTYPE html>
<html lang="en">
    <head>
        <meta charset="UTF-8">
        <title>Carter Dome</title>
        <meta description="Carter Dome is a mountain located
in New Hampshire.">
        <link rel="stylesheet" href="style.css">
    </head>
    <body>

        <h1>Carter Dome</h1>

        <img src="images/Carter-Dome.jpg" height="600"
width="800" alt="A picture of Carter Dome">

        <p>See <a href="#stats">statistics</a> or find <a
href="#additional">additional reading</a> on Carter Dome.</p>

        <p><span class="bold-text">Carter Dome</span>, or
simply The Dome, is a mountain located in <span class="blue-
text">Coos County, New Hampshire</span>. The mountain is
part of the <span class="blue-text">Carter-Moriah Range</
span> of the <span class="blue-text">White Mountains</
span>, which runs along the northern east side of <span
```

```html
class="blue-text">Pinkham Notch</span>. <span class="bold-
text">Carter Dome</span> is flanked to the northeast by <span
class="blue-text">Mount Hight</span> and to the southwest by
<span class="blue-text">Wildcat Mountain</span> (across <span
class="blue-text">Carter Notch</span>).</p>

        <p>The origins of <span class="bold-text">Carter
Dome's</span> name are unknown. Local folklore suggests
that it was named after a hunter named Carter, while a
neighboring peak is named after his hunting partner, Hight.</
p>

        <p>The mountain is ascended from the west by the
<span class="blue-text">Carter Dome Trail</span> and <span
class="blue-text">Nineteen Mile Brook Trail</span>, and from
the east by the <span class="blue-text">Black Angel Trail</
span>.</p>

        <hr>
        <div id="stats">
            <h2>Statistics</h2>
            <ul>
                <li><span class="cat">Elevation:</span> 4,832 ft
(1,473 m)</li>
                <li><span class="cat">Prominence:</span> 2,821
ft (860 m)</li>
                <li><span class="cat">Coordinates:</span>
44°16'02"N 71°10'44"W</li>
            </ul>
            </div>
            <hr>
            <div id="additional">
                <h2>Additional Reading</h2>
                <p>For more information, please see the <a
href=" https://en.wikipedia.org/wiki/Carter_Dome">Wikipedia
article on Carter Dome</a>

            </div>
    </body>
</html>
```

This page is full of text, so it's an excellent canvas on which to apply the text formatting processes we've learned. In addition to some span elements, a relative link containing a reference to style.css has been added to the head element. In the same directory, create a file called style.css and put some text formatting CSS rules in it, as shown:

CSS

```css
body {
    font-family: Arial, Helvetica, sans-serif;
    font-size: 12px;
}


h1 { font-size: 22px; }
h2 { font-size: 18px; }


.bold-text { font-weight: bold; }
.blue-text { color: blue; }
```

When you reload the Carter Dome HTML file, you will notice it now displays in Arial font with more precisely sized headers and colored text highlighting locations and key terms in the article. Try experimenting with various font names, colors, and other styles.

LOOK AND FEEL

Our client isn't a fan of the gray color scheme of the ClydeBank Coffee Shop website. They inform us that it should be brown, not gray. Since the colors were specified in css/style.css (the css/ denotes that the style sheet is in the CSS folder), we can easily change this.

If you haven't yet downloaded the ClydeBank Coffee Shop website, please do so from www.github.com/clydebankmedia/clydebank-coffee-shop.

In the style.css file, there are several places where the client's chosen colors are defined. Rather than specifying them all, we're not giving you any hints this time. Try to change these colors on your own.

>> Change the header background color to a light brown color named "sienna."

>> Change the navigation menu background color to "chocolate" and the text color to white.

>> Change the footer background color to chocolate.

These colors are just our recommendations; you don't have to use those values. Feel free to experiment with different colors.

Once you've made the changes, open `index.html` (or refresh, if you have it open already) and see the changes. Thanks to your hard work, the site is already looking a lot better! As always, if you get stuck, the answers are in appendix V.

Chapter Recap

>> Fonts are grouped into families, and similar fonts can be specified for your text via the font-family property.

>> Web designers used to be restricted to the fonts installed on the visitor's computer, but now fonts can be loaded from the web server and displayed on the page.

>> Font, size, color, decorations, boldness, shadow, and more can be added to your text.

| 9 |
Layout/Format

Chapter Overview

>   » CSS allows elements to be positioned in a variety of ways.
>   » Elements can float and deviate from the normal flow of HTML.
>   » CSS Flexbox allows for dynamic positioning of elements.

In this chapter, we will explore how to lay out your web page. Until now, we have been using simple elements to put content on the page, assign those elements ids and classes, and style them with CSS. Now it's time to explore how objects are sized and positioned, and how to use "floating" to break free from the linear style of development and create regions of content on your page.

Position

The CSS position property tells the browser how an element should be positioned on the page. There are four possible values for position: static, relative, fixed, and absolute.

static

The default setting, static, tells the browser to follow the normal flow of the page. Elements will appear in the order they are presented in the HTML code. Since this is the default, you only need to set the position to static if you are changing the position attribute of a nested element (for example, a `<p>` inside a `<div>`) and you want the inner element to deviate from its container.

relative

Relative position specifies that any formatting we provide for an element will be relative to its normal position. When we set a position to relative, we usually define additional properties like top, right, bottom, and left. This lets us describe the desired position in relation to the normal position. Here's an example:

CSS

```css
.relative-position {
    position: relative;
    left: 20px;
}
```

HTML

```html
<div>
    I have a hard time relating to this div.
</div>
<div class="relative-position">
    I can relate to this div.
</div>
```

This CSS rule will move the div 20 pixels left of its normal position.

fixed

Elements given a position of "fixed" will hold their position on the page relative to the viewport. In other words, even if you scroll the page, the item will stay in place. This can be useful for keeping a static link menu on the page, keeping a "Back to Top" link in the bottom right corner, or keeping a footer from disappearing when the visitor scrolls. Remember our #top-ad element? Let's make it "stick" to the top:

CSS

```css
#top-ad {
    position: fixed;
    top: 0;
    right: 0;
    width: 640px;
    background-color: yellow;
    color: red;
}
```

HTML

```html
<div id="top-ad">This ad not only catches your attention
but insists on sticking around!</div>
```

The class "top-ad" sets the top and right positions to 0 and sets the fixed position attribute. This will always keep the footer at the top of the view, regardless of how much the user scrolls.

absolute

If we want an element to be fixed in relationship to its containing element rather than to the viewport, then we use absolute position. When we set an element to absolute, it will look for the nearest ancestor (that is, any element that contains it) with a position property not set to "static" and will position itself to be fixed in relation to that element.

Let's consider the following code:

HTML

09-05.html

```
<div class="the-parent">
    This is the parent (ancestor) element, called the-
parent, which is set to relative.
    <div class="the-child">
    This child element, called the-child, is set to
absolute. Its properties will be in relationship to the
parent element.
    </div>
</div>
```

Next, we will apply the CSS:

CSS

09-06.css

```
div.the-parent {
    position: relative;
    background-color: #CCCCCC;
    width: 400px;
    height: 200px;
    border: 1px solid black;
}

div.the-child {
    position: absolute;
    background-color: #ffffff;
    top: 80px;
    right: 0;
```

```
        width: 200px;
        height: 100px;
        border: 1px solid black;
    }
```

The resulting layout will look something like this (figure 68):

fig. 68

This is the parent (ancestor) element, called the-parent, which is set to relative.

> This child element, called the-child, is set to absolute. Its properties will be in relationship to the parent element.

Floating Elements

With the position attribute, we can move elements around on a page and specify where we want them based on the page, viewport, or parent element. Rather than assigning specific locations, we may want an element to flow with the text. We use the float property to accomplish this.

float

Let's look at this HTML code:

HTML

09-07.html

```
<div class="sidebar">
<p>Excerpt from: A Floating Home by Cyril Ionides & J. B.
Atkins</p>
</div>
<div class="main-text">
<h1>A Floating Home</h1>
<p>One winter I made up my mind that it was necessary
to live in some sort of vessel afloat instead of in a house
on the land. This decision was the result, at last pressed
```

```
on me by circumstances, of vague dreams which had held my
imagination for many years.</p>
    <p> These dreams were not, I believe, peculiar to myself.
The child, young or old, whose fancy is captive to water,
builds for castles in Spain houseboats wherein he may spend
his life floating in his element. His fancy at some time
or other has played with the thought of possessing almost
every type of craft for his home—a three-decker with a
glorious gallery, a Thames houseboat all ready to step into,
a disused schooner, a bluff-bowed old brig. He will moor
her in some delectable water, and when his restlessness
falls upon him he will have her removed to another place.
Civilization shall never rule him. As though to prove it he
will live free of rates, and weigh his anchor and move on
if the matter should ever happen to come under dispute. Nor
will he pay rent resentfully to a grasping landlord. For a
mere song he will pick up the old vessel that shall contain
his happiness. Her walls will be stout enough to shelter him
for a lifetime, though Lloyd's agent may have condemned her,
according to the exacting tests that take count of sailors'
lives, as unfit to sail the deep seas.</p>
    </div>
```

Now let's style the "sidebar" and "main-text" divs with CSS:

CSS

09-08.css

```
.sidebar {
    float: right;
    height: 100px;
    width: 200px;
    padding: 5px;
    border: 1px solid black;
}


.main-text { border: 1px solid #333333; }
```

Our resulting display will look like this (figure 69):

fig. 69

A Floating Home

Excerpt from: A Floating Home by Cyril Ionides & J. B. Atkins

One winter I made up my mind that it was necessary to live in some sort of vessel afloat instead of in a house on the land. This decision was the result, at last pressed on me by circumstances, of vague dreams which had held my imagination for many years.

These dreams were not, I believe, peculiar to myself. The child, young or old, whose fancy is captive to water, builds for castles in Spain houseboats wherein he may spend his life floating in his element. His fancy at some time or other has played with the thought of possessing almost every type of craft for his home—a three-decker with a glorious gallery, a Thames houseboat all ready to step into, a disused schooner, a bluff-bowed old brig. He will moor her in some delectable water, and when his restlessness falls upon him he will have her removed to another place. Civilization shall never rule him. As though to prove it he will live free of rates, and weigh his anchor and move on if the matter should ever happen to come under dispute. Nor will he pay rent resentfully to a grasping landlord. For a mere song he will pick up the old vessel that shall contain his happiness. Her walls will be stout enough to shelter him for a lifetime, though Lloyd's agent may have condemned her, according to the exacting tests that take count of sailors' lives, as unfit to sail the deep seas.

At first glance, float may seem like the other relative positioning methods previously described. But with float we don't specify any specific location or offset information—we only tell the browser to place the element on the right or left of other elements.

clear

Float allows us to shift elements to the left or right, but once multiple elements are involved it's easy to experience overlapping or unexplained results. To prevent this, we use the clear property. When we set clear, we are telling the browser to start over with float positioning. Let's add a clear property to the main-text div, like so:

09-09.css

```
.main-text {
    border:1px solid #333333;
    clear: right;
}
```

Here we are telling the browser that no floating element can exist to the right of the main-text element, thus resetting the float until the next row (figure 70).

fig. 70

Excerpt from: A Floating Home by Cyril Ionides & J. B. Atkins

A Floating Home

One winter I made up my mind that it was necessary to live in some sort of vessel afloat instead of in a house on the land. This decision was the result, at last pressed on me by circumstances, of vague dreams which had held my imagination for many years.

These dreams were not, I believe, peculiar to myself. The child, young or old, whose fancy is captive to water, builds for castles in Spain houseboats wherein he may spend his life floating in his element. His fancy at some time or other has played with the thought of possessing almost every type of craft for his home—a three-decker with a glorious gallery, a Thames houseboat all ready to step into, a disused schooner, a bluff-bowed old brig. He will moor her in some delectable water, and when his restlessness falls upon him he will have her removed to another place. Civilization shall never rule him. As though to prove it he will live free of rates, and weigh his anchor and move on if the matter should ever happen to come under dispute. Nor will he pay rent resentfully to a grasping landlord. For a mere song he will pick up the old vessel that shall contain his happiness. Her walls will be stout enough to shelter him for a lifetime, though Lloyd's agent may have condemned her, according to the exacting tests that take count of sailors' lives, as unfit to sail the deep seas.

CLEAR VALUES	
none	the default setting, allowing elements to float on either side
left	no elements can float to the left
right	no elements can float to the right
both	no floating elements will appear on either side of the specified element
inherit	the element will inherit the clear value from its containing element

GRAPHIC

fig. 71

As you can see, using float and clear in concert gives us a lot of control in the layout of our page.

When we set up floating elements, we can run into issues when content (usually an image) is larger than its container. Float, like other relative positioning methods, can allow the image to bleed over the edge of its container.

Consider this example:

HTML

SNIPPET

09-10.html

```
<div class="carter">
    <img src="images/carter_dome_view.jpg" id="carter-
pic" alt="Carter Dome" height="120" width="160">
    This is a picture of Carter Dome.
</div>
```

Now let's add a basic CSS float.

CSS

SNIPPET

09-11.css

```
.carter {
    border: 1px solid #000;
    padding: 5px;
}


#carter-pic { float: right; }
```

Our rendering will look something like this (figure 72):

IMAGE

fig. 72

This is a picture of Carter Dome.

Had there been enough text, the image would be fully contained within the div. To handle this situation, we can assign "auto" to the overflow property in our div, like so:

SNIPPET

09-12.css

```css
.carter {
    border: 1px solid #000;
    padding: 5px;
    overflow: auto;
}
```

Now the image fits within the element (figure 73):

IMAGE

fig. 73

This is a picture of Carter Dome.

This will work in many cases, but you may run into issues where the margin or padding of one of the elements causes a display issue. A better way to handle this is to use a CSS technique called "clearfix":

SNIPPET

09-13.css

```css
.carter {
    border: 1px solid #000;
    padding: 5px;
    overflow: auto;
}

.carter::after {
    content: "";
    clear: both;
    display: table;
}
```

The `::after` suffix allows you to append properties to the content after the element. In this case, we're adding an empty string ("") and a `clear: both` to prevent overlap. The `display: table` (that is, the display property set to table) causes the additional empty content to be displayed as though it were a table. We'll dive into the display property in the next section.

Float and clear allow for some interesting page layouts. For example, we can create a horizontal grid of three boxes.

HTML

09-14.html

```html
<div class="grid">
    <div class="box">
        <p>Box 1</p>
    </div>
    <div class="box">
        <p>Box 2</p>
    </div>
    <div class="box">
        <p>Box 3</p>
    </div>
</div>
```

CSS

09-15.css

```css
.box {
    float: left;
    width: 33.33%;
    padding: 50px;
    border: 1px solid #000000;
}

.grid::after {
    content: "";
    clear: both;
    display: table;
}

.box, .grid, .grid::after { box-sizing: border-box; }
```

This HTML/CSS will render this layout (figure 74):

First, we created classes for box and grid (specifically `grid::after`), then told the browser, via the box-sizing property set to the value `border-box`, to include border and padding in the element's calculated width and height.

ADVERTISEMENT

The ClydeBank Coffee Shop is running a promotion this month—free delivery on all orders over $15. You can't beat that. Since it's such a great deal, we're going to add it to the ClydeBank Coffee Shop website via a banner at the top of the page. Though you can use the yellow background color we used in the previous absolute positioning example, feel free to experiment with various background and text colors.

You might think that `position: absolute` would be ideal for this, but unfortunately that will cut off the top part of the header. To fix this, you can set `top`, `left`, and `right` to 0 and use `position: relative`.

Try this on your own. If you get stuck, you can always refer to the answer key in appendix V.

Display

The display property, as its name suggests, specifies how an element is to be displayed, if at all. There are lots of values in this property, so we'll now focus on the most frequently used.

Check out go.quickstartguides.com/htmlcss for some additional display properties. The link you're looking for is called "Display Properties." Go figure.

none

If the display property is set to "none," the element will not display on the page. You might wonder why you would go to the trouble of defining an element in HTML only to prevent it from being displayed. The most common use case for this is when you need to hide an element initially (for example, an error box), then display that element after a certain condition has been met. This is usually paired with JavaScript code.

09-16.css

For instance, consider a class defined as follows:

```
.error-message { display: none; }
```

Now let's create an error message:

09-17.html

```
<div class="error-message">
    <p>Something went wrong!</p>
</div>
```

The error message won't be shown until the display property is changed, via JavaScript, to anything but "none."

inline

An inline display will show all elements as part of one line, regardless of their normal HTML attributes.

For instance:

09-18.html

```
<div>
    This is some text.
    <p class="inline-paragraph">This is a paragraph.</p>
    And here is some more text
</div>
```

If we define the following CSS:

09-19.css

```
.inline-paragraph { display: inline; }
```

Then the paragraph element will be treated as part of the same line, like this (figure 75):

fig. 75

This is some text. This is a paragraph. And here is some more text

block

A display value set to "block" will treat each element of text as its own separate block on its own line.

09-20.css

```
.block-paragraph { display: block; }
```

The same HTML will display like this (figure 76):

This is some text.
This is a paragraph.
And here is some more text

fig. 76

While this is expected behavior in HTML, allowing the developer to assign this value is helpful when they need to revert to block layout inside containing elements that use a different display property.

> I usually force elements to behave like blocks via the `display: block` attribute when converting links to navigation—especially for mobile, when the links need to stack.

inline-block

The inline-block value defines the display layout as a hybrid of the block and inline styles. In this case, an element with this value will display inline but as part of a block layout.

HTML

09-21.html

```
<div>
    This is some text.
    <p class="inline-text">This is a paragraph.<br>It has a
line break, but is still part of this block</p>
    And here is some more text
</div>
```

CSS

```
.inline-text { display: inline-block; }
```

This will display as follows (figure 77):

> This is a paragraph.
> This is some text. It has a line break, but is still part of this block And here is some more text

Navigation Bar

Until now, the display property may have seemed abstract and theoretical, but in page navigation, the display property is invaluable. It was noted in chapter 5 that, in addition to providing bullets and numbered lists, navigation bars also benefit from the list element. Let's put that functionality to use.

Say we have a simple list of pages we want to use in our site:

```
<ul>
    <li><a href="/">Home</a></li>
    <li><a href="about.html">About</a></li>
    <li><a href="learn.html">Learn More</a></li>
    <li><a href="contact.html">Contact</a></li>
</ul>
```

By default, it would look like this (figure 78):

- Home
- About
- Learn More
- Contact

In some situations, this might be useful, but we can make it far more interesting. Let's add a little bit of styling using some of the CSS techniques we have learned in this chapter:

CSS

```css
.main-nav {
    font-family: verdana, sans-serif;
    font-size: .8rem;
    list-style-type: none;
    margin: 0;
    padding: 0;
    overflow: hidden;
    background-color: #333333;
}

.main-nav li { float: left; }
.main-nav li a {
    display: block;
    color: #EEEEEE;
    text-align: center;
    padding: 10px 12px;
    text-decoration: none;
}
```

Now we need to modify our HTML to include the class names. Note that in the previous CSS the `li` and `a` elements are listed after `.main-nav`, so rather than all `li` and `a` elements being redefined, only those inside a containing element with the `main-nav` class will be affected.

HTML

```html
<ul class="main-nav">
    <li><a href="/">Home</a></li>
    <li><a href="about.html">About</a></li>
    <li><a href="learn.html">Learn More</a></li>
    <li><a href="contact.html">Contact</a></li>
</ul>
```

The result is a stylish navigation bar (figure 79):

Using the float property, we told the browser to have all list elements forgo their usual vertical arrangement and horizontally align to the left. The overflow property set to "hidden" on the main nav prevents a new line on the navigation bar from being created by the browser. Setting `text-decoration: none` on an element in the list prevents links from being underlined, giving the overall design a nicer look.

CSS Flexbox

In previous versions of HTML and CSS, page layout tended to follow a grid pattern. There were essentially four different element-arrangement strategies: "block" for handling blocks of content within a web page, "inline" for handling strings of text, "table" for representing two-dimensional data, and "positioned" for specifying the explicit position of items on a page. Now that pages are being viewed on a wider variety of devices, this grid lacks the flexibility needed to automatically arrange elements on multiple screens.

Recently, the concept of "flex" or "flexbox" layout has emerged. The flexbox strategy expands on the four traditional layout display values with additional values that instruct the browser on how to stack, wrap, and arrange elements. This model allows for layout without using floats or relative positioning, thereby avoiding the dreaded overlap issues associated with these techniques.

Imagine a bag of marbles. If you lay the bag on the table, the marbles will align in a roughly horizontal fashion. Putting the bag of marbles in your pocket forces the marbles into tighter arrangement. The marbles will remain in the bag but will reorient themselves to fit the available area.

To construct flexbox-style layouts, we begin by defining an HTML structure with a container and then add a few internal elements.

HTML

09-26.html

```
<div class="flex-container">
    <div>1</div>
    <div>2</div>
    <div>3</div>
    <div>4</div>
    <div>5</div>
</div>
```

Visual Studio Code has a nifty shortcut for designing multiple elements that is most useful for creating divs and spans. Type `div*3`, then hit ENTER and three div elements will appear. Replace `div` with the element and `3` with the number of elements you want to create.

In our CSS, we set the display property of the parent element "flex-container" to flex. Let's give it a light gray background color:

CSS

```css
.flex-container {
    display: flex;
    background-color: #CCCCCC;
}
```

We can now define the behavior of any div elements within our flex-container class.

```css
.flex-container > div {
    background-color: #ffffff;
    margin: 10px;
    padding: 20px;
    font-size: 30px;
}
```

The resulting display will look something like this (figure 80):

Flex also allows us to alter the way the content displays. We can change the display to a column format using the flex-direction property (figure 81):

```css
.flex-container {
    display: flex;
    flex-direction: column;
    background-color: #CCCCCC;
}
```

fig. 81

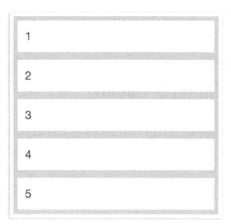

Sometimes content will not fit in a single line. If we set the flex-wrap property to "wrap," the browser will display the layout in a line if there is enough room; if not, it will create a new line to display the remaining content. This allows us to adapt to a wide variety of screen widths (figure 82).

fig. 82

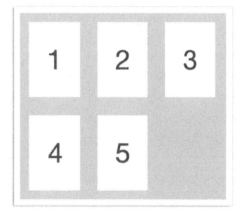

There are many more CSS flex properties. For a complete listing, check out the full "Flex Container List" list linked in the Web Developer Resource Library included with the free digital assets for this book at go.quickstartguides.com/htmlcss.

Moving Forward

In part II, we've covered the basics of HTML and CSS. With this knowledge, you can build simple and attractive web pages. In part III, we'll cover more advanced topics to help you style your pages to look great on all devices, including tablets and phones. We'll also explore HTML forms, allowing you to collect data from your visitors.

You've done a great job! See you in part III!

Chapter Recap

»   With CSS, we can position HTML elements in a variety of ways. In addition to altering the flow and order of presentation, we can make elements float outside their normal position, stick to a side of the window, or even disappear.

»   The list element can be used to build an attractive and functional navigation bar.

»   CSS Flexbox allows elements in a container to adapt to the size of the screen on which they are being displayed, giving the designer tremendous layout flexibility.

PART III

ADVANCED

| 10 |
HTML Junk Drawer

Chapter Overview

» HTML/CSS provides a cornucopia of bells and whistles.
» Learn to use emojis, multimedia, tables, and more.

In part II, we covered the basics of HTML and CSS. With practice, the concepts discussed will become second nature to you.

Since web design is a broad topic covering many different techniques and technologies, it's impossible to memorize every component. Part III will cover more advanced topics that you will need to reference but might not use in your everyday web design work.

You might wonder why we called this chapter the "HTML Junk Drawer." Every home, from a tiny house on wheels to a sprawling estate, has a junk drawer—that place where we stash anything and everything we don't know where else to put. And the word *junk* is actually a misnomer, as we regularly turn to our junk drawer when we need a paperclip, a twist tie, or some other mundane but valuable tool that helps us solve a problem. The topics we'll cover in this cornucopia of a chapter are incredibly useful tidbits of web design knowledge. Let's get started!

Superscript and Subscript

You can add superscript and subscript text to a web page via the `<sup></sup>` and `<sub></sub>` elements (figure 83).

10-01.html

```
<p>The quick brown fox jumped over the lazy red dog. The
quick brown fox <sup>jumped</sup> over the lazy red dog. The
quick brown fox jumped over the lazy red dog. The quick
brown fox jumped over the <sub>lazy red</sub> dog.</p>
```

The quick brown fox jumped over the lazy red dog. The quick brown fox ^{jumped} over the lazy red dog. The quick brown fox jumped over the lazy red dog. The quick brown fox jumped over the _{lazy red} dog.

The sup (superscript) and sub (subscript) elements in action

It's important to note that adding superscript and subscript text can adjust the containing line down or up depending on font size and line height. To mitigate this, you can increase the line height for all text so the browser doesn't need to offset that value for just one line.

Abbreviations

The `<abbr></abbr>` element allows you to add abbreviations to your HTML documents. When you use abbr, the browser will underline the abbreviation with a dotted line and display the value of the title attribute as a hint when the mouse hovers over the text (figure 84).

```
<p>The quick brown fox jumped over the <abbr title="Lazy
Red Dog">LRD</abbr>. The quick brown fox jumped over the
lazy red dog. The quick brown fox jumped over the lazy red
dog. The quick brown fox jumped over the lazy red dog.</p>
```

The quick brown fox jumped over the LRD. The quick brown fox jumped over the lazy red dog. The quick brown fox jumped over the lazy red dog. The quick brown fox jumped over the lazy red dog.

Lazy Red Dog

The abbr element underlines and defines the LRD abbreviation.

Blockquotes and Cite

The `<blockquote></blockquote>` element indents the content it contains and provides an optional cite attribute. Web designers often use it to display quotes from other sources. If desired, you can put the exact quote within the `<q></q>` element, and the citation (usually used as a footnote) can be displayed with the `<cite></cite>` element (figure 85).

```
<p>The quick brown fox jumped over the lazy red dog. The
quick brown fox jumped over the lazy red dog. The quick
brown fox jumped over the lazy red dog. The quick brown fox
jumped over the lazy red dog.</p>

<blockquote cite="Mr. Fox, The Quick Silver Anthology,
1999">
<p><q>The quick silver fox jumped over the lazy yellow
dog. The quick silver fox jumped over the lazy yellow dog.
The quick silver fox jumped over the lazy yellow dog.</q></p>
</blockquote>
<p>The quick brown fox jumped over the lazy red dog. The
quick brown fox jumped over the lazy red dog. The quick
brown fox jumped over the lazy red dog. The quick brown fox
jumped over the lazy red dog.</p>

<cite>Mr. Fox, The Quick Silver Anthology, 1999</cite>
```

The quick brown fox jumped over the lazy red dog. The quick brown fox jumped over the lazy red dog. The quick brown fox jumped over the lazy red dog. The quick brown fox jumped over the lazy red dog.

"The quick silver fox jumped over the lazy yellow dog. The quick silver fox jumped over the lazy yellow dog. The quick silver fox jumped over the lazy yellow dog."

The quick brown fox jumped over the lazy red dog. The quick brown fox jumped over the lazy red dog. The quick brown fox jumped over the lazy red dog. The quick brown fox jumped over the lazy red dog.

Mr. Fox, The Quick Silver Anthology, 1999

The second paragraph is contained within the block quote element.

At the time of publication, Chrome and Firefox do not do anything special with the block quote, cite, and q elements beyond indenting the block quote, italicizing the cite, and putting quotes around the q element. You may wonder why one would bother with these elements at all if the browser won't fully utilize them. Using HTML5-compliant elements, even if the browser doesn't do anything special with them at the moment, helps to "future-proof" your website and aids browser plugins, screen readers, and other tools. By coding for upcoming features, you'll have a jump-start on the next generation of browser technology.

You can override the handling of these (or any other) elements via CSS. For instance, a trade journal may want to use its house style, which involves drawing a thick border to the left-hand side of the block quote, highlighting quotes (via the q element) by setting the background-color attribute of q to yellow, and positioning the cite in the footer or setting it to use a smaller font.

10-04.css

```
/* Add a thick border to the left of blockquote */
blockquote { border-left: 3px solid black; }

/* Give quote (q) a neon-yellow background */
q { background-color: #FFFF33; }

/* Make cite a smaller font and a lighter color */
cite { font-size: 80%; color: gray; }
```

Pre and Code

There are times when you want to display programming code on a web page. Fortunately, HTML has a solution—the `<pre></pre>` and `<code></code>` elements.

The `<pre>` tag (short for preformatted) opens a section of code, and the `</pre>` tag closes it. Anything in between is displayed in a monospaced font— where each letter and character occupies an equal amount of horizontal space (figure 86).

10-05.html

```
<pre>
    This is an example of computer code.
</pre>
```

If you press the ENTER key while typing text, the text will be wrapped to the next line both in your HTML file and when displayed in the browser.

fig. 86

```
This is an example of computer code.
```

Using the pre element

The `<code>` tag opens a section of code in much the same way as `<pre>`, but `<code>` is intended for inline use, much like `<span>`. Just like `<pre>`, the browser renders `code` in a monospaced font, but the formatting is a bit different (figure 87).

```
<p>Enter <code>dir</code> on the command line to see a
list of files.</p>
```

Enter `dir` on the command line to see a list of files.

Using the code element

Special Characters

The symbols on top of the number keys on a standard keyboard are the most frequently used non-alphanumeric characters. However, in some cases, you'll want to use characters that aren't on a standard keyboard. While you can insert them from a character map application on your computer or copy and paste them from another page, this won't work if the page character set (configured via the charset meta tag) doesn't match the inserted character. It isn't practical to change this every time you want to use a special character, so the safest and most compatible method of adding a unique symbol is to use an HTML entity code.

An HTML entity code starts with an ampersand followed by a word and ends with a semicolon. This unlikely combination tells the browser to render the unique character instead of the code symbols (figure 88).

```
<p>&copy; Copyright 2020, ClydeBank Media, All Rights
Reserved.</p>
```

The copyright sign is a commonly used symbol. Sometimes you'll see an open parenthesis, the letter C, and a closed parenthesis, like this: (C). That's adequate but doesn't look as good as an actual copyright symbol.

© Copyright 2020, ClydeBank Media, All Rights Reserved.

The copyright symbol in action

There are hundreds of special characters you can use in your HTML documents. Several of the most commonly used are featured in figure 89.

SYMBOL	NAME	HTML ENTITY CODE
©	Copyright	&copy;
™	Trademark	&trade;
®	Registered Trademark	&reg;
€	Euro Currency	&euro;
←	Left Arrow	&larr;
→	Right Arrow	&rarr;
↑	Up Arrow	&uarr;
↓	Down Arrow	&darr;
N/A	Non-Breaking Space	

GRAPHIC

fig. 89

10-08.html

To grab the code from figure 89, visit the GitHub code repository at www.github.com/clydebankmedia/htmlcss-quickstartguide and locate Snippet_10-08.html.

Emojis

Emojis have become an indispensable part of life. Odds are you've used one today in a text, message, or social media post. Fortunately, adding emojis in HTML is as easy as adding a named HTML entity. Emojis are inserted by inserting an ampersand prefix followed by the pound sign and the number of the emoji entity. The code is closed with a semicolon (figure 90).

10-09.html

```
<p>Would you like a &#127803;?</p>
```

Emojis, like all HTML entities, are simply characters in the UTF-8 character set. Since they are like any other character, they can be manipulated with CSS (figure 91).

10-10.html

```
<p>Would you like a <span style="font-size:
50px;">&#127803;</span>?</p>
```

fig. 90

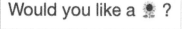

The rendered display of the flower emoji

fig. 91

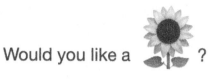

The flower, rendered in a 50-pixel font size

Since HTML emojis are displayed via an HTML entity code, you might be wondering if you can use entity code numbers instead of words for all HTML special characters. As you might suspect, you can. For example, the copyright symbol can also be shown with `&#169;`. Still, it's much easier to remember `&copy;`, so it's generally best to use the named HTML entities when possible.

Audio and Video

Adding audio and video to a web page used to be an involved affair, with web designers usually resorting to third-party plugins like RealPlayer™ and Adobe Flash™. Fortunately, HTML5 includes audio and video elements that make it easy to add multimedia content to your web page.

Audio

The aptly named `<audio></audio>` element lets us insert an audio player with a specified file directly into the web page. The audio element expects a contained `<source>` element to specify the file to play:

10-11.html

```
<audio controls>
    <source src="assets/welcome.mp3" type="audio/mp3">
</audio>
```

fig. 92

An audio control

The controls property of audio enables the "audio control" display in the browser with play, time, volume, mute, and index for scrubbing through the audio content (figure 92). If you omit controls, it will not be displayed, and JavaScript code will be required to control the player. For the sake of user sanity, browsers usually require some action (mouse-clicking, key-pressing, etc.) before music can be played.

You can specify multiple sources in different formats. MP3 is generally well-recognized, but you can use OGG, MP4, AAC, and others. In this example, the browser will first try to use the MP3 file specified. If it doesn't have support to play MP3s, the browser will load and play the OGG file.

10-12.html

```html
<audio controls>
    <source src="assets/welcome.mp3" type="audio/mp3">
    <source src="assets/welcome.ogg" type="audio/ogg">
</audio>
```

Video

The `<video></video>` element works much the same as the `<audio>` element in that it permits playback of multiple video types and has a display that can be toggled via HTML attributes. However, the video tag adds a few more properties, including support for various subtitle tracks and a resizable screen (figure 93).

10-13.html

```html
<video width="640" height="480" controls>
    <source src="welcome.mp4" type="video/mp4">
    <track src="welcome_en.vtt" kind="subtitles"
srclang="en" label="English">
    <track src="welcome_es.vtt" kind="subtitles"
srclang="es" label="Spanish">
    Your browser doesn't support video playback.
</video>
```

fig. 93

A video control

The width and height attributes allow you to specify the size of the video. If possible, use the exact dimensions of the video with matching aspect ratio (that is, ratio-consistent width and height values) for the best performance and appearance. To enable controls, ensure that the `controls` attribute is present in the video opening tag.

If you want to display subtitles, add the `<track>` element, as previously shown. A VTT file represents subtitles in the WebVTT format, a W3C standard for subtitles. Various software programs allow for editing these files or creating one from scratch in a text file.

Finally, you can specify the text you want to display if the video element isn't supported in a user's browser. In this example, it will say: "Your browser doesn't support video playback."

Embedding a YouTube Video

You might think the video tag would be the natural choice for embedding a YouTube video on a web page. While that works for an MP4 video file, it doesn't work with a YouTube video, because YouTube includes its own custom player, advertising, and other code along with the video.

Fortunately, YouTube provides an easy way to grab the HTML code necessary to show a video on your page. Just click the Share button underneath the video and choose the Embed option. A window will appear with options that will let you customize the player, along with a box displaying the code for you to paste onto your web page.

Image Sets

When the `<img>` element was introduced in chapter 5, the `src` attribute was described as the method of specifying the URL of the image to display. This is entirely correct, but we cautioned you to avoid using pictures sized differently than the intended size on the screen, to save bandwidth and reduce page load time. Image resizing and optimization is an excellent strategy. Still, users with large screens may see a poor-quality image, and pages with high-quality images may waste bandwidth on small screens.

Enter the `<picture>` element. Just like the `<audio>` and `<video>` elements, `<picture>` allows you to specify multiple file sources for the image to be displayed. This ensures that the browser will load the correctly sized image for the device.

10-14.html

```
<picture>
    <source media="(min-width: 1024px)" srcset="/images/
flower-1024.jpg">
    <source media="(min-width: 640px)" srcset="/images/
flower-640.jpg">
    <source media="(min-width: 320px)" srcset="/images/
flower-320.jpg">
    <img src="/images/flower.jpg">
</picture>
```

In this example, browsers on devices with screens at least 1024 pixels wide will load the `/images/flower-1024.jpg` image file. Browsers on smaller devices will load the appropriate file depending on the media attribute. Resizing the browser window will load the proper image for the minimum width specified. Finally, the `img` tag inside the picture element will load the `/images/flower.jpg` in the rare case that the browser doesn't support the picture element.

There's one additional trick you can use with the source element that allows you to specify different versions of a file to meet different size requirements without having to use multiple source lines. Let's use the `srcset` attribute to condense our previous example into more concise code.

10-15.html

```
<picture>
    <source srcset="=/images/flower-320.jpg, /images/
flower-640.jpg 640w, /images/flower.jpg 1024w" media="(min-width:
320px)">
    <img src="/images/flower.jpg">
</picture>
```

In our reworked example, we specify, via the media attribute, that the minimum width must be 320 pixels, the size of the smallest image, `/images/flower-320.jpg`. Then, `/images/flower-640.jpg` should be shown on screens with a width of 640 pixels and, finally, `/images/flower.jpg` should be used on screens with 1024-pixel width or greater.

While this may seem like a lot more work, using the picture element will help you design more responsive pages that use images suited to the size of the screen. As a bonus, you'll save bandwidth and reduce the page load time of your website.

Tables

Tables are quite useful for displaying tabular, spreadsheet-like data. At one time, before div and CSS, some coders used tables to form the layout of web pages. Using tables for layout is outdated, doesn't scale on different devices, and is very frowned upon by modern web designers. But the table element still provides a fantastic way to display data.

Consider this screenshot example of retail sales data (figure 94).

fig. 94

Year	Shirts	Shoes	Pants
2017	$420,392	$18,304	$34,912
2018	$480,221	$17,952	$36,112
2019	$491,919	$16,844	$46,924
2020	$501,029	$15,124	$39,947

A table made with Microsoft Excel

You could simply save the screenshot as a JPG or PNG file and insert it into your web page, but this isn't good practice, for a variety of reasons. An image takes a separate HTTP or HTTPS request to the web server, increasing download and rendering time in the browser. If, for example, you wanted to add a new row for 2021's sales figures, you'd have to update the data in Excel, take a new screenshot, and upload the new image to your web server.

The simpler and better approach is to use the `<table></table>` element. Here's an unstyled HTML rendition of the data in figure 94.

10-16.html

```
<table>
    <tr>
        <th>Year</th>
        <th>Shirts</th>
        <th>Shoes</th>
```

```
        <th>Pants</th>
      </tr>
      <tr>
        <td>2017</td>
        <td>$420,392</td>
        <td>$18,304</td>
        <td>$34,912</td>
      </tr>
      <tr>
        <td>2018</td>
        <td>$480,221</td>
        <td>$17,952</td>
        <td>$36,112</td>
      </tr>
      <tr>
        <td>2019</td>
        <td>$491,919</td>
        <td>$16,844</td>
        <td>$46,924</td>
      </tr>
      <tr>
        <td>2020</td>
        <td>$501,029</td>
        <td>$15,124</td>
        <td>$39,947</td>
      </tr>
</table>
```

Parts of a Table

As you can see, the table element contains the headers, rows, and columns of all the data to be displayed. Let's explore the related elements in detail.

tr: Tables are composed of rows that run horizontally. The `<tr></tr>` element (short for table row) marks the start and end of a new row.

td: The `<td></td>` element (short for table data) contains the contents of a column. Each row can have one or multiple columns, but every row should have the same number of columns. In situations where you wish columns to span more than one cell, you can use the `colspan` attribute.

```
<td colspan="2"></td>
```

In this example, two columns are spanned, but you can use as many columns as you wish as long as it doesn't exceed the table's total number of columns.

th: The `<th></th>` element (short for table header) acts just like a `<td></td>` column except its contents are bolded and set apart from a normal column. This is often used to name a column.

thead: The `<thead></thead>` element is used to group header columns, similar to the `<head></head>` element in an HTML document.

tbody: The `<tbody></tbody>` element is used to group content columns, similar to the `<body></body>` element in an HTML document.

tfoot: The `<tfoot></tfoot>` element is used to group footer columns, similar to the `<footer></footer>` element in an HTML page.

NOTE

The th, thead, tbody and tfoot elements are not required but are available to be used if the layout calls for them.

Styling the Table

In figure 94, the table's top row and border were slate gray. We can easily accomplish a similar look with CSS.

```css
table { border: 1px solid blue; }
th {
    background-color: darkblue;
    color: white;
    font-weight: bold;
}
td { padding: 5px; }
```

For easier reading, you can set the background color of every other row to gray, with the `nth-child` selector applied to even-incremented `tr` elements.

```css
tr:nth-child(even) { background-color: lightgray; }
```

Now let's add the CSS shown previously and slightly modify our example to demonstrate `colspan` and alternating odd/even rows. To center the text in a cell with `colspan`, we'll create a class called `center-cell` (figure 95).

CSS

SNIPPET

10-20.css

```css
table { border: 1px solid blue; }
th {
    background-color: darkblue;
    color: white;
    font-weight: bold;
}
tr:nth-child(even) { background-color: lightgray; }
td { padding: 5px; }
.center-cell { text-align: center; }
```

HTML

SNIPPET

10-21.html

```html
<table>
    <tr>
        <th>Year</th>
        <th>Shirts</th>
        <th>Shoes</th>
        <th>Pants</th>
    </tr>
    <tr>
        <td>2017</td>
        <td>$420,392</td>
        <td>$18,304</td>
        <td>$34,912</td>
    </tr>
    <tr>
        <td>2018</td>
        <td colspan="2" class="center-cell">$480,221</td>
        <td>$36,112</td>
    </tr>
    <tr>
        <td>2019</td>
        <td>$491,919</td>
        <td>$16,844</td>
        <td>$46,924</td>
    </tr>
```

```
    <tr>
        <td>2020</td>
        <td>$501,029</td>
        <td>$15,124</td>
        <td>$39,947</td>
    </tr>
</table>
```

Year	Shirts	Shoes	Pants
2017	$420,392	$18,304	$34,912
2018	$480,221		$36,112
2019	$491,919	$16,844	$46,924
2020	$501,029	$15,124	$39,947

A table styled with CSS demonstrating alternating row highlighting and a
`colspan="2"` on the 2018 row

IFrames

The `<iframe></iframe>` element, short for *inline frame*, allows you to embed HTML code from another website or page.

You should use care when embedding an iframe on your page. If you use an iframe to include content from another site, you do not have any control over what content the web browser fetches in the frame. If the site changes the URL or blocks your site from including the content, your frame will be broken, at best, and could possibly display unexpected content. Additionally, frames are vulnerable to a type of attack known as ***cross-site scripting***, so you're opening the door to potential security issues.

If you find yourself reaching for an iframe to solve a problem, there are likely better ways to address your issue. Consider using a scripting language like JavaScript or backend code like PHP. Nevertheless, despite their disadvantages, iframes can be useful in some situations. Even if you elect not to use them in your own builds, you may encounter them if you maintain other websites, so it's helpful to know how they work.

```
<iframe src="https://www.clydebankmedia.com" width="640"
height="480"></iframe>
```

In this example, the front page of ClydeBankMedia.com will load inside the frame. You don't have to reference an external website—an iframe can reference a file on the same site.

```
<iframe src="menu.html" width="640" height="480"></iframe>
```

You aren't required to use width and height attributes, but if you don't, the browser will define these values.

Chapter Recap

- » Elements like sup, sub, abbr, blockquotes, and cite allow you to add features frequently found in professional documents and white papers.

- » Use pre and code elements to display code on your web pages.

- » HTML supports special characters and emojis.

- » Multimedia features can be added to your web pages via the audio and video elements.

- » HTML tables are ideal for displaying tabular data but should not be used for general layout.

| 11 |
HTML Forms

Chapter Overview
» Forms allow user input.
» The input element provides for data entry.
» HTML5 has built-in input validation.

You have likely used countless HTML forms while browsing the internet. Forms are used for search boxes, contact pages, logins, registrations, and checkout pages, and are combined in complex arrangements to form applications like webmail and social media platforms.

Forms Overview

Forms employ both frontend code for display and backend code to process and use the submitted data. Since this book focuses on HTML and CSS, we can't cover the backend code, but as a web designer, you'll often be called on to design the form while a programmer is tasked with making use of the submitted data to perform tasks on the web server.

Recall from chapter 1 that backend languages, like PHP and Python, run on the web server and perform functions that both process user data and display dynamic content to the user. Forms play an integral role in connecting the user with the databases and functionality of the server.

An HTML form is a group of elements that allow user input. These elements can accept a wide variety of input types, including name, email, phone number, option selections, and even file uploads. These input elements are given a name, and the data entered by the user is associated with that element name and is either sent to another URL, processed by JavaScript code on the page, or both.

Forms are set apart from other parts of the page via a `<form>` tag. At the end of the form, a closing `</form>` tag is used. The `<form>` tag has several attributes that are important in instructing the browser in how to handle the submission of the data entered by the user (figure 96).

NOTE

The examples in this section will work fine in your browser for testing, but until a backend script is added to process the input and do something with it, they won't do anything on their own. These code snippets will just be used for illustrative purposes. The "Processing Form Input with PHP" section of this chapter provides some sample PHP code that will send this form's input to an email address.

fig. 96

Send Us The Details
and let one of our trained professionals get right back to you...

Name *		Email *
Phone		Preferred Contact Method...
Domain		Subject *
Comments *		

Send Now

An example contact form, styled with CSS

Action

The "action" attribute of the form is perhaps most important. It instructs the browser where to send the data submitted by the user. If this attribute is omitted, the data is sent to the same page. The URL can be either an absolute or a relative URL.

SNIPPET

11-01.html

```
<form action="contact.html">
```

NOTE

If the form is to perform some task, like send an email, add data to a database, or something similar, then the action must point to a page (usually a PHP script or other backend language file) that actually processes the data from the form. In this example, without extra code, an HTML page like contact.html can only use JavaScript to parse form input variables.

Method

The "method" attribute instructs the browser as to what kind of request will be used to submit the form's data. This can be either GET or POST. If the method is not specified, GET is used.

11-02.html

```
<form action="contact.html" method="POST">
```

Both GET and POST requests receive responses from the server. The difference between them is in how the user-provided data is sent. To illustrate both points, we'll display an example form and explain how user-submitted variables are handled with both methods.

GET: When form data is sent via GET, the browser simply requests the URL specified in the action attribute with an HTTP/S GET request. This request merely asks for the page or file to download, without any additional HTML headers. User data is added to the end of the URL.

GET FORM

11-03.html

```
<form action="contact.php" method="GET">
    <label for="name">Name</label><br>
    <input type="text" name="name" required><br><br>
    <label for="message">Message</label><br>
    <textarea name="message" rows="5" cols="60"
maxlength="2000"></textarea><br><br>
    <input type="submit" name="submit" value="Send
Message">
    </form>
```

GET URL AFTER SUBMIT

```
https://www.yoursite.com/contact.php?name=Jim&message=He%20
is%20dead
```

A question mark is added after the file name, then, for each input element within the form, the name attribute from the form is specified, followed by an equals sign and then the content of the field as submitted by the user. Any special characters, including spaces, are "escaped," that is, transformed into a number sequence, so that they don't interfere with browser or server parsing of the URL. Any spaces are replaced with `%20`, where the percent sign denotes the start of a special sequence and 20 is the number of the space character. `%20` is by far the most common URL code used in HTML to accommodate input that would disturb the structure of the URL.

POST: Forms with their method attribute set to POST will instruct the browser to send the form data to the web server via an `HTTP/S` POST request. This type of request sends the form input data to the web server, and the server usually responds with HTML content. This keeps all input data out of the URL and facilitates more complex input, such as when the user uploads a file to your form.

POST FORM

11-04.html

```
<form action="contact.php" method="POST">
    <label for="name">Name</label><br>
    <input type="text" name="name" required><br><br>
    <label for="message">Message</label><br>
    <textarea name="message" rows="5" cols="60"
maxlength="2000"></textarea><br><br>
    <input type="submit" name="submit" value="Send
Message">
</form>
```

POST URL AFTER SUBMIT

```
https://www.yoursite.com/contact.php
```

Note that the URL is simply `contact.php`—no variables are appended to it. Instead, the `name=Jim` and `message=He%20is%20dead` are POSTed to the server as headers. Headers are additional pieces of data that are sent along with each request to a web server and that aren't shown in the URL.

The GET method is fine for simple forms with one or two input elements, but if a lot of user data is submitted via the form, the resulting URL can become quite unwieldy. I recommended using POST in those cases.

Name

The "name" of the form is optional but helpful, especially when several forms exist on the same page. Form names can be referenced by JavaScript or server-side languages like PHP to determine which form inputs should be processed.

11-05.html

```
<form name="contact" action="contact.html" method="POST">
```

Id

As with all HTML elements, an id attribute can be specified. This is helpful for using the form with JavaScript code. The id attribute is not passed to the server. It is optional.

Target

With the "target" attribute, you can instruct the browser to submit the page in a new window by setting the target to _blank.

11-06.html

```
<form action="contact.html" method="POST" target="_blank">
```

Key Elements

Now that we've explored the form element and its attributes, it's time to dive into the building blocks of forms—the HTML components that provide opportunities for user interaction. In these examples, we will omit the form opening and closing tags for the sake of brevity, but on a real web page they would almost always be part of a form.

Input

An `<input>` element provides a way for a user to enter data into your form. It has a wide variety of attributes that control the display and functionality of the form.

Before we get into the types of input (text, email addresses, files, etc.), we should explore its traditional attributes. In the following examples, we'll assume that the type attribute is set to text, which allows for generic input with characters and numbers. Later, we'll dive into more specific types of input.

Name: The "name" attribute provides a way to reference the data entered into the input element. The name of the input element is used when sending GET or POST data to the web server (figure 97).

11-07.html

```
Subject:
<input type="text" name="subject">
```

fig. 97

A text input box

If the user specifies "A Summer Day" in this field and it's used in a GET form (figure 98), then upon submission the URL becomes:

```
https://www.yoursite.com/contact.html?subject=A%20Summer%20Day
```

fig. 98

A text input box named "subject" filled in with the text "A Summer Day"

Id: The "id" attribute of the input element isn't required but is helpful for use in JavaScript.

Style: An input element can be styled with a CSS class. If we wanted to bold the text of the input box, we could create a class and attach it to the input box via the class attribute.

11-08.css
and
11-09.html

```
.subject { font-weight: bold; }
```

```
<input type="text" name="subject" class="subject">
```

Type: The "type" attribute allows you to specify the format of input that will be accepted in the field. In the previous examples, we've assumed "text," which is the most generic specification. However, there are a wide assortment of types that allow you to define precisely the kind of data you want to accept. Some of the input types provide user interface elements that help the user specify the desired value. For example, the *range* type displays a slider, the *date* and *time* types display formatting helpers and up/down arrows to toggle months and years, and radio and checkbox fields are sized appropriately on each device.

VARIOUS INPUT TYPES	
TEXT	
text	Generic text
number	Generic number (no letters allowed)
email	Email address
tel	Phone number
url	Website address (URL)
search	Search input (behaves like text)
password	Behaves like text but obscures characters for more secure entry
DATE AND TIME	
month	Provides for month and year input
week	Provides for week and year input
time	Provides for time input in `hh:mm:ss AM/PM`
date	Provides for `mm/dd/yyyy` input, adjusting for localized international variants
datetime-local	Provides for `mm/dd/yyyy` date and `hh:mm:ss AM/PM` time input, adjusting for localized international variants
MULTIPLE CHOICE / CHECK	
radio	Displays circular buttons to select from multiple options. Text for options is supplied via a `<label>` element. If selected by user, *value* attribute is sent to server. To force selection among multiple elements, give each input radio element the same *name* attribute.
checkbox	Displays a checkbox the user can toggle on and off. Text for the option is supplied via a `<label>` element, and the value is specified via the *value* attribute.

GRAPHIC

fig. 99

SUBMISSION	
button	Displays a button. The *value* attribute is displayed as the button text. By itself, it doesn't do anything, but when paired with JavaScript it can trigger action on the page.
reset	Displays a button that resets all input elements to their default or preselected values. Text on the button is taken from the *value* attribute. Use this element with caution on long forms, as accidentally clearing a long form can raise a user's blood pressure to dangerous levels.
submit	Displays a submit button, allowing for submission of the form given the *action* and *method* values.
image	Same as submit but the *src* attribute of the input element is used to specify the URL of an image to use instead of the submit button. You need to specify *width* and *height* attributes of the image.
SPECIAL PURPOSE	
range	Displays a slider allowing for a range of numbers. Requires *min* and *max* input attributes to be set with a minimum and a maximum number.
color	Provides a color selection box, allowing the user to specify a particular color. Value becomes the hex color code of the user-selected color.
file	Displays a file upload box, allowing the user to upload a file. Parsing of the file must be done by backend server code.
hidden	This input element is not displayed on the page. Instead, the *name* and *value* attributes are used to pass a variable to the processing page.

Readonly: Specifying the "readonly" (read only) attribute tells the browser to prevent the user from changing the field.

SNIPPET

11-10.html

```
<input type="tel" name="phone" value="123-456-7890"
readonly>
```

While not absolutely required, it doesn't make much sense to use the readonly attribute without specifying a value. This is often done on forms to indicate that the user can't change some parts of it but can change others. The field is still displayed, and the user can click the input box, but they cannot change the value. Input fields marked as readonly are still sent to the server in a GET or POST request.

Disabled: This is similar to readonly, except the field will not be selectable and will not be sent to the server. Most browsers will set the background to gray to indicate it cannot be clicked on or changed (figure 100).

fig. 100

A disabled input text box

Placeholder: This attribute's value tells the browser to display text that hints as to the type of input the user should enter into the field (figure 101).

11-11.html

```
<input type="text" name="name" placeholder="Please enter
your name">
```

By default, most browsers will display this text in a lighter shade than usual and will clear the placeholder text when the user clicks in the field or starts to enter data. The placeholder value is not sent to the server, even if the field is empty.

fig. 101

Name: | Please enter your name |

An input text box with a placeholder

The placeholder can be styled as a pseudo-element using the `::placeholder` selector.

11-12.css

```
::placeholder {
    color: darkgray;
    font-style:italic;
}
```

Required: Specifying the "required" attribute on an input element instructs the browser to require the user to put a value in the field. We'll cover this topic later in this chapter under "HTML5 Validation."

11-13.html

```
<input type="text" name="name" required>
```

In this case, the text box called "name" would have to have some text entered before submission was possible.

Autofocus: When this attribute is set, the field will automatically become the input focus when the page loads. This means that a user can simply start typing when the page loads and this input field will start receiving the data. You should only specify one autofocus on a page.

11-14.html

```
<input type="text" name="name" autofocus>
```

Autocomplete: This instructs the browser to enable or disable autocomplete. By default, autocomplete is on. A browser does not have to honor this, and limiting your users' choices for inputting data may cause user frustration, so judicious use of this attribute is advised.

11-15.html

```
<input type="text" name="username" autocomplete="off">
```

Step: For certain input types, namely range, number, and the date/time types, specifying "step" allows you to adjust the increment and decrement values when the user toggles through the acceptable choices. It is best used with *min* and *max*.

11-16.html

```
<input type="range" name="pressure" min="0" max="100"
step="5">
```

Pattern: The "pattern" attribute allows you to create special restrictions on input. We'll cover this in the "HTML5 Validation" section of this chapter.

Submit: Every HTML form must have a way for a user to input and then submit the data. While input elements are usually used to collect data, the "submit" type is used to create a submit button the user can click to trigger the form's submission.

```
<input type="submit" name="submit" value="Send Message">
```

In this example, a submit button is created with the text "Send Message."

Labels

Label elements are used to display text alongside most input elements; they are generally used right before an input element. They make it easier for screen readers and some browser add-ons to identify form input elements and can also help mobile users by providing a larger area to tap to select the input field in question.

Specifying the "for" attribute on the label element allows you to tell the browser exactly which input field the label should be associated with.

```
<label for="email">Your Email</label><br>
<input type="email" name="email">
```

Placeholder attributes (discussed in the previous section) can eliminate the need for labels with some text fields, but labels are extremely useful elsewhere, such as with radio selection input types:

```
<p>What is your favorite color?</p>

<input type="radio" name="color" value="Red">
<label for="Red">Red</label><br>
<input type="radio" name="color" value="Blue">
<label for="Blue">Blue</label><br>
<input type="radio" name="color" value="Green">
<label for="Green">Green</label>
```

Fieldset and Legend

Complicated forms can be intimidating and cumbersome for the user. Breaking the form into smaller related groups makes it easier to fill. The `<fieldset></fieldset>` element can encapsulate input fields and labels, allowing you to display your form data logically. The `<legend></legend>` element gives the fieldset a name, allowing the user to separate it from the rest of the fields (figure 102).

```
<form>
    <fieldset>
        <legend>Personal Details</legend>
        <label for="name">Name:</label>
        <input type="text" id="name" name="name"><br><br>
        <label for="age">Age:</label>
        <input type="text" id="age" name="age"><br><br>
    </fieldset>

    <fieldset>
        <legend>Company Details</legend>
        <label for="company">Company Name:</label>
        <input type="text" id="company"
name="company"><br><br>
    </fieldset>

    <br>
    <input type="submit" value="Submit">
</form>
```

Personal Details

Name: [   ]

Age: [   ]

Company Details

Company Name: [   ]

[Submit]

Two groups of input elements separated by fieldsets with legends

The two fieldsets contain the inputs and labels for each group, and the legend element provides a name for the fieldset. The fieldset and legend elements, like all other HTML elements, can be styled with CSS to provide an even more visually appealing layout of your form.

Textarea

A textarea is essentially a text type of input that accepts multiple lines of text. It has most of the same attributes as an input element, with a few specific options that cater to longer text input. The textarea tag is different from the input element in that it has a closing tag and has no value attribute. The predefined value of a textarea element, which you would normally set with `value=""`, is simply the content between the opening `<textarea>` tag and the closing `</textarea>` tag.

In this example, we'll use all of the special attributes and explain them in detail.

```
<textarea name="message" rows="5" cols="60"
maxlength="2000" wrap="hard"></textarea>
```

11-21.html

Rows: With the rows attribute, you can specify the "height" of the text box in rows. The text area will accept more rows of text than are specified in "rows," but at least the specified number of rows will be displayed. The height of a row is determined by the height of the font of the text box. This can be overridden with CSS by overriding the textarea element or attaching an id or class to it.

Cols: The cols attribute allows you to specify the "width" of the text box in columns. A column is simply one character width and, as with rows, this adjusts according to the size of the text box's font. It can be refined in CSS by overriding the textarea element or attaching an id or class to it.

Maxlength: If you set the maxlength attribute, you can limit the total number of characters that can be entered by the user into the textarea field.

Wrap: Text entered into a textarea element is wrapped to the next line for the user but is not wrapped in the data submitted to the server. This is the default behavior and is defined by setting "wrap" to "soft." Specifying the "hard" setting for wrap inserts new-line characters (returns) after each wrapped line before sending it to the server.

Resize (via CSS): Many browsers allow users to resize a text area in both height and width. Because of this, the page formatting can be affected negatively. To avoid this, consider using the CSS resize property:

```css
resize: vertical; /* allows resizing only for the height */
resize: horizontal; /* allows resizing only for the width */
resize: none; /* allows no resizing */
```

Select: The select element creates a dropdown list of several options. It shares many of the input attributes but has a special syntax for multiple choice elements. Here's an example:

```html
<select name="return">
    <option value="Email">Email</option>
    <option value="Phone">Phone Call</option>
</select>
```

In this case, the name of the element is "return" and a dropdown menu is displayed with the visible options "Email" and "Phone Call." However, the name value will be set to "Email" or "Phone," depending on which they select. The *value* attribute allows you to specify a value that differs from the displayed value, but if you omit it, then the exact text between the `<option>` and `</option>` elements is used.

If you want to specify a default option, use the *select* attribute. This takes no parameters and will preselect the option when the page loads.

```html
<select name="return">
    <option value="Smoke" disabled>Smoke Signals</option>
    <option value="Email">Email</option>
    <option value="Phone" selected>Phone Call</option>
</select>
```

In this example (figure 103), "Phone Call" will be selected by default.

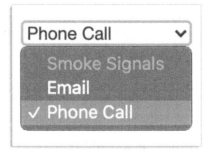

A select box with a "selected" default value

HTML5 Validation

Validation is the process of ensuring the user has entered the required data into your form fields.

Historically, JavaScript and server-side code were used to check data the user submitted before the form was sent to the server. While this approach is perfectly acceptable, it is no longer necessary to use JavaScript to validate input.

Adding the "required" attribute to an input tag will tell the browser to check the field to ensure it contains content and, if that check fails, to block submission of the form.

SNIPPET

11-25.html

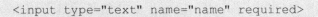

```
<input type="text" name="name" required>
```

In this example, the field will be selected and, depending on the browser, a visual indicator will be displayed prompting the user to fill in the field (figure 104).

IMAGE

fig. 104

Google Chrome displays this graphic pointing to the invalid field.

Input validation goes beyond a simple check to make sure text is in a box. If you specify it on a special type of input, like email, it will ensure that a valid email address is entered (figure 105).

SNIPPET

11-26.html

```
<input type="email" name="email" required>
```

IMAGE

fig. 105

On an email field, Google Chrome will prompt the user to enter a valid email address.

Select elements can also use validation. You can force the user to select a value from a select box in two different ways. First, you can specify a default option with no value and put a required attribute on the select tag.

11-27.html

```
<select name="reply" required>
    <option value="" selected>Please select...</option>
    <option value="Email">Email</option>
    <option value="Phone" selected>Phone Call</option>
</select>
```

In this example, the user will be forced to choose "Email" or "Phone Call." You can also omit the "selected" attribute altogether, like this:

11-28.html

```
<select name="reply" required>
    <option value="Email">Email</option>
    <option value="Phone" selected>Phone Call</option>
</select>
```

While this method ensures you'll get a value, it is not guaranteed to capture the user's attention, as the field can simply be left to its default value. The choice of approach in this matter will depend on your preference, the audience, and the business requirements of the form.

The "min" and "max" attributes can be used to ensure a number entered by the user was within the desired range. The "maxlength" attribute, as the name suggests, controls the maximum length of text, text area, and related fields. But what if you want to make sure a particular type of data is entered, like a social security number or a United States telephone number? That's where pattern matching comes in.

The "pattern" attribute can be paired with the "required" attribute to indicate that a pattern of text should be used to validate the input field. This is done using a syntax known as regular expressions, or regex for short. Regular expressions are extremely powerful; a proper discussion of this syntax would easily fill an entire book. For now, we'll focus on a few simple values you may need.

11-29.html

```
<input type="text" name="ssn" pattern="^(\d{3}-?\d{2}-?\d{4})$" required>
```

The pattern value contains a regular expression to validate a US social security number. It may seem extremely complex, but breaking it down into its individual components makes it a bit easier to understand.

- » `^` signifies the start of the string
- » `(` notes the start of the data to be matched
- » `\d{3}` the `\d` indicates digit, and `{3}` means 3, so this means 3 digits
- » `?` match the previous character literally (that is, the dash is not part of a special instruction)
- » `\d{2}` match 2 digits
- » `?` as before, ignore the previous dash (–)
- » `\d{4}` match 4 digits
- » `)` closes the definition of data to be matched
- » `$` signifies the end of the string

If your form asks for sensitive data, like a social security number or credit card information, you must make certain that the form is delivered via an HTTPS (SSL) page. If you are coding the backend processing of this sensitive information, you must also encrypt and protect it. Moreover, with sensitive data you should always use the `POST` method, to avoid the data being inserted into the URL.

11-30.html

Let's validate a two-letter country code, like "US" or "CA."

```
<input type="text" name="country" pattern="^([A-Z]{2})$"
required>
```

This validates correctly with an entry like "US" but would not allow "USA" or "Canada." Here's a breakdown of the regex:

- » `^` signifies the start of the string
- » `(` notes the start of the data to be matched
- » `[A-Z]{2}` indicates capital letters A through Z are accepted and we require two of them
- » `)` closes the definition of data to be matched
- » `$` signifies the end of the string

Don't worry if you don't understand regular expressions. You can use HTML and CSS without even knowing they exist (aside from pattern matching in input fields). However, knowledge of regular expressions is beneficial in programming languages, including JavaScript.

It should be noted that, although validating user data with HTML5 or JavaScript is a good practice, it doesn't replace the need for server-side data input validation. Malicious or malformed data sent to a backend script can cause a compromise of your website or security issues for your web server. In the following section, we'll explore some simple ways to validate data in PHP.

Processing Form Input with PHP

Though there are many options for handling user input, PHP is a reasonable choice because it's a simple and common backend language used on most Linux and Windows web servers. Since your web hosting company will almost certainly support it, powering a contact form with PHP is a good choice. In this section, you'll find an example PHP contact form handler and some introductory details about PHP. For more information on web hosting, please consult the more comprehensive discussion about web hosting in appendix I.

An HTML file is simply a text file with an `.html` extension, and the same principle applies to PHP files. For the server to execute a text file as a PHP script, the file must have a `.php` extension.

To signify the file will contain PHP code, we place `<?php` at the beginning of the file. We can return to HTML mode by closing the PHP mode with `?>`. The opening and the closing of a section of PHP code are similar to the opening and closing tags of an HTML element. Any line of PHP code that starts with `//` or `#` is a comment and is not processed.

11-31.php

```php
<?php
// This is some PHP code
?>
<p>This will be shown on the page.</p>
```

When a contact form (or any form) is submitted via a web browser to a PHP script, PHP places the value of the input fields (that is, `<input>`, `<textarea>`, `<select>`, etc.) in a unique structure called an "array" that we can access from code.

Recall that a form can be submitted via GET or POST. PHP makes both available to the script, like this:

11-32.php

```php
<?php
// Place value of HTML input field "name" in variable
called "name"
$name = $_GET['name'];
```

This script will take the value of the HTML input field called "name" and assign it to the variable `$name`. In PHP, all variables start with a dollar sign. Variables are a container in which to store a value for later processing. The $_GET array is a special variable that contains other variables within it. These variables are accessed by a "key." In this case, "name" is the key, denoting that we want the input field "name" from the array.

What if the form is posted? In that case, we can use the $_POST array.

11-33.php

```php
<?php
// Place value of HTML input field "name" in variable
called "name"
$name = $_POST['name'];
```

If we don't care which method is used, we can use the $_REQUEST array. This is preferable in most cases because it can handle either GET or POST.

11-34.php

```php
<?php
// Place value of HTML input field "name" in variable
called "name"
$name = $_REQUEST['name'];
```

You'll also note that in the three previous examples, each line of PHP code shown has a semicolon at the end. In PHP, every line of code must end in a semicolon. If you omit it, you'll receive an error.

Placing the value of the input element in a variable doesn't accomplish much in the real world. For our script to handle the code, it needs to do something with the data.

But first, we should make sure the data is valid. HTML provides validation, as we discussed in the previous section. Still, malicious users and spammers can use GET and POST variables through external scripts and can force values into the input fields that would bypass our validations. In our example code, we'll use the filter_var PHP function to ensure the data is coherent or "sane."

11-35.php

```php
<?php
// Replace with your email address
$you = "you@youremail.com";

// Place HTML input fields into variables
$name = $_REQUEST['name'];
$email = $_REQUEST['email'];
$phone = $_REQUEST['phone'];
```

```
$country = $_REQUEST['country'];
$subject = $_REQUEST['subject'];
$reply = $_REQUEST['reply'];
$message = $_REQUEST['message'];

// Validate email address
if (filter_var($email, FILTER_VALIDATE_EMAIL)) {
    die("Invalid email.");
}

// Build the message to send
$content = "
Name: $name
Email: $email
Phone: $phone
Country: $country
Subject: $subject
Best Method to Reply: $reply

Subject:
$subject

Message:
$message";

// Build mail headers
$headers = "Reply-to: $email";

// Send the message
mail($you, $you, $subject, $headers);
?>
<p>Your message was sent successfully.</p>
```

This code will work in most simple configurations, but it lacks several important features, including anti-spam protection and validation for variable length. A spammer could submit this form many times with promotional or abusive messages. Since this form sends the mail to your address, this kind of misuse could become annoying. Additional validation and CAPTCHA (Completely Automated Public Turing Test to tell Computers and Humans Apart) challenges may be necessary.

This code may not work on all web hosting servers, as each host has different restrictions and rules about sending emails via PHP code. The PHP `mail()` function usually works, but if not, you may have to use custom code. Your web host should be able to point you in the right direction.

The purpose of this example code is not to provide a complete solution to all your contact form needs but rather to serve as a starting point for you to learn more about backend programming languages like PHP.

Putting It All Together

Now that we've explored HTML forms, let's build a contact form with validation. In your text editor, create the following file and view the results in your browser. Note that you won't be able to submit the form because there's no backend code, but you'll be able to see and interact with the form elements.

11-36.html

```
<!DOCTYPE html>
<html lang="en">
    <head>
        <meta charset="UTF-8">
        <title>Contact Us</title>
    </head>
    <body>

        <h1>Contact Us</h1>

        <form action="contact.php" method="POST">

            <label for="name">Name</label><br>
            <input type="text" name="name" required><br><br>

            <label for="email">Email</label><br>
            <input type="email" name="email" required><br><br>

            <label for="phone">Phone</label><br>
            <input type="tel" name="phone"><br><br>

            <label for="country">Country</label><br>
            <input type="text" name="country" pattern="^([A-Z]
{2})$" required><br><br>
```

```
        <label for="name">Subject</label><br>
        <input type="text" name="subject" required><br><br>

        <label for="reply">Desired Reply</label><br>
        <select name="reply" required>
          <option value="" selected>Please select...</
option>
          <option value="Email">Email</option>
          <option value="Phone" selected>Phone Call</
option>
        </select><br><br>
        <label for="message">Message</label><br>
        <textarea name="message" rows="5" cols="60"
maxlength="2000"></textarea><br><br>
        <input type="submit" name="submit" value="Send
Message">
      </form>

  </body>
</html>
```

In this example, we ask for the user's name, email, phone, country, subject, and desired reply method, and we provide a space for them to enter a message. We validate the name, email, country, subject, message, and reply method, but we do not require the phone number, because they may choose "Email" as their desired reply method.

The form will POST to `contact.php`, which can be filled with the PHP example code we provided in the previous section to process the message.

You don't have to use PHP—you can use Ruby, Python, or any other backend scripting language. Covering these other languages is beyond the scope of this book. Still, as a web designer, you may need to integrate with several backend languages, and knowing how to build forms and send them to the appropriate URL will be an invaluable skill.

NOTE

The following form is functional but is rather plain-looking. Why not try to spruce it up by using CSS to decorate the heading, input fields, select box, and labels?

CONTACT FORM

The `contact.html` page of the ClydeBank Coffee Shop website is missing a contact form. Let's add one, so visitors can contact the coffee shop.

You can use the PHP file `contact.php` described in this chapter to send the email. Our client has informed us that a developer will do that for us. All we need to do is create the form and add validation.

If you haven't yet downloaded the ClydeBank Coffee Shop website, please do so from www.github.com/clydebankmedia/clydebank-coffee-shop.

We already have a working example of a form in the "Putting It All Together" section of this chapter. However, it is more detailed than we need. The client informed us that we only need ask for their name, email address, and message. Try to copy the form element, the relevant input fields, and the submit button into the `contact.html` file. Don't forget to validate each field. If you don't want to use the `contact.php` included in this chapter, then you can leave the action to reference contact.html, as a developer will adjust this after we're done.

While we encourage you to try this task on your own, you can consult appendix V if you get stuck. Once you're done, patrons will have an easy way to reach the coffee shop via email. Fantastic work!

Chapter Recap

» HTML forms allow users to provide input on a web page.

» The input element is the primary method of data entry. It provides many options for accepting text, numbers, email addresses, website URLs, and more.

» HTML5 provides methods of validating the data that users enter into your form, including the required attribute and pattern matching.

» Backend languages like PHP can process your contact form data and send an email to you with its contents.

| 12 |

Cool Tricks

Chapter Overview

» Using CSS enables creativity and efficiency.
» Use overlays to grab attention.
» Calculated values make for fast and flexible coding.

The HTML and CSS we've learned up until this point covers common elements and CSS selectors you'll use every day in web design. Since you've progressed to a more advanced stage in your learning, it's time to go over some exciting tricks and techniques that can add additional visual interest and flexibility to your work while allowing you to save coding time and enhance your users' experience.

CSS Gradients

A gradient is a transition between at least two colors. The change can be gradual or abrupt, but a gradient differs from a border between two colors in that there is a space where the colors mingle with one another. There are two primary types of gradients: linear and radial.

You may wonder why you would use CSS to create a gradient when one is so easily made in Photoshop, GIMP, or pretty much any graphics program. Until gradients were added to CSS, that's what web designers had to do.

There's nothing wrong with that approach, but adding an image to a page, especially an image that includes important text, puts an extra burden on the web designer: if you want to change the text, you must change the entire image. And with CSS, you can style an element with a gradient in a fraction of the time it takes to download even the smallest image.

Linear Gradients

A linear gradient is a transition of colors along a single line. In figure 106, we have a square div element with two colors, white and black.

LINEAR GRADIENT
TOP TO BOTTOM

fig. 106

Here's the CSS and HTML code:

12-01.css

CSS

```css
#linear-gradient {
    width: 500px;
    height: 150px;
    background-color: black;
    background-image: linear-gradient(black, white);
}

#linear-gradient p {
    text-align: center;
    vertical-align: middle;
    line-height: 150px;
    color: white;
}
```

HTML

```html
<div id="linear-gradient">
    <p>Linear Gradients</p>
</div>
```

The div with the "linear-gradient" id has several important definitions.

Even though we're using a gradient, we are still specifying a background color in case the browser is too old to support gradients. This is rare, as all browsers in modern use have this ability, but it's a good idea to add this for backward compatibility.

The actual gradient is created in the "background-image" attribute. This is done via the linear-gradient keyword. At a minimum, you must specify two colors. In this case, we've chosen black and white. But you can specify additional colors. For example, you could create a rainbow:

```
#linear-gradient {
    width: 500px;
    height: 150px;
    background-color: black;
    background-image: linear-gradient(red, orange, yellow,
green, blue, indigo, violet);
    }
```

We have embedded a paragraph of text inside the div. Because we want to style this paragraph differently, we specify the p selector after the id definition:

```
#linear-gradient p {
    text-align: center;
    vertical-align: middle;
    line-height: 150px;
    color: white;
    }
```

Only the paragraph(s) inside this specific div will be styled in this definition.

Additionally, we centered the text in the div, both horizontally and vertically, using the "vertical-align" and "text-align" attributes of the paragraph element. We specified the line-height to match the height of the containing div so that the vertical alignment would be centered based on the full size of the div, not just the pixel size of the paragraph element font. This technique perfectly centers the text in both dimensions.

Even though the linear gradient follows a straight line, it can go in different directions. We can specify this in our definition:

```
#linear-gradient {
    width: 500px;
    height: 150px;
    background-color: black;
    background-image: linear-gradient(to right, black,
white);
    }
```

In this case, we specify that the gradient should move from left to right, with black on the left and white on the right (figure 107).

fig. 107

LINEAR GRADIENT
LEFT TO RIGHT

If we specify "to left" instead, the white will be displayed on the left side and the black on the right side.

If we specify "to bottom right," the gradient will move from the top left corner to the bottom right corner. You can use "to bottom left," "to top right," or any other similar variant to create a diagonal linear gradient.

If you want finer control over the angle, you can specify it in degrees:

```
background-image: linear-gradient(45deg, black, white);
```

You can even provide a negative angle to reverse the direction:

```
background-image: linear-gradient(-45deg, black, white);
```

12-05.css
and
12-06.css

Use the web page starter template (`starter.html`) and experiment with the different gradient options to create your own interesting patterns. You will need to create a div element, then give it an id with a meaningful name. In CSS, assign it a width and height, and apply a gradient of your choice. Now is the perfect time to check out and experiment with the "Fun with Layering Gradients" link in your Digital Assets. Go to go.quickstartguides.com/htmlcss.

Radial Gradients

Radial gradients are a transition of colors in a circular or elliptical shape. In figure 108, we have a square div element with two colors, white and black, in a radial gradient.

fig. 108

Here is the CSS and HTML code:

CSS

12-07.css

```css
#radial-gradient {
    width: 300px;
    height: 300px;
    background-color: black;
    background-image: radial-gradient(black, white);
}
```

HTML

12-08.html

```html
<div id="radial-gradient"></div>
```

By default, the shape is circular, but we can create an ellipse by specifying it before the colors.

```css
background-image: radial-gradient(ellipse, black, white);
```

We can also specify the center point of the radial gradient:

12-09.html
and
12-10.css

```css
background-image: radial-gradient(circle at top right,
orange, yellow, black);
```

Using the same techniques as with the linear gradient, we can create a bigger transition with the yellow color and a smaller transition of the orange color, creating an even nicer gradient:

```css
background-image: radial-gradient(circle at top right,
orange 10%, yellow 30%, black);
```

12-11.css

Create the gradient as shown in the last two examples, and you'll be treated to a vibrant gradient that looks like the sun in space. Remember to name the div, assign it a width and height, and specify its name as an id in your CSS rule.

Sprites

A sprite is usually a small graphic that is used in a larger image. Video games use sprites to allow the computer to "paint" the screen with ready-made images from a palette of sprites. It may help to think of sprites like letters in an alphabet. Instead of painting the screen with letters, the game (or, in our case, the web browser) can display sprites from a larger palette.

CSS allows you to use one file, composed of multiple images, as separate graphics. This helps speed up your website by eliminating the need for multiple requests to the web server. Instead, all necessary graphics are downloaded in one image (figure 109).

GRAPHIC

fig. 109

An image composed of sprite images as used in the ClydeBank Coffee Shop

Sprites are often used for buttons, navigational icons, and other small images that are used frequently throughout a site.

CSS

SNIPPET

12-12.css

```css
#palette {
    width: 40px;
    height: 40px;
    padding: 0;
    border: none;
    background: url('/img/sprites.png') 0 0;
}
#guitar {
    width: 40px;
    height: 40px;
    padding: 0;
    border: none;
    background: url('/img/sprites.png') -40px 0;
}
```

```
#mask {
    width: 40px;
    height: 40px;
    padding: 0;
    border: none;
    background: url('/img/sprites.png') -80px 0;
}
```

HTML

SNIPPET

12-13.html

```
<form>
    <input id="palette" type="submit" name="smile"
value="">
    <input id="guitar" type="submit" name="envelope"
value="">
    <input id="mask" type="submit" name="tag" value="">
</form>
```

In this example, we have three buttons—a palette, a guitar, and a mask. They are wrapped in a form element and each is a submit button, so clicking on any of them will submit the form. Padding and borders have been set to 0 to hide the traditional submit button effect, and a background image, /img/ sprites.png, has been specified.

At first, you might wonder how this will work. Won't all three elements show the same background image? If we didn't specify the background-position-x and background-position-y attributes, it would, but by defining the width and height and specifying these x and y offsets, we can cycle through the image and display any part of it we wish.

Recall the shorthand method of specifying borders and padding from chapter 7. In this case, we used the same shorthand approach by appending these two values, first the x (left) value and second the y (top) value, to the end of the URL definition in the background attribute. This shorthand method leads to less typing and a smaller CSS file.

The first image is the palette, and thus the offset, defined by 0 0 in the palette example, tells the browser that it will find the image at left 0 and top 0. The second image, a guitar, is found at 40px left and 0 top. The mask image is found at 80px left and 0 top. Since every image is the same width, we simply add the width of an image to move from image to image (from left to right). When we use negative numbers for the y offset, we're moving the background to the left. Imagine the element as a window through which we view various parts of the background image that moves in accordance with our instructions.

You can also use multiple rows of images. If you do this, you must increment the top offset to match the row. For example, if we had a graphic with two rows of three images, and all were 40 pixels by 40 pixels, we would specify `url('/img/sprites.png') -80px -40px;` to show the third image on the second row.

It is not necessary to specify a unit (px, em, etc.) when specifying a zero width or height for this or any other position or size element in CSS.

SPRITES

By astounding coincidence, the owner of the ClydeBank Coffee Shop discovered that you recently learned about sprites. He wants you to use your newfound knowledge to convert the icons used throughout the site into `<span>` elements with various class names that point to the sprite in question, eliminating the need to load multiple images on each page and, in turn, hopefully speeding up the website.

If you haven't yet downloaded the ClydeBank Coffee Shop website, please do so from www.github.com/clydebankmedia/clydebank-coffee-shop.

In the images folder of the coffee shop website, you'll find a file called `sprite.png` that contains all of our icons and the ClydeBank logo. Create the necessary CSS additions so that the following `<span>` elements will display an inline representation of the image.

12-14.html

```
<span class="sprite-palette"></span>
<span class="sprite-guitar"></span>
<span class="sprite-mask"></span>
<span class="sprite-controller"></span>
<span class="sprite-mic"></span>
<span class="sprite-quill"></span>
<span class="sprite-cup"></span>
<span class="sprite-utensils"></span>
<span class="sprite-milk"></span>
```

The names I have assigned for the span classes in this exercise have the word *sprite* followed by a dash (`sprite-`) before the name of the icon. This technique is called namespacing (the process of creating namespaces). Namespaces are used to separate names in code to avoid name collisions with other existing (or future) additions to your code. For example, without this technique, naming a CSS class "milk" would work for now but would pose a problem if we later wanted to add a div with an id of milk.

Once you have created the classes in CSS to enable use of various parts of this collection of sprites, you will need to change the `<img>` elements in the HTML pages to use these `<span>` elements instead.

HINT: The icons in the sprite image are 40 px wide and 40 px tall.

Try this exercise on your own. If you run into problems, you can refer to the answer key in appendix V.

HINT: The CSS file, style.css, is in the CSS folder, and the sprite image is in the images folder. The two-dot shortcut (..) (see the "Images" section of chapter 5) will be useful here to instruct the browser to go up one directory before trying to check the images folder for sprite.png.

Transitions

You can add dynamic motion and effects to your HTML elements via CSS transitions. Transitions allow you to define an initial state, an end state, and how quickly the change between those states occurs. This basic form of animation is a bit too abstract to explain in words, so let's illustrate it with a practical example.

Say you have an image that you'd like to enlarge when the user hovers over it. To make this happen, you'll need to use an initial value and a pseudo-class variant, `:hover`, on the element with the image.

CSS

12-15.css

```
#car {
    width: 320px;
    height: 240px;
}
#car:hover {
    width: 640px;
```

```
        height: 480px;
        transition: width 2s, height 2s;
    }
```

12-16.html

HTML

```
<img id="car" src="images/car.jpg" alt="A car">
```

In this example, the hover size is twice as big as the normal size. Additionally, the transition attribute is assigned a two-second width and a two-second height transition time. The image will be resized when the user hovers with their mouse, and the transition will take two seconds. The time in seconds doesn't have to match—you can specify four seconds for height and two seconds for width if you like.

You can also transition just width (or just height):

12-17.css

```
#car {
    width: 320px;
    height: 240px;
}
#car:hover {
    width: 640px;
    transition: width 2s;
}
```

Notice that in this example the height for the hover pseudo-class was omitted. If it had been left in, the image would have instantaneously resized to the larger height and, over two seconds, resized to the new width, because no height transition time was specified.

You can add a delay on the transition so that the resize won't start for a certain number of seconds.

12-18.css

```
#car {
    width: 320px;
    height: 240px;
}
#car:hover {
    width: 640px;
    transition: width 2s;
    transition-delay: 1s;
}
```

By default, the resize is eased in, meaning it starts a bit slow, gets faster as it proceeds, then slows again as it ends. If this isn't what you want, you can change the behavior of the default "ease" value via the transition-timing-function attribute.

12-19.css

```
#car {
    width: 320px;
    height: 240px;
}
#car:hover {
    width: 640px;
    transition: width 2s;
    transition-timing-function: linear;
}
```

A linear behavior will eliminate the slow start and finish. You can also specify ease-in, ease-out, and ease-in-out to further modify this effect.

Transforms

You can animate elements with CSS transformations. Various attributes allow you to rotate, scale, and even move elements across the page. You can pair these effects with events, like :hover, to create a truly dynamic experience for your users.

There are many different CSS transforms, both two and three dimensional. We'll cover the most common ones here, but you can see them all in our "2D and 3D Transforms Index" found in your Digital Assets at clydebankmedia. com/htmlcss-assets.

Rotation

Recall our car example from the "Transitions" section. To demonstrate rotation, let's shift the car 45 degrees to the right.

CSS

12-20.css

```
#car {
    width: 320px;
    height: 240px;
    transform: rotate(45deg);
}
```

12-21.html

HTML

```
<img id="car" src="images/car.jpg" alt="A car">
```

To use this example on your local workspace, you'll need an image. It doesn't specifically have to be a car, but if you use a different file name, change the image source to match. After you save this to an HTML file, you'll see the car has been tilted. We can animate this with `:hover` as well. When you hover your mouse over the image, the car will rotate.

12-22.css

```
#car:hover {
    width: 320px;
    height: 240px;
    transform: rotate(45deg);
}
```

Scale

Scaling allows you to expand or contract an element based on a decimal value. Remember when we increased the size of the car from 320x240 to 640x480 in the beginning of this chapter? You may have noticed that we doubled the dimensions. It's important to keep the same aspect ratio, which is the proportion of the width and height, to avoid distorting an element (especially an image). Using the scale transform allows us to specify this multiplier for the width and height of an object.

12-23.css

```
#car:hover { transform: scale(2, 2); }
```

In this example, we have removed the expanded size and specified that when the user hovers over the car it will multiply the width and height times two. You can specify different values for each if you wish, and you can also use numbers smaller than 1, like `0.5, 0.5`, for example, to shrink the image's width and height by half.

Skew

To skew an element along both its *x* and *y* axes, you can use the `skewX`, `skewY`, or `skew` transforms. `skewX` and `skewY` allow you to alter the applicable axis, and skew takes both axes as values (figure 110).

12-24.html

HTML

```
<div id="warning">This element is a bit off its rocker!</div>
```

CSS

```css
#warning {
    width: 250px;
    height: 30px;
    background-color: gray;
    color: white;
    text-align: center;
    line-height: 30px;
    transform: skew(45deg, 30deg);
}
```

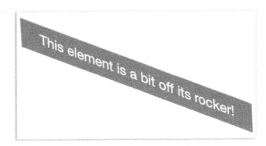

Note that in this example we could have specified the `skewX` and `skewY` separately, but using skew is easier if you are going to adjust both axes.

Overlay/Modal Without JavaScript

You have likely run across a website that darkens the view and forces you to click "OK" or something similar before you can proceed. This is called a modal overlay and is usually used to hide content behind a terms of service agreement or a newsletter registration. Modal interfaces, like an overlay, limit the user's input to a given set of options, creating a very effective technique for requesting your user's attention.

To construct an example of this technique, we'll use gradients to create the overlay.

CSS

```css
/*  */
.overlay{
    background: rgba(0,0,0, 0.8);
    position: fixed;
    top: 0;
    right: 0;
```

```
        bottom: 0;
        left: 0;
        display: none;
    }


    /* Checkbox */
    #onOff{
        position: fixed;
        clip: rect(0,0,0,0);
    }


    #onOff:checked ~ .overlay { display: block; }


    /* Buttons */
    .overlayButton{
        display: inline-block;
        margin-left: auto;
        margin-right: auto;
        background: steelblue;
        border-radius: 8px;
        padding: 10px;
        color: #fff;
        font-weight: bold;
        text-transform: uppercase;
        margin-left: 50%;
        margin-top: 40px;
        text-align: center;
    }
    .overlay .overlayButton { background-color: darkred; }


    /* Background and Fonts */


    body{
        font-family: sans-serif;
        background-color:#556;
    /* Set a linear gradient as the background image
*/    background-image: linear-gradient(30deg, #445 12%,
transparent 12.5%, transparent 87%, #445 87.5%, #445),
        linear-gradient(150deg, #445 12%, transparent 12.5%,
transparent 87%, #445 87.5%, #445),
```

```
        linear-gradient(30deg, #445 12%, transparent 12.5%,
transparent 87%, #445 87.5%, #445),
        linear-gradient(150deg, #445 12%, transparent 12.5%,
transparent 87%, #445 87.5%, #445),
        linear-gradient(60deg, #99a 25%, transparent 25.5%,
transparent 75%, #99a 75%, #99a),
        linear-gradient(60deg, #99a 25%, transparent 25.5%,
transparent 75%, #99a 75%, #99a);
        background-size:80px 140px;
        background-position: 0 0, 0 0, 40px 70px, 40px 70px, 0
0, 40px 70px;
}
```

HTML

```
<input id="onOff" type="checkbox">

<!-- Overlay -->
<label for="onOff" class="overlay">
    <label class="overlayButton" for="onOff">
      Overlay Off
    </label>
</label>

<!-- Button -->
<label class="overlayButton" for="onOff">
    Overlay On
</label>
```

NOTE

You'll notice that the class names are composed of two words without a space, with the first letter of the second word capitalized. This is camel case, as we introduced in the "Elements" section of chapter 4. When using longer words to describe classes and ids, it's good to use camel case or dashes between the words to make the names easier to read.

In this example, you can toggle the overlay with the button provided in the middle of the page. This provides interactive functionality without your having to use JavaScript, offering faster performance and helping to ensure that add-ons that block JavaScript won't interfere with the overlay.

Keyframe Animation

When web designers wanted to animate parts of their web pages, they used to turn to plugins like Adobe Flash™. Now it's possible to animate elements via CSS.

CSS animation is an in-depth topic, so we won't be able to go over every detail of it in this book. Regardless, we can meet most common animation needs with a discussion and example of keyframes and a few animation functions.

Animations are simply a series of images (frames) that, when displayed in rapid sequence, give the impression of seamless movement. Storing or rendering every frame (25 or more per second) can be taxing on the browser and bandwidth. Keyframes are frames that define a specific state of the animation, and the browser uses the properties in these keyframes to construct the animation between the keyframes. Keyframes can be defined for the beginning and end of the animation or for points in between. Since the duration of the animation is controlled separately, the keyframes are identified by percentage of the total animation (0%, 20%, 80%, 100%, etc.).

That's a technical explanation, so let's consider a real-life situation using our car example. Let's say we want to move the car image across the screen. If we had to construct an image of the car's position at each moment, it might take hundreds or even thousands of separate images to give the illusion of movement. A much simpler approach is to give the browser a "start" keyframe and an "end" keyframe and provide instructions on how to handle the rest.

CSS

12-28.css

```css
#car {
    width: 320px;
    height: 240px;
    position: relative;
    animation-name: zoom;
    animation-duration: 5s;
    animation-iteration-count: 2;
    animation-direction: alternate;
}

@keyframes zoom {
    from { left: 0px; }
    to { left: 500px; }
}
```

HTML

```
<img id="car" src="images/car.jpg" alt="A motorized
conveyance.">
```

In this example, the image of the car will move from the left to the right and back again, over a span of five seconds in each direction. The "from" and "to" states of the animation define starting and ending positions. In this case, we're using the left relative position, but you could use many other CSS attributes. We assign this keyframe definition with `animation-name`, and in the example, "zoom" after `@keyframes` defines the name of the set of keyframes we create within the brackets of that selector.

We specify the duration by setting `animation-duration` to five seconds. The animation is repeated twice; this is defined by `animation-interaction-count`. If you set animation-interaction-count to "infinite," then the animation will be repeated infinitely. And the animation is alternated (reversed) each time via `animation-direction`.

Another example can be created using the "percent complete" keyframe option. This works almost identically but allows us to track multiple properties animated at the same time for one element on the page. In this example, the CSS properties of the element remain the same, but adjustments are made to the keyframe animation.

CSS

```css
#car {
    width: 320px;
    height: 240px;
    position: relative;
    animation-name: zoom;
    animation-duration: 5s;
    animation-iteration-count: 2;
    animation-direction: alternate;
}

@keyframes zoom {
    0%{ left: 0px; }
    20% { transform:rotate(-45deg); }
    100%{ left: 500px; }
}
```

HTML

```
<img id="car" src="images/car.jpg" alt="A motorized
conveyance.">
```

In this example, the keyframes "from" and "to" were replaced with the percent equivalents, 0% and 100%, respectively. Also added is a 20% keyframe that changes the rotation of the car, leveraging the transform property we discussed earlier to rotate the car 45 degrees counterclockwise by the 20% mark of duration. The browser will start this rotation at 0% and return to the default of 0 degrees rotation by the time the animation is 100% complete. How is this better? The car does a wheelie! This same technique could be used if we needed an element to change color and then change back again, or perhaps have something move in a different axis, as if it was thrown. With the correct combination of properties you could "throw" a stick across the screen, changing the distance from the left and having the distance from the bottom increase and then peak at 50% before coming back down. You could even add a subtle rotation (as in the previous example).

One other piece of CSS magic that makes this animation work is `position: relative`. In this case, the left position is relative to the body element, but you could wrap this in a div and it would be relative to that. You can even run multiple animations at once with elements using keyframe definitions that are different from their containing elements. This advanced feature would allow you, for example, to animate the wheels of a moving car if the wheels were a div element within the moving car div. Relative positioning makes this possible by eliminating the need to specify (and thus keep track of) the exact pixel-perfect position of every element on the page.

Experiment with various values for the animation settings. You can also specify background colors and other CSS attributes like size, font, and even CSS transforms. Just for fun, grab a photo of a family member and animate them across the page. The opportunities for creativity with CSS keyframe animation are nearly limitless!

Calculated Values

So far, whenever we have coded an example with a specified size, we have used absolute values. For example, our car image is 320 pixels wide by 240 pixels high.

```css
#car {
    width: 320px;
    height: 240px;
}
```

CSS has a built-in function for calculating values on the fly. We could use this:

```css
#car {
    width: calc(300px + 20px);
    height: calc(200px + 40px);
}
```

The browser would add the values together as directed and use them for the width and height. The previous two examples will produce the same results. You can add (with +), subtract (with -), multiply (with *), or divide (with /).

You may wonder why someone would use the `calc()` function when they could simply specify the total value. If you're just adding pixels, there isn't much of an advantage. The true power of using calculated values is in the ability to compute *unlike* values.

Let's say you want a div to be not quite the width of the screen.

CSS

```css
#mydiv {
    width: calc(100% - 50px);
    background-color: black;
    color: silver;
}
```

HTML

```html
<div id="mydiv">I'm wide, but not too wide!</div>
```

Here, we told the browser to make the width 100% but then to subtract 50 pixels from that. The div will always be 80 pixels less than its container's size.

GRADIENTS

In chapter 8, our client had us give the ClydeBank Coffee Shop website a new look and feel. Unfortunately, they have grown tired of the color scheme we implemented and want a new, fresh look for the header.

They still like the sienna-colored header, so after some thought you decide to add a gradient to the header. You can start with `sienna` and work in the color from the menu, `saddlebrown`. The header is styled in the style.css file, so your work will focus there. Try to add the gradient on your own. If you get stuck, the solution is in appendix V.

KEYFRAME ANIMATION

Our client wants to show off work they have done in the coffee shop. They've shared a large image, named background.jpg, that captures the whole space. You will find background.jpg in the images folder of the ClydeBank Coffee Shop website.

Using keyframe animation, apply a "camera pan"-style effect to the `<main>` element by adjusting the `background-position` to move the image right and left. Since we only have one `<main>` element on the page, we can get away with applying the CSS animation to it. That said, you may want to consider assigning the `<main>` element an id and adding the CSS animation to it rather than redefining the element.

We want this animation to continue to move, but select an appropriate timing function to ensure smooth motion. You can test various durations to avoid a distracting background. Try this on your own first, but if you get stuck, a solution can be found in appendix V.

If your screen is larger than fifteen inches, the keyframe animation effect may be less pronounced (or not at all pronounced). But fear not—even if you have a huge screen, you can simply resize the window to experience the animation in all its glory! We'll teach you more about adjusting your website for various device sizes in the following chapter on media queries.

Chapter Recap

» Various CSS features can enliven otherwise static web content.

» Gradients allow for beautiful and expressive coloring of your web pages.

» Sprites allow a single image file to act as the source file for many images.

» Becoming proficient in keyframe animation and calculated values enables CSS coders to be flexible, creative, and efficient.

| 13 |
Media Queries

Chapter Overview
» Media queries adjust elements for various devices.
» Printers and screen readers use media queries.

Designing a web page that looks great on all devices can be quite a challenge. You have undoubtedly seen web pages that worked just fine on a laptop but were nearly impossible to use on a phone. Fortunately, responsive design provides a solution. ***Responsive design*** is a philosophy of using relative sizing, positioning, and media queries to make your page look good on all devices (figure 111).

UNRESPONSIVE DESIGN   **RESPONSIVE DESIGN**

fig. 111

The difference between a responsive site and an unresponsive site

So far, we've learned various techniques for addressing sizes in a relative fashion. You can use percentages for width and height to scale to any screen. But even for simple web pages, this relative position and sizing just isn't enough for every device. On certain screen sizes, some elements, like sidebars and navigation menus, look better hidden or stacked in a different order. Navigation menus and advertisements often look terrible when printed.

With media queries, we can assign different rules to various screen sizes. On a phone, we can collapse the top navigation menu into a small dropdown menu or move the sidebar to the bottom. On large screens, we can include a right sidebar or add additional screen elements that would never fit on smaller devices. And on printers or screen readers, we can omit difficult-to-represent elements and prioritize useful content.

Structure

There are two primary ways to introduce media queries on your web page. First, you can use the `<link>` tag to reference a CSS file for a specific device and/or size via the media attribute.

13-01.html

```
<link rel="stylesheet" media="screen and (max-width:
600px)" href="mobile.css">
<link rel="stylesheet" media="screen and (min-width:
600px)" href="style.css">
<link rel="stylesheet" media="print" href="print.css">
```

In this case, we have defined three CSS files—one for mobile, one for regular screens, and one to use when the user prints the web page.

We'll get into the specific syntax for the media attribute in a moment, but for now let's examine the alternative approach: the single-file CSS method. In this example, the main style sheet, often called style.css, handles all three definitions.

13-02.css

```
/* For small screens like phones */
@media only screen and (max-width: 1000px) {
    background-color: darkgray;
        color: white;
        font-size: 16px;
}
    /* There are, of course, more elements than color and
font size, but we are just using these two attributes for our
```

```
example */
   /* For larger tablets, laptops, and desktops */
   @media only screen and (min-width: 1000px) {
      background-color: darkgray;
         color: white;
         font-size: 12px;
   }
   /* For the printed page */
   @media print {
      background-color: white;
         color: black;
         font-size: 12px;
   }
```

In this example, all screens will have a dark gray background and white text. Smaller screens will have a larger font (16px) and larger screens will have a smaller font (12px). And the printed page will contain a white background and black text to avoid wasting ink.

Though we specified only colors and font sizes, you can use any valid CSS rule inside the `@media { }` block that you want to apply to that device or size.

The `min-width: 1000px` and `max-width: 1000px` keywords in the size definitions tell the browser to apply the rules for that query only on screens that are at least 1000 pixels wide and at most 1000 pixels wide, respectively. You can use any number of pixels for these definitions, but there are recommendations based on common screen sizes that we'll explore in the "Choosing Breakpoints" section in this chapter.

You may notice the "only" keyword used in the previous example. This makes the media query apply only to a certain device. If we didn't use it, our queries would also modify printer and screen reader devices.

On devices with screens that rotate (phones and tablets), we can assign a query to match a certain orientation.

13-03.css

```
   @media screen and (orientation: landscape) {
      /* CSS rules here apply to landscape mode (device on
its side) */
   }
   @media screen and (orientation: portrait) {
      /* CSS rules here apply to portrait mode (device
upright) */
   }
```

We can use this same technique to adjust our page, depending on the orientation selected during print setup. It's impossible to print in both orientations at once, so only one of these will be used.

```
@media print and (orientation: landscape) {
    /* CSS rules here apply to printing in landscape mode */
}
@media print and (orientation: portrait) {
    /* CSS rules here apply to printing in portrait mode */
}
```

Choosing Breakpoints

Device screen size varies wildly, but a general rule of thumb is that devices with widths *under* 1000 are phones or tablets, and screen sizes larger than that usually belong to laptops or desktops. There are exceptions to this rule, especially with high-resolution screens, but for optimum readability for your users, it's best to use mobile-style menus (that is, the "hamburger menu") for screens less than 1000 pixels in width (figure 112).

fig. 112

The hamburger menu

For a list of common device sizes, please reference Screen Sizes on Popular Devices found at go.quickstartguides.com/htmlcss.

Content Fit/Feel

You've likely been frustrated with a website not working exactly as intended on your mobile device. You don't want annoyed users, so always remember to give some thought to the types of devices your visitors are likely to use. Various third-party "web analytics" platforms will allow you to view data on which types of devices are being used to access your website.

Placing buttons or selectable elements too close together can present a usability challenge on phones. Since mobile users *tap* rather than *click*, objects must be spaced far enough apart so that a tap not precisely on center doesn't accidentally select something else on the page. This small area around selectable elements is known as a "tap target" and requires special consideration on touch screens. You can use additional padding on input boxes, buttons, and links in your lower-width media queries to provide a wider area for a user to tap.

As you can see, media queries enable a tremendous amount of customization and flexibility. Paired with relative sizing, carefully sized **breakpoints**, and comfortable tap targets, your website can look pixel-perfect on any device.

Google encourages websites to be "mobile friendly" (that is, responsive) and publishes their own guidelines on this topic. Those interested in search engine optimization and optimal user experience should review the Mobile Friendly guidelines at developers.google.com/search/mobile-sites.

Viewport Meta Tag

The viewing area of a web browser is called the viewport. Viewports vary with the size of the screen and, in the case of a desktop or laptop, the browser window. For the sake of brevity, we have omitted the viewport meta tag in most examples, but it should be used on all your web pages.

13-05.html

```
<meta name="viewport" content="width=device-width,
initial-scale=1.0">
```

In this default example, the width is set to the device width, and the scaling (zoom) is set to 1.0. Decimal numbers below 1 instruct the browser to zoom away from the page, or shrink, making content smaller but fitting more on the screen at once. Larger numbers will zoom in to the content.

Simulating Screen Sizes

Testing a web design can be challenging, especially considering the vast array of screen sizes and browsers. There's nothing like testing on the actual device, but when you don't have that luxury, browser development tools can help make quality assurance a breeze.

To activate the device toolbar in Chrome-based and Firefox web browsers, open the development tools with F12, then click on the device icon in the top right, as shown in figure 113.

fig. 113

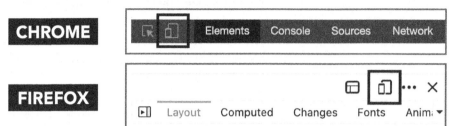

The toggle icon for the device toolbar in both Chrome and Firefox. (The design of this icon may change in future browser versions.)

The left-hand pane displaying the web page will shrink. This will display the responsive toolbar, allowing you to select from an array of devices and screen sizes (figure 114). The responsive toolbar is invaluable for testing media queries and page compatibility with various screen widths and heights.

fig. 114

The responsive toolbar and view in Chrome

GOING MOBILE

Our ClydeBank Coffee Shop website is looking better on the desktop but does not scale well at all on mobile devices. In this exercise, we're going to fix that. Making the website look good on every type of device would take a while, so we're going to focus on the most popular device: the modern cell phone. Of course, sizes vary considerably, so we'll focus on an average size range that should work well on most screens. For the purposes of this task, let's assume our device has a minimum screen width of 375 pixels and a maximum width of 725 pixels.

Using media queries added to the bottom of our style.css file, adjust the various elements on the coffee shop website to look good both on mobile and laptop/desktop screens. Solutions can vary slightly depending on the approach, but we want the navigation, front page elements, and both header and footer to look good on either device.

Try this on your own first, but if you get stuck, a solution can be found in appendix V.

Since this is the last of our coffee shop site-building exercises in the text, I wanted to give you the opportunity to go the extra mile with me. I've expanded on this design with some of my own special enhancements. Feel free to download the code and explore my version of the ClydeBank Coffee Shop site. All site files can be downloaded from our GitHub account. The main repository is called "David's Perfect Cup." Access it directly here: www.github.com/clydebankmedia/davids-perfect-cup.

Chapter Recap

» Your users will display your site on a wide variety of devices, so making your site responsive using media queries and relative sizing is essential for a good user experience.

» Media queries allow printed web pages and screen readers to ignore certain parts of the page to focus on the appropriate content for those devices.

| 14 |
Bootstrap

Chapter Overview
» Bootstrap is a popular HTML and CSS framework.
» Bootstrap is fully responsive by default.

For years, web designers have been struggling to keep up with continually evolving standards and browser capabilities. As additions were made to CSS standards, browsers used ugly hacks and incompatible methods of support to account for these upgrades. When mobile devices became commonplace and websites adapted to fit the needs of various screen sizes, CSS frameworks began to fill the void with a standard, responsive interface to ease development burdens.

In this chapter, we'll cover Bootstrap, an HTML and CSS framework that removes a lot of the time-consuming labor from designing responsive, modern websites. As of this publication, it is one of the most popular CSS frameworks in use. It was initially developed by designers at Twitter and was open-sourced in 2011 on GitHub. Bootstrap provides classes and design paradigms that free the developer from having to think too much about responsive design and instead allows them to focus on their content. In fact, with Bootstrap, it's possible to build a website that works great on all devices and screen sizes without writing a single media query.

Despite the popularity and usefulness of Bootstrap, we almost didn't include it in the book. It might seem strange to omit such a powerful tool from this text, but the reason is purely instructive. I didn't want my readers to have to rely on a third-party library for all their web design needs. Libraries and frameworks come and go, but HTML and CSS are here to stay. Teaching you the fundamentals of HTML and CSS gives you timeless knowledge that you can take to any framework, or use to create a website with no third-party software at all.

Furthermore, knowing the nuts and bolts of HTML and CSS arms you with skills that you could use to create your own library of code that you use to build websites. By the time you've finished reading this book, and with some experience, you could write a framework like Bootstrap yourself. Your commitment to mastering these fundamentals—and not being overly dependent on a specific framework or library—will secure your future as a web designer. Your repertoire of personal skills and tools will never be supplanted by the new framework that comes along.

For these reasons, we've waited to introduce this chapter until after you were given a chance to learn and develop some solid fundamental HTML and CSS skills. Nevertheless, don't let these words of caution stop you from using and enjoying excellent frameworks like Bootstrap. Even if you stick to pure HTML and CSS code, you can still incorporate shortcuts and ideas from other frameworks.

We'll be using Bootstrap version 4 in this book, but the techniques discussed here should apply, at least in large part, to future releases.

Installing Bootstrap

"Installing Bootstrap" is a bit of a misnomer, as there is nothing to install!

While you can download the CSS and JavaScript files that enable Bootstrap for your website, several ***CDNs (content delivery networks)*** host frameworks like Bootstrap for free. As of this writing, you can use these lines of code from StackPath:

14-01.html

Place in Head Element

```
<!-- Add Bootstrap stylesheet using Stackpath CDN -->
<link rel="stylesheet" href="https://stackpath.
bootstrapcdn.com/bootstrap/4.5.0/css/bootstrap.min.css">
```

14-02.html

Place Before Closing Body Element

```
<!-- Add jQuery, a JavaScript library used by Bootstrap -->
<script src="https://code.jquery.com/jquery-3.5.1.slim.min.
js"></script>
<!-- Add the Popper JavaScript library -->
<script src="https://cdn.jsdelivr.net/npm/popper.js@1.16.0/
dist/umd/popper.min.js"></script>
<!-- Add Bootstrap JavaScript code last so it can benefit
from the above script inclusions -->
<script src="https://stackpath.bootstrapcdn.com/
bootstrap/4.5.0/js/bootstrap.min.js"></script>
```

If you want to download the CSS and JavaScript files, visit www. getbootstrap.com/docs/4.5/getting-started/download and download the ZIP file with compiled CSS and JS. If you choose this method of installation, you'll need to reference the CSS and JavaScript files from your local site rather than using the URLs from a CDN like StackPath. Once the files are in your `css` and `js` folders, you can include them via `link` and `script` tags just like you would any other external asset.

If you use the CDN method of installation, your simple Bootstrap-enabled web page will look something like this example:

14-03.html

```html
<!doctype html>
<html lang="en">
    <head>
        <meta charset="utf-8">
        <meta name="viewport" content="width=device-width,
initial-scale=1, shrink-to-fit=no">
        <title>Example Bootstrap Page</title>
        <link rel="stylesheet" href="https://stackpath.
bootstrapcdn.com/bootstrap/4.5.0/css/bootstrap.min.css">
    </head>
    <body>

        <main role="main">

            <!-- Web Page Content Goes Here -->

        </main>

        <script src="https://code.jquery.com/jquery-3.5.1.slim.
min.js"></script>
        <script src="https://cdn.jsdelivr.net/npm/popper.
js@1.16.0/dist/umd/popper.min.js"></script>
        <script src="https://stackpath.bootstrapcdn.com/
bootstrap/4.5.0/js/bootstrap.min.js"></script>
    </body>
</html>
```

The necessary CSS and JavaScript is loaded at the beginning and end of the document, and the main element contains your website HTML code.

Layout Grid

Bootstrap uses a grid system that allows you to divide the page into rows and columns. Let's examine a simple demonstration and then dig into the mechanics of this incredibly easy and flexible page layout system.

The row/column layout functionality is simple to use and extremely useful.

14-04.html

```
<div class="container">
    <!-- Start a row -->
    <div class="row">
        <!-- Start a column -->
        <div class="col">
            <!-- Contents of column -->
            The first column
        </div>
        <!-- Start a second column -->
        <div class="col">
            The second column
        </div>
    </div>
</div>
```

fig. 115

| The first column. | The second column. |

Web browser display of the container, row, and column layout

In this example, a two-column layout is presented encased in a container and a horizontal row (figure 115). The columns will be automatically resized and, if needed, stacked vertically to adjust for the size of the screen. If we need to add a third column, it's as easy as adding another div (figure 116).

14-05.html

```
<div class="container">
    <div class="row">
        <div class="col">
            The first column
        </div>
        <div class="col">
            The second column
```

```
        </div>
        <div class="col">
            The third column
        </div>
    </div>
</div>
```

fig. 116

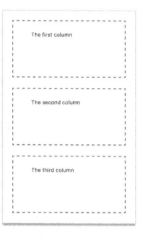

Columns will stack vertically when shown on a smaller screen.

You can add additional rows by specifying another div with the row class. Each row doesn't have to have the same number of columns. Here's an example with two columns on the first row and three columns on the second row (figure 117).

14-06.html

```
<!-- The text-center class is added to set text-align:
center; for all contents of the container div -->
    <div class="container text-center">
        <!-- This row has two columns -->
        <div class="row">
            <div class="col">
                The first column on the first row.
```

```
      </div>
      <div class="col">
        The second column on the first row.
      </div>
    </div>
    <!-- This row has three columns -->
    <div class="row">
      <div class="col">
        The first column on the second row.
      </div>
      <div class="col">
        The second column on the second row.
      </div>
      <div class="col">
        The third column on the second row.
      </div>
    </div>
  </div>
```

The `text-center` class, a built-in CSS class of Bootstrap, was added to the row/column container so that the text would be centered.

The first column on the first row.   The second column on the first row.
The first column on the second row.   The second column on the second row.   The third column on the second row.

Two Bootstrap rows, the first with two columns, the second with three

If you want to make one (or more) of the columns larger, you can specify a number from one to twelve after the column (figure 118).

14-07.html

```
<div class="container text-left">
  <div class="row">
    <div class="col-3">
      The first column.
    </div>
    <div class="col-9">
        The second column.
    </div>
  </div>
</div>
```

In this case, we've used the `text-left` class, another predefined CSS class in Bootstrap, to left-align the text so that you can more easily see the size of each column. The `col-3` column is much smaller than the `col-9` column. This technique is handy for creating side menus.

A Bootstrap row with two columns sized with numbers

I didn't just pick three and nine out of thin air. The two numbers, added together, are twelve—the number of units Bootstrap uses for the sizing of columns in its layout grid. If I had used two and ten, the left-hand column would be smaller, and the right-hand column would be larger. Specifying six and six would have resulted in two columns of the same size, but with two elements, the six could be omitted, because Bootstrap will size the columns evenly.

If you use three columns and wish to size them differently, you could use three, three, and six, for example, and you'd end up with a larger right-hand column with two equally sized smaller columns on the left. You can use any number of columns you wish (up to twelve) as long as the numbers after the `col-X` class specification add up to twelve. If you go over twelve, the CSS classes that Bootstrap uses for layout will produce unexpected results.

It's important to note that these twelve units don't correspond to a specific number of pixels. Instead, they are proportional sizes that Bootstrap uses to adjust the columns to fit within the available screen real estate of any given device. Columns will be displayed horizontally in a row unless the screen size is too small, in which case it shifts the columns to a vertical display. A tablet or phone might show the columns horizontally when in *landscape mode* (oriented for a wider display), then stack them vertically when changed to portrait (oriented for a taller display).

Bootstrap's breakpoints allow us to specify at what screen size column classes are activated. The default breakpoint for extra-small screens for the `col` class is 576 pixels, below which we receive a single-column layout. But we can adjust this by using the various column breakpoints.

```
<div class="container">
   <div class="row">
      <div class="col-sm-3">
         The first column
   </div>
   <div class="col-sm-9">
     The second column
      </div>
   </div>
</div>
```

In this example, we specify `col-sm-3` and `col-sm-9` as the column classes. These will function identically to `col-3` and `col-9`, respectively, except the two-column layout will only activate once we reach a "small" screen width of 576 pixels or more. If we use `col-md-3` and `col-md-9`, the two-column layout activates at Bootstrap's "medium" screen size of 720 pixels.

There are some cases when we would wish to change the columns specified at different screen sizes. Perhaps one column of content has an image we want to feature, and the other has some additional information about that image. In this case we can specify multiple column classes.

```
<div class="container">
   <div class="row">
      <div class="col-sm-6 col-md-9 col-lg-10">
         Image
      </div>
      <div class="col-sm-6 col-md-3 col-lg-2">
         Image Data
      </div>
   </div>
</div>
```

In this example, the left column receives six columns starting at the small screen size (576 pixels), nine at medium (768 pixels), and ten when at large or above (992 pixels). This enables a flexible layout similar to what we can achieve with custom media queries but without needing to create these ourselves. Media queries are, of course, used in the background by Bootstrap to enable this functionality.

If you don't want to specify a size, you can simply use the `col` and `col-X` (where X is a number from 1 to 12) classes, and Bootstrap will try to size things automatically. In all cases, a gutter width of fifteen pixels will be applied to the left and right sides of a column to provide padding. This ensures that columns aren't jammed beside one another. If you want to remove gutters, simply add the `no-gutters` style to the column, row, or container in question.

fig. 119

	MAX CONTAINER WIDTH	CLASS PREFIX	OTHER
EXTRA SMALL <576px	None (auto)	`.col-`	GUTTER WIDTH: 30 px (15px on each side of column) ———— NUMBER OF COLUMNS: 12
SMALL ≥576px	540px	`.col-sm-`	
MEDIUM ≥768px	720px	`.col-md-`	
LARGE ≥992px	960px	`.col-lg-`	
EXTRA LARGE ≥1200px	1140px	`.col-xl-`	

Bootstrap layout grid column classes

Color Styles

Bootstrap comes with a variety of color styles for text, buttons, borders, and other components. These styles apply to both foreground and background colors and are handy for adding a bit of color to user interface elements. These color schemes are technically a "utility," which we'll discuss later in this chapter, but since color schemes can be used to style nearly anything in Bootstrap, I wanted to cover them here first.

The name of a color class is constructed from the name of the Bootstrap component, like text, buttons, alerts, etc., and the name of the style, with a separating dash. For example, if you wanted to use the `primary` color scheme on a button, it would be called `btn-primary`. The `success` style text would be called `text-success` (figure 120).

You aren't limited to these colors with Bootstrap, but each color scheme has been specifically designed to work with the components contained in the framework. Just like anything with HTML, you can recolor one, all, or certain parts of an element with CSS.

COLOR SCHEME	BACKGROUND	FOREGROUND	USE CASE
Primary	Blue	White	Brings attention to primary elements. Default buttons are often styled with the btn-primary class.
Secondary	Gray	White	Often used to visually deemphasize elements.
Success	Green	White	Denotes a successful operation. Commonly used with alerts via the alert-success class.
Danger	Red	White	Indicates something failed or is of great importance. Commonly used with alerts via the alert-danger class.
Warning	Yellow	Black	Warns the user about a potential issue.
Info	Cyan	White	Informs the user.
Light	Light Gray	Dark Gray	Provides a pleasing, softer palette for general information.
Dark	Dark Gray	Near White	Often used to provide a "dark" theme to an element.
White	White	Black	Provides a default color scheme.

Bootstrap color schemes

fig. 120

Components

Bootstrap also offers components that are easy to use and come with full device flexibility right out of the box. In this section, we will go over the most frequently used components.

Keep in mind that nearly all components in Bootstrap can be themed with the color styles discussed in the "Color Styles" section of this chapter.

Alerts

You can use the alert feature to display simple boxed messages on top of your site. You've undoubtedly seen these kinds of messages alerting you to a particular status message or important announcement.

14-10.html

```
<div class="alert alert-warning" role="alert">
    This is a warning! Please pay attention to it.
</div>
```

There are a wide variety of colors and styles—too many to list here. One commonly used alternative to the warning alert is the success alert:

14-11.html

```
<div class="alert alert-success" role="alert">
    You're learning about Bootstrap. Great job!
</div>
```

As you can see, they are both nicely styled and are sure to grab the user's attention (figure 121).

fig. 121

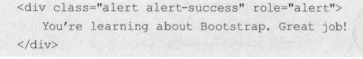

A warning alert and a success alert in Bootstrap

The warning alert has a yellow background, and the success alert has a green background.

Badges

A badge is a small bit of text that usually sits to the top right of text or an icon. Badges create a focal point for the user's attention. The number of unread messages in your phone's text messaging app is an excellent example of this concept.

To use a badge, add the `badge` class in a span, like this:

```
<h4>Inbox <span class="badge badge-danger">4</span></h4>
```

I selected `badge-danger` because I wanted white text against a red background, but you can use any of the Bootstrap color schemes. A badge can be a number or text (figure 122).

A badge used within an H4 tag. In this example, the badge will render with white text on a red background.

As you know, your email inbox is capable of having more or less than four items in it. Badge labels can be dynamically updated when JavaScript, or a backend language like PHP, makes changes. JavaScript and backend languages can change anything on the page, including the number in the badge.

Buttons

Buttons are usually created with the input element with the type attribute set to "submit." But in HTML5, you can use the button element to create a button that can be used outside a form. This is especially handy when invoking JavaScript functions (figure 123).

A primary-styled Bootstrap button

```
<button type="button" class="btn btn-primary">Click Me!</button>
```

The button can also be used as a submit button for a form.

```
<button type="submit" class="btn btn-primary">Submit</button>
```

You can style links as buttons, producing an element that looks identical to figure 123 but serves as a regular link that takes the user to another page when clicked.

```
<a href="contact.html" class="btn btn-primary">Contact</a>
```

If you want a smaller button, use the `btn-sm` class; larger buttons can be created with the `btn-lg` class (figure 124).

```
<button type="submit" class="btn btn-sm btn-
primary">Small Submit</button>
<br>
<br>
<button type="submit" class="btn btn-lg btn-primary">Big
Submit</button>
```

A `btn-sm` and a `btn-lg` button

You can create an outline button—that is, a button with no background color and only a border—with the `btn-outline` class (figure 125).

```
<button type="submit" class="btn btn-outline-
primary">Submit</button>
```

A `btn-outline` button styled with the primary color scheme

Cards

A Bootstrap card is a flexible container that can serve in a wide variety of roles. In its simplest form, a card is merely a box around an element—usually text and image (figure 126).

```
<!-- Start the card and apply the text-center class to
center everything in this card -->
  <div class="card text-center">
    <!-- Start the card body -->
    <div class="card-body">
      <p>This is a very simple card.</p>
    </div>
  </div>
```

This is a very simple card.

A simple example of the card component

In this example, the `text-center` class is added to the card div, ensuring that any elements, including the paragraph element, are centered. This isn't required but creates a pleasing appearance.

A card can also serve as an interesting page element, like this card featuring an ad for employment (figure 127).

```
<div class="card">
    <!-- Add the employee image outside the card-body so
it isn't affected by the padding and margins it adds. -->
    <img src="/images/next-employee.jpg" class="card-img-
top" alt="Our Next Employee">
    <!-- Start the card-body -->
    <div class="card-body">
      <h5 class="card-title">Our Next Employee</h5>
```

```
        <p class="card-text">Do you have what it takes to
work at the ClydeBank Coffee Shop?</p>
        <a href="#" class="btn btn-primary">Apply Today!</a>
    </div>
</div>
```

fig. 127

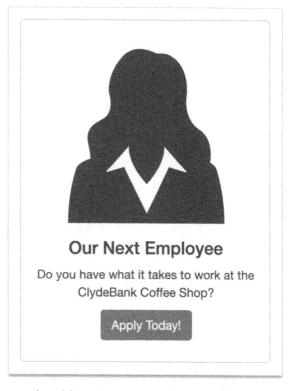

A card featuring an image, title, text, and button

This elaborate example showcases the various elements that are often contained in a card. Let's examine each part in detail. The div styled by the `card-body` class serves as the container for the content of the card. In our example, the image `next-employee.jpg` is loaded outside the card body. This way, the image is visually set apart from the rest of the content within the card. Were we to enclose the image inside the `card-body`, it would have more padding.

The `card-title` class is usually paired with an `<h>` tag and serves to highlight the title of the card. The `card-text` class is typically applied to a `<p>` tag. Call-to-action buttons (in this case, the "Apply Today!" button), exist outside the `card-text` but are within the `card-body`.

You aren't limited to these classes. Cards can contain other elements or even other Bootstrap components.

Carousel

You've undoubtedly seen slideshows of images decorating web pages you've visited. Before Bootstrap, web designers frequently used third-party JavaScript and CSS slideshow libraries or manually coded solutions to fit their site. Fortunately, Bootstrap includes a slideshow carousel that is simple to use and works great on all devices.

Let's say we want to add a slideshow featuring various blends of coffee. Here's an example:

SNIPPET

14-20.html

```
<div id="featured-blends" class="carousel slide" data-
ride="carousel">
    <div class="carousel-inner">
        <!-- Since this div is given the active class, it
will be shown by default -->
        <div class="carousel-item active">
            <img src="/images/columbian.jpg" class="d-block
w-100" alt="Columbian Blend">
        </div>
        <div class="carousel-item">
            <img src="/images/arabica.jpg" class="d-block
w-100" alt="Arabica Blend">
        </div>
        <div class="carousel-item">
            <img src="/images/robusta.jpg" class="d-block
w-100" alt="Robusta Blend">
        </div>
    </div>
</div>
```

Using this code, the browser will display a beautiful slideshow of coffee blends. The first slide shown is given the `active` class. Carousel components must have a unique id (in this case, `featured-blends`).

By default, the images will cycle every five seconds. You can change this by adding the `data-interval="X"` attribute to the carousel div (changing X to the number of seconds for the desired delay, multiplied by 1000, since the value is specified in milliseconds).

If you want "previous" and "next" controls, it's easy to add them via links styled with the `carousel-control-prev` and `carousel-control-next` classes.

14-21.html

```html
<!-- In this example, set data-interval to 5000 (5 seconds,
or 5000 milliseconds) to specify the time between slide
changes -->
    <div id="featured-blends-controls" class="carousel slide"
data-ride="carousel" data-interval="5000">
        <div class="carousel-inner">
            <div class="carousel-item active">
                <img src="/images/columbian.jpg" class="d-block
w-100" alt="Columbian Blend">
            </div>
            <div class="carousel-item">
                <img src="/images/arabica.jpg" class="d-block
w-100" alt="Arabica Blend">
            </div>
            <div class="carousel-item">
                <img src="/images/robusta.jpg" class="d-block
w-100" alt="Robusta Blend">
            </div>
        </div>
        <!-- Within the carousel, show the controls. Bootstrap
positions these automatically by setting the location
relative to the containing div--the carousel container. -->
        <a class="carousel-control-prev" href="#featured-
blends-controls" role="button" data-slide="prev">
            <span class="carousel-control-prev-icon" aria-
hidden="true"></span>
            <span class="sr-only">Previous</span>
        </a>
        <a class="carousel-control-next" href="#featured-
blends-controls" role="button" data-slide="next">
            <span class="carousel-control-next-icon" aria-
hidden="true"></span>
            <span class="sr-only">Next</span>
        </a>
</div>
```

Collapse

The collapse component provides a simple way to show and hide other elements. The JavaScript that makes this possible is contained within the Bootstrap framework, leaving you to focus on the HTML. Collapsed content is usually shown or hidden using a link or button element.

14-22.html

```html
<p>
    <a class="btn btn-primary" data-toggle="collapse"
href="#Robusta" role="button" aria-expanded="false" aria-
controls="Robusta">
        Robusta
    </a>
</p>
<!-- This div is hidden by default but becomes visible
when the above link (styled as a button) is clicked -->
<div class="collapse" id="Robusta">
    <div class="card card-body">
        Robusta has twice the caffeine content of Arabica
but a less-refined taste. It is usually used for instant
coffee.
    </div>
</div>
```

fig. 128

The collapse component is applied to a button and is used to toggle the display of a card.

In our example, we have a link styled with the `btn` class (button) to convert it into a button. The `data-toggle` attribute of the link is set to collapse, and the `href="#Robusta"` attribute is set to the id of the card div containing our hidden content. When the page is loaded, the content is initially hidden, but upon clicking the button link, the card is displayed. This can be toggled by clicking the button again (figure 127).

The hidden content can be anything—it doesn't have to be a card. This technique is extremely useful for hiding not-often-needed information and for providing interesting user interaction on the page.

Jumbotron

The jumbotron is a simple Bootstrap component that displays a large notice to the user. It is similar to a card but contains options for an attention-grabbing title and lead text that is hard to miss. The container `jumbotron` class, when paired with a `container`, an `h1` tag (usually styled with the Bootstrap utility class `display-4` for a larger size), and a paragraph tag styled with `lead`, are all it takes to display a convincing message on your page (figure 129).

14-23.html

```html
<div class="jumbotron">
    <div class="container">
        <h1 class="display-4">The Jumbotron</h1>
        <p class="lead">Text here is sure to be noticed.</p>
    </div>
</div>
```

fig. 129

The jumbotron—a big sign your visitors won't miss

Lists

You're already familiar with the `ul` (unordered list) and `ol` (ordered list) elements that we covered in chapter 5. Bootstrap's list component enhances these elements with a pleasing style and additional functionality.

Here's a simple example of the list component in action (figure 130):

14-24.html

```
<ul class="list-group">
    <li class="list-group-item">First Item</li>
    <li class="list-group-item">Second Item</li>
    <li class="list-group-item">Third Item</li>
</ul>
```

fig. 130

A basic list component example

In this case, the list is made more attractive than the one in figure 46 in chapter 5. Now, let's highlight one of the items (figure 130).

14-25.html

```
<ul class="list-group">
    <!-- This will be styled differently as it has the active
class -->
    <li class="list-group-item active">First Item</li>
    <li class="list-group-item">Second Item</li>
    <li class="list-group-item">Third Item</li>
</ul>
```

fig. 131

A list component example with an active item

Swapping the `active` class with the `disabled` class will fade the list item per the selected Bootstrap color theme, so users know that item is no longer available.

If you want a horizontal menu, add the `list-group-horizontal` class (figure 132).

```
<ul class="list-group list-group-horizontal">
    <li class="list-group-item active">First Item</li>
    <li class="list-group-item">Second Item</li>
    <li class="list-group-item">Third Item</li>
</ul>
```

A list component example with an active item displayed horizontally

Modals

A modal dialog in computing is a window or box that asks the user a question and cannot be dismissed without an answer. Bootstrap offers the modal component that allows you to construct a pop-up window that asks a user a question or shows a critical alert.

Modal components are broken into two main parts—the trigger and the modal itself. The trigger is usually a button or a button-styled link that, when clicked, displays the modal interface (figure 133). You might see HTML attributes here we haven't covered yet, but we'll explain them after the code sample.

```
<!-- Button Trigger -->
<button type="button" class="btn btn-primary" data-
toggle="modal" data-target="#modal-example">Launch Modal
Demonstration</button>

<!-- Modal Dialog -->
<div class="modal fade" id="modal-example" tabindex="-1"
role="dialog" aria-labelledby="modal-example-label" aria-
hidden="true">
    <div class="modal-dialog">
        <div class="modal-content">
            <div class="modal-header">
                <h5 class="modal-title" id="modal-example-
label">This Page Contains Classified Information</h5>
            </div>
```

```
        <div class="modal-body">
            <p>You must have a super secret clearance to
access this page.</p>
        </div>
        <!-- Here the buttons are placed in the modal-
footer -->
        <div class="modal-footer">
            <!-- A button-styled link is used here since it
goes to another site. -->
            <a href="https://www.google.com/" class="btn btn-
secondary" >I Was Just Leaving</a>
            <!-- This button dismisses the modal dialog -->
            <button type="button" class="btn btn-primary"
data-dismiss="modal">I Understand</button>
        </div>
    </div>
  </div>
</div>
```

fig. 133

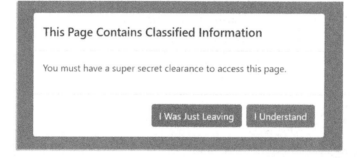

The modal dialog box that appears when the button is clicked

The trigger portion of the modal is straightforward. The `data-toggle="modal"` and `data-target="#modal-example"` attributes of the button describe the action and target element id to activate when clicked.

The dialog itself contains several key parts: the containing class that is given the `modal` class, and the `modal-dialog` class that contains the `modal-content`, `modal-header`, `modal-title`, `modal-body`, and `modal-footer`. The `modal-header` serves as a container for the `modal-title`, often filled with heading text. The `modal-body` contains the descriptive text (or other elements) in the modal, and the `modal-footer` contains the action elements—in this case, a link styled with the `btn` class that sends the user to Google and a button with the `data-dismiss="modal"` attribute. When you set `data-dismiss` to modal, Bootstrap knows that this button, when clicked, should close the modal dialog box.

The `tabindex` attribute tells the browser the order in which to focus (or highlight) the element when the user presses TAB on the keyboard. Setting this to -1 prevents the element (in this case, our modal div) from being reachable via the pressing of TAB. This is to stop our modal dialog from accidentally being triggered before it's requested.

In our example, the `fade` class is applied to the primary modal container to instruct Bootstrap to fade the modal into view. Without this, the dialog box instantly appears. In either case, the background behind the dialog is overlaid with a semi-transparent div to partially obscure the contents.

Navigation

Navigation menus are a critical part of your website. Without them, your visitors couldn't navigate to other pages. While navigation has always been important on the web, mobile devices have made responsive design a requirement for browsing multipage websites on cell phones and tablets.

As with most challenges in responsive design, Bootstrap has a ready-made solution using predefined classes and the semantic `nav` element. On laptops and desktop computers, the menu will appear as a long horizontal bar. On smaller screens, a *hamburger menu*, a button styled with a three-line vertically stacked icon that opens a menu, is presented on the right-hand side of the navigation bar (figure 136). When the visitor clicks the hamburger, a menu appears with the navigation links (figure 137).

The best way to explain the multiple parts of a navigation bar is to show an example. You'll see that the `nav` component uses an assortment of HTML elements to present navigation. We'll dive into the sample first, then show some screenshots, and finish with an explanation of the code.

Even though this example is related to the ClydeBank Coffee Shop website, it will not work on the original website because that site doesn't have Bootstrap. You can add Bootstrap to the coffee shop website if you wish and then use this navigation bar or any other component from Bootstrap.

```
<nav class="navbar navbar-expand-lg navbar-dark bg-dark">
    <!-- The navbar-brand class defines the title (or logo) of
the navigation bar -->
    <a class="navbar-brand" href="#">ClydeBank Coffee Shop</a>
    <!-- This button is transformed (when needed) into the
"hamburger" icon for mobile devices -->
    <button class="navbar-toggler" type="button" data-
toggle="collapse" data-target="#MainNavbar" aria-
controls="MainNavbar" aria-expanded="false" aria-
label="Toggle Navigation">
        <span class="navbar-toggler-icon"></span>
    </button>
    <div class="collapse navbar-collapse" id="MainNavbar">
        <ul class="navbar-nav mr-auto">
            <!-- Since this is styled "active", it will be
displayed with white text, indicating this is the page we
are on. -->
            <li class="nav-item active">
                <a class="nav-link" href="#">Home <span
class="sr-only">(current)</span></a>
            </li>
            <li class="nav-item">
                <a class="nav-link" href="#">About</a>
            </li>
            <!-- The dropdown class tells Bootstrap that this
menu item will trigger a dropdown menu. The dropdown menu
to expand has the id of navbarDropdown. -->
            <li class="nav-item dropdown">
                <a class="nav-link dropdown-toggle" href="#"
id="navbarDropdown" role="button" data-toggle="dropdown"
aria-haspopup="true" aria-expanded="false">
                Events
                </a>
                <!-- This is the dropdown menu itself, described
by navbarDropDown. Bootstrap ties these two together so that
this div is expanded when the user clicks the appropriate
menu item. -->
                <div class="dropdown-menu" aria-
labelledby="navbarDropdown">
                    <a class="dropdown-item" href="#">Music</a>
                    <a class="dropdown-item" href="#">Comedians</a>
```

```
              <!-- Place a line between Comedians and
Exhibits. This is similar to an hr element -->
              <div class="dropdown-divider"></div>
              <a class="dropdown-item" href="#">Exhibits</a>
              </div>
          </li>
          <li class="nav-item">
              <a class="nav-link" href="#" tabindex="-
1">Contact</a>
          </li>
      </ul>
  </div>
</nav>
```

fig. 134

The Bootstrap navigation bar in desktop/laptop mode

fig. 135

The Bootstrap navigation bar in desktop/laptop mode after the events menu is opened

fig. 136

The Bootstrap navigation bar in mobile mode

fig. 137

The Bootstrap navigation bar in mobile mode after the hamburger menu is clicked

The nav semantic element contains the navigation menu. In this example, we have styled it with the `navbar`, `navbar-expand-lg`, `navbar-dark`, and `bg-dark` classes. The `navbar` class tells Bootstrap to style the navigation bar, while the other three classes define the size and color scheme. The div styled with `navbar-brand` that contains the text "ClydeBank Coffee Shop" tells Bootstrap to enlarge the font and make this text the left-most and the featured item in the bar. Web designers usually place the name of the company in this location.

The button styled with `navbar-toggler` becomes the hamburger menu icon used to collapse and expand the menu in mobile mode. If the `data-target` attribute matches the id of the `navbar-collapse` div, Bootstrap will take care of the JavaScript necessary to facilitate the animation.

The menu itself is essentially an unordered list (`ul`) styled with the `navbar-nav` class. This class transforms the list into a horizontally oriented list that was hinted at in chapter 5. Each list item (`li`) styled with the `nav-item` class is a menu item. The menu item given the `active` class is styled with a more prominent font color.

A list item styled with the `dropdown` class creates a dropdown menu. This functionality is extremely useful for creating nested menus for sites with complex page structures. A link (`<a>`) styled with both `nav-link` and `dropdown-toggle` becomes the menu item that visitors can click to expand the menu, and a new div contained within this list, styled with `dropdown-menu`, presents a submenu to the user. Links given the `dropdown-item` class become new menu items. A divider is placed in the example's dropdown menu with a div using the `dropdown-divider` class.

Though the navigation component may seem complicated, it follows a logical, nested structure and makes creating responsive menus a snap.

Pagination

In addition to site navigation bars, Bootstrap can restyle the `nav` element to present a pagination menu to your users. This is useful if you have a website with exceedingly long content that you wish to split over several pages (figure 138).

```
<nav aria-label="Page Navigation">
    <ul class="pagination">
        <li class="page-item"><a class="page-link"
href="#">Prev</a></li>
        <li class="page-item"><a class="page-link" href="#">1</
a></li>
        <li class="page-item"><a class="page-link" href="#">2</
a></li>
        <li class="page-item"><a class="page-link" href="#">3</
a></li>
        <li class="page-item"><a class="page-link"
href="#">Next</a></li>
    </ul>
</nav>
```

The Bootstrap pagination component

In this example, the nav element contains an unordered list (ul) that is styled with the pagination class. The list items (li) in the unordered list have the page-item class, and links inside the list items have the page-link class. Though the href attribute is set to #, you can change the links to match other web pages or on-page page anchor target ids (discussed in chapter 5).

Progress Bars

Progress bars are most often used in complex forms or reports. Bootstrap makes it easy to create an attractive progress bar with two simple divs.

To demonstrate, we've assembled four bars of varying states of progress.

```
<div class="progress">
    <div class="progress-bar" role="progressbar" style="width:
25%;" aria-valuenow="25" aria-valuemin="0" aria-
valuemax="100">25%</div>
</div>
<br>
```

```
<div class="progress">
  <div class="progress-bar" role="progressbar" style="width:
50%;" aria-valuenow="50" aria-valuemin="0" aria-
valuemax="100">50%</div>
</div>
<br>
<div class="progress">
  <div class="progress-bar" role="progressbar" style="width:
75%;" aria-valuenow="75" aria-valuemin="0" aria-
valuemax="100">75%</div>
</div>
<br>
<div class="progress">
 <div class="progress-bar" role="progressbar" style="width:
100%;" aria-valuenow="100" aria-valuemin="0" aria-
valuemax="100">100%</div>
</div>
```

fig. 139

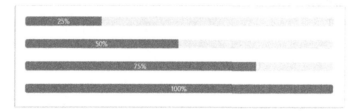

Various scroll bar components

Tables

Remember our sales figures table example from chapter 10? Let's let
Bootstrap make it more appealing by adding the `table` class to the table.

14-31.html

```
<table class="table">
    <tr>
        <th>Year</th>
        <th>Shirts</th>
        <th>Shoes</th>
        <th>Pants</th>
    </tr>
    <tr>
        <td>2017</td>
        <td>$420,392</td>
```

```
            <td>$18,304</td>
            <td>$34,912</td>
        </tr>
        <tr>
            <td>2018</td>
            <td>$480,221</td>
            <td>$17,952</td>
            <td>$36,112</td>
        </tr>
        <tr>
            <td>2019</td>
            <td>$491,919</td>
            <td>$16,844</td>
            <td>$46,924</td>
        </tr>
        <tr>
            <td>2020</td>
            <td>$501,029</td>
            <td>$15,124</td>
            <td>$39,947</td>
        </tr>
</table>
```

Bootstrap decorated our tabular display with comfortably spaced rows, a well-designed header, and an overall appealing style. As a bonus, the table is now responsive—looking great on all devices (figure 140).

fig. 140

Year	Shirts	Shoes	Pants
2017	$420,392	$18,304	$34,912
2018	$480,221	$17,952	$36,112
2019	$491,919	$16,844	$46,924
2020	$501,029	$15,124	$39,947

The sales figure table from chapter 10 styled with the `table` class

Utilities

Bootstrap offers "helper" CSS classes that expand functionality to both Bootstrap and non-Bootstrap components on your web page. These can be very helpful in page layout and formatting.

As an added benefit, these helper utilities save keystrokes. As we go over these classes, try to recall how you would use manual CSS to accomplish the same sort of style.

Borders

To add a border to an element, use the border class.

14-32.html

```
<div class="border"></div>
<div class="border-top"></div>
<div class="border-right"></div>
<div class="border-bottom"></div>
<div class="border-left"></div>
```

The border class will add a full border around the element. The top, right, bottom, and left variations will add a border only on the applicable portion of the element. By default, a faint-gray border is drawn, but you can change the color by using one of Bootstrap's color schemes.

14-33.html

```
<div class="border border-primary"></div>
```

This div would be surrounded by Bootstrap "primary" blue borders.

You can give an element a rounded border by including the rounded class. A subtle variation of this, the rounded-circle class, is most attractive on images—especially portraits (figure 141).

fig. 141

An img element with the rounded-circle class

```
        <img src="/images/john.jpg alt="Our CEO, John!"
. class="rounded-circle"></div>
```

14-34.html

Clearfix

You may remember the clearfix technique from "Floating Elements" in chapter 9. Bootstrap makes using clearfix a breeze.

```
<div class="clearfix"></div>
```

14-35.html

Float

Floating divs, as discussed in chapter 9, is simple with Bootstrap. Simply apply the float-left, float-right, or float-none CSS class, and Bootstrap will handle the rest.

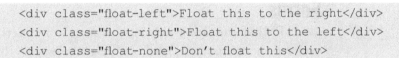

```
<div class="float-left">Float this to the right</div>
<div class="float-right">Float this to the left</div>
<div class="float-none">Don't float this</div>
```

14-36.html

Sizing

Bootstrap offers a system of helpers for defining the width of a div. The width of an element, when specified in a percentage, is relative to its containing element. That containing element may be the body tag or a div nested among other elements.

Using the width selector is easy, but Bootstrap makes it even simpler by providing a shortcut class.

```
<div class="w-25">This div will be set to width: 25%</div>
<div class="w-50">This div will be set to width: 50%</div>
<div class="w-75">This div will be set to width: 75%</div>
<div class="w-100">This div will be set to width: 100%</div>
```

14-37.html

Height is also defined by simple helper classes.

```
<div class="h-25">This div will be set to height: 25%</div>
<div class="h-50">This div will be set to height: 50%</div>
<div class="h-75">This div will be set to height: 75%</div>
<div class="h-100">This div will be set to height: 100%</div>
```

14-38.html

14-39.html

You can set `max-width` and `max-height` with ease.

```
<div class="mh-25">This div will be set to max-height: 25%</div>
<div class="mw-50">This div will be set to max-width: 50%</div>
```

Overflow

In chapter 9, we discussed the overflow CSS selector, which allows you to set an overflow policy for an element. Overflow occurs when the content won't fit inside its container. Bootstrap provides two handy CSS classes that save some typing.

14-40.html

```
<div class="overflow-auto"></div>
<div class="overflow-hidden"></div>
```

Forms

HTML forms are a website's gateway to its users. In chapter 11, we explored the form, input, label, and related elements that enable web pages to collect and process visitor data. You may recall a suggested exercise at the end of that chapter to style the HTML form elements with CSS. If you did this exercise, you might have noticed how challenging it can be to acquire consistent, good-looking input elements.

Bootstrap has made styling forms easy and intuitive. When the additional CSS rules are applied to form elements, they not only look great but are extremely adaptive to mobile devices, making it easier for your users to interact with your website.

Consider this simple and clean form (figure 142).

14-41.html

```
<form>
    <div class="form-group">
        <label for="name">Name</label>
        <input type="text" class="form-control" id="name">
    </div>
    <div class="form-group">
        <label for="email">Email</label>
        <input type="email" class="form-control" id="email">
    </div>
    <div class="form-group">
        <label for="message">Message</label>
        <textarea name="message" class="form-control"
id="message"></textarea>
```

```
      </div>
      <button type="submit" class="btn btn-primary">Submit</
button>
    </form>
```

fig. 142

A simple Bootstrap contact form

In this example, the form code isn't radically different from a standard HTML form, but there are two key exceptions: the form-group and form-control classes.

The form-group class creates a logical structure for each form element and its accompanying label. The form-control class applies a variety of styles to the input element to ensure device compatibility and proper spacing within the form-group.

With a bit of magic from Bootstrap's layout grid and label-less input boxes, we can put form elements on the same row to better utilize space for complex forms and similar groups of data (figure 143).

14-42.html

```
<form>
  <div class="form-row">
    <div class="col">
      <input type="text" name="first-name" class="form-control"
placeholder="First Name">
    </div>
    <div class="col">
      <input type="text" name="last-name" class="form-control"
placeholder="Last Name">
    </div>
        <div class="col">
      <button type="submit" class="btn btn-primary">Submit</
button>
```

```
    </div>
   </div>
</form>
```

An inline Bootstrap form

If you want to add a bit of help text below an input field, Bootstrap has you covered (figure 144).

14-43.html

```
<form>
    <div class="form-group">
        <label for="name">Name</label>
        <input type="text" class="form-control" id="name">
    </div>
    <div class="form-group">
        <label for="email">Email</label>
        <input type="email" class="form-control" id="email"
aria-describedby="email-help">
        <!-- Display small text that provides additional
information to the user about this input element -->
        <small id="email-help" class="form-text text-muted">
            We will never share your email address with anyone!
        </small>
    </div>
    <div class="form-group">
        <label for="message">Message</label>
        <textarea name="message" class="form-control"
id="message"></textarea>
    </div>
    <button type="submit" class="btn btn-primary">Submit</
button>
</form>
```

The email help is contained within a `<small></small>` element and is given the id `email-help`. You'll notice the email input is decorated with the `aria-describedby="email-help"` attribute. This is done to tell accessibility software like screen readers that the input element has instructions to be read to the user via the element with the matching id—in our case, the small element with text.

fig. 144

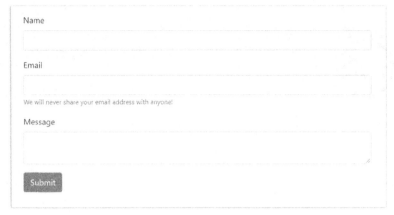

A contact form with help text below the email field

Typography

Bootstrap includes a definition for a set of fonts carefully selected to look great on every device. Since every device has a serif and a sans-serif default font option, Bootstrap overrides this with fonts like Segoe UI on Windows, Noto Sans on Linux, Roboto on Android, and Apple System on iOS and macOS. It also creates a more pleasing set of sizes for headings and overrides the default pure black text color for specific elements for a smoother, print-like appearance.

Headings

As mentioned in the introduction, Bootstrap redefines heading elements with a better scale of font sizes and an ever-so-slightly lightened black color that looks great on modern screens (figure 145).

fig. 145

h1. This is a Bootstrap heading.
h2. This is a Bootstrap heading.
h3. This is a Bootstrap heading.
h4. This is a Bootstrap heading.
h5. This is a Bootstrap heading.
h6. This is a Bootstrap heading.

Bootstrap headings. It's difficult to tell in the image, but the text isn't exactly black— it's a slightly softened version of black.

Color

In addition to overall color styles, Bootstrap provides helpful CSS classes for text colors.

```html
<!-- This paragraph has blue text on a white background -->
<p class="text-primary">.text-primary</p>

<!-- This paragraph has gray text on a white background -->
<p class="text-secondary">.text-secondary</p>

<!-- This paragraph has green text on a white background -->
<p class="text-success">.text-success</p>

<!-- This paragraph has red text on a white background -->
<p class="text-danger">.text-danger</p>

<!-- This paragraph has yellow text on a white background -->
<p class="text-warning">.text-warning</p>

<!-- This paragraph has light blue text on a white
background -->
<p class="text-info">.text-info</p>

<!-- This paragraph has light text on a dark background -->
<p class="text-light bg-dark">.text-light</p>

<!-- These paragraphs have dark text on a white background -->
<p class="text-dark">.text-dark</p>
<p class="text-body">.text-body</p>

<!-- This paragraph has gray text on a white background -->
<p class="text-muted">.text-muted</p>

<!-- This paragraph has white text on a dark background -->
<p class="text-white bg-dark">.text-white</p>

<!-- This paragraph has gray text on a white background -->
<p class="text-black-50">.text-black-50</p>

<!-- This paragraph has gray text on a dark background -->
<p class="text-white-50 bg-dark">.text-white-50</p>
```

Weight, Style, and Decoration

14-45.html

Bootstrap has a simple shortcut for bolding text.

```
<p class="font-weight-bold">Bold text.</p>
```

You can remove the underline for a particular link with `text-decoration-none`.

14-46.html

```
<a href="https://www.clydebankmedia.com/" class="text-decoration-none">This link to CBM is not underlined</a>
```

The `<code></code>` and `<pre></pre>` elements are redefined to provide a more attractive presentation of code on a web page.

14-47.html

```
<code>This is a sample of code.</code>
<pre>This is a sample of preformatted text.</pre>
```

The `code` text is displayed in light red, and the `pre` text is shown in a dark gray font (figure 146).

fig. 146

```
This is a sample of code.
This is a sample of preformatted text.
```

Bootstrap's enhanced `code` and `pre` elements.

Alignment

Bootstrap has built-in classes for easy text and object alignment. These can be applied to most elements, and if you include the class in a div, all elements contained within that div will default to that alignment.

14-48.html

```
<p class="text-left">This text will be left-aligned.</p>
<p class="text-center">This text will be center-aligned.</p>
<p class="text-right">This text will be right-aligned.</p>
```

Wrapping

If text is too long to fit in an element, it will wrap. You can prevent this with these helpful Bootstrap utility classes.

```
<p class="text-wrap">This text will be wrapped.</p>
<p class="text-nowrap">This text will NOT be wrapped.</p>
```

Additional Learning

Bootstrap can make your forms look beautiful and help you create attractive and responsive tables. It provides a plethora of additional helpful tools to use in your website's design. Covering every detail of Bootstrap's functionality would require a book of its own, so if you're interested in quickly creating responsive websites, I encourage you to check out the Bootstrap website and documentation at www.getbootstrap.com.

Moving Forward

In part III, we've covered advanced HTML and CSS. Armed with this knowledge, you can create semantically designed pages and contact forms, and you can transform and animate with CSS. With media queries, you can ensure your site looks impressive on all devices. With just a few lines of code, Bootstrap lays the foundation for a beautiful site and makes responsive web design simple. In part IV, we'll detail how to set up a project to arrange all these pieces into a living, breathing website.

You've come a long way. Keep up the great work. See you in part IV!

Chapter Recap

» Bootstrap provides a CSS framework on which to build responsive websites featuring cross-browser and cross-device compatibility with clean code.

» Bootstrap can provide many enhancements to your website out of the box, including normalized fonts, heading sizes, and colors, and various CSS utility classes.

» Bootstrap saves keystrokes and eliminates some redundant code, allowing you to focus on your layout.

PART IV

THE WORK ENVIRONMENT

| 15 |
Workflow

Chapter Overview
» Clean, organized project structure is vital.
» Use scaffolding and wireframing to plan projects.
» Content management systems help to customize existing code.

In the previous chapters, we have covered the nuts and bolts of HTML and CSS. At this point, you should be able to construct a web page from scratch and add text, images, and visual styling, and adjust it to look good on all devices.

In part IV, we'll explore the workflow and tools of a web developer. Workflow is simply the steps and procedures you take to design a website—from the first HTML file and line of code to the ongoing maintenance of the site throughout its lifetime. A good workflow, paired with your new HTML and CSS skills, is the last piece of the puzzle, allowing you to unlock your full potential as a web designer.

Project Setup and Management

There is no perfect way to set up a structure for a website. Every site will have different requirements, and every web designer has their preferred style of organization. In this section, my goal is not to force you to follow a particular method. Instead, I want to help you establish your own comfortable and productive workflow by providing examples and recommendations with instructions on how to adjust them to suit your needs.

Folder Structure
HTML has no specific requirements for file and folder placement. In fact, in the early days of web design, I saw websites with all HTML, CSS, image, and other related files in the same folder! This layout would be unthinkable today, especially on a complex website. Managing more than just a few pages and images would quickly become a chore.

Over the years, folder and file name conventions have evolved. Following these conventions is helpful but not required. Here is a list of standard file and folder names used in modern web design.

» **HTML Files**: Pages usually reside in the main folder of the site. It is possible to store pages in subfolders, but keep in mind that doing so makes using relative paths for CSS, JavaScript, and images a more tedious process.

» **Images**: A folder called `images` usually stores the graphic elements for the website.

» **Audio/Video**: If present, this content is usually contained in the media folder. Sometimes the `media` folder also contains images.

» **CSS Files**: If a site uses just one style sheet, it is often named style.css and located in a folder called `css`. On small sites, you may see the style.css file placed in the home folder.

» **JavaScript Files**: These usually sit in a folder called `js` or `javascript`.

» **Favorite Icon (Favicon)**: A favicon.ico file is a special kind of image file shown as an icon on the tab or bookmark of your website. It isn't required, but it's a good idea to use one. It *must* be in the main folder of the site.

» **PDF, Text, and Downloads**: Files intended to be downloaded, like PDFs, text files, executables, ZIP files, and the like, are generally found in a folder called `assets` or `downloads`.

Scaffolding

It's helpful to have gathered all the text, images, and layout details you'll need before you start to design a website. If all the data is there, you can arrange it without having to break your workflow to obtain more information from your client or team. Unfortunately, this rarely happens. You'll often receive an overall idea of what is needed on the website but few pieces of content. Text and images will trickle in as you progress through the project, and pages may be added just before the site is complete.

When you design a website, get in the habit of paying attention to future expansion—it will save you hours of work in the long run. The goal isn't to try to think so far ahead you are paralyzed in the present, but rather to consider possible upgrades and additions to your design so that you don't have to rework the entire site just to add a page. In programming terminology, this attribute is referred to as *scalability*; a site that "scales" well handles additions without significant problems.

Construction crews use framing to support additional building materials when a house is under construction. The framers may not know what color the homeowner will paint the walls, but that data isn't needed at that stage of building. In web design, scaffolding (also known as "wireframing") provides placeholder content, so the overall layout of the site can be constructed without finalizing details.

Recall the empty anchor links on the ClydeBank Coffee Shop website. The original designer wasn't sure what the page names would be, so they used # as a placeholder link. When a visitor clicked the link, they would be directed to the top of the current page, but this was preferable to triggering a 404 Not Found error or being taken to a page not yet finished.

Lorem Ipsum text is an excellent way to provide scaffolded text content, enabling you and the client to envision the page layout with full text. Sample images can fill in empty areas, and empty divs with their height and width set to match the eventual size can provide spacing for future content.

In some cases, a client may provide a sketch of a website on paper. Translating this into a web design layout can be challenging, but remember that most pages use a similar structure. Pages usually contain a header, often with an embedded navigation element; the main content area, sometimes with a div floating left or right for a sidebar; a content div; some kind of separation after the div break; and then a footer with links, copyright, and contact information.

Testing and Debugging

Testing can be just as challenging and time-consuming as designing the website. We'll get into some specific techniques you can use to test and debug, but the most important thing to remember about producing a problem-free website is to test early and often. By testing as you go, you avoid having to make massive "all or nothing" changes. A series of small tweaks and improvements with feedback from colleagues or your client along the way generally works best. You don't want to put a lot of work into something that might not be what the client wants, so it's better to know sooner rather than later, when it's still possible to make changes without undoing a lot of work.

Browser Development Tools

We've been working with local HTML files throughout this book, so testing has not been a cumbersome task. Making a change in your editor and then refreshing the web page in your browser has been sufficient. The process is similar when working with a remotely hosted website via file transfer protocol (FTP), with the added step of uploading the saved file to the server and testing it on the live site. But this testing workflow has significant drawbacks.

The biggest problem with live testing is that you are making changes to a website in real time. Visitors will be able to see these changes and possibly inaccurate, incomplete, or broken HTML content. This isn't a big deal for a personal or hobby page, but it is highly undesirable for a company site. This issue can mostly be eliminated with the use of a *staging site* (a private site for testing or showing work to others), but this can incur extra cost with your web hosting company and still requires uploading the changed file to your web server via FTP. If it takes one hundred changes to make a complex element render correctly in the browser, you will be wasting a lot of time re-uploading your work.

This is where browser-based testing and debugging comes into the workflow. Rather than using your code editor to change the file, re-upload, refresh, and hope for the best, you can use the live development tools in modern web browsers, including Mozilla Firefox and Google Chrome (and derivates like Microsoft Edge, Brave, and Chromium). You can access this toolbox via the F12 key on the keyboard or by right-clicking on an element and clicking *Inspect* in Chrome or *Inspect Element* in Firefox.

Figure 147 shows the Chrome inspector, but other browser development tools are similar and follow the same basic layout. The left pane shows the website, and the right pane displays the source code and property inspectors. The inspector frame is further divided into multiple sections—the most important two being the source code (left) and the CSS properties (right).

If you double-click on the source code, you can edit it directly in the browser. If you click on the empty CSS rule that looks like this...

```
element.style {

}
```

…you can add CSS rules to the highlighted element. The results of your edits are displayed in real time, and no changes are made to the files, so you don't have to worry about messing up a live website. This development environment isn't suitable for adding enormous amounts of content and HTML code, but it can speed up a lot of small, incremental changes with instant feedback.

fig. 147

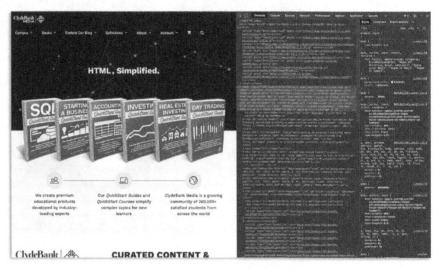

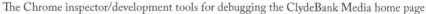

The Chrome inspector/development tools for debugging the ClydeBank Media home page

The JavaScript console, usually found within the development tools in a tab titled *Console*, shows any warning or error messages from the JavaScript code executed on the page and provides a command line for manually entering JavaScript code. This is incredibly useful for debugging JavaScript.

You can use the *Network* tab to see a waterfall display of the various page assets (CSS files, images, etc.) that are loaded on the site, as well as their attributes and the time it took to load them. If you have a slow-loading website, this view can show you which files are taking the longest to load, providing a handy report for website speed optimization (figure 148).

The Chrome inspector/development tools with the Network tab selected

fig. 148

Going Live

Until now, you have been designing your website on your hard drive. This is effective but provides no way for others to see your work. If you are in the middle of a design and need to showcase your work to a client or other interested party, you *can* compress the files and send the resulting ZIP archive to them via email, but this isn't very efficient. Large sites can exceed the storage limit on most email accounts.

A *shared web hosting* provider might be a good choice for showcasing and ultimately *deploying* your work. Once you purchase the account, you'll need to upload your files via an FTP client. Instructions vary with different FTP software packages, but we've covered the basics in appendix II, "FTP."

Development, Staging, Production

On simple sites, using FTP is probably enough, but complex sites may need a source code control system like Git (see chapter 16) or a method of first uploading changes to a staging server for approval before making it live.

Using multiple websites, usually named `dev.yourwebsite.com`, `new.yourwebsite.com`, or `staging.yourwebsite.com`, provides an excellent way to test changes before going live. If you are working as part of a larger team, consult your system administrator for instructions on uploading to a development or staging server.

Customizing Existing Code

If no CMS software like WordPress is used, files for the website will likely be in plain HTML format. You may also find HTML code in PHP files with the .php extension.

A freelance web designer who picks up a job will often be able to jump right into the work after the client provides them with FTP access. We'll cover FTP in appendix II.

WordPress

WordPress allows you to add and edit pages and posts via the administration dashboard. Posts (which include blog posts) are dated content that can be accessed under *Posts*. Pages, located under the *Pages* menu, contains content like the home page, about pages, contact pages, and perhaps other static, non-blog text. Custom themes and plugins may change this behavior.

Construction of posts and pages and the adjusting of options and themes in WordPress is done in the administration panel. This is almost always located at `yoursite.com/wp-admin` (replace yoursite.com with your domain name). Only those with an administrator account have full access to the administrative backend, so if you aren't the site owner, you'll need to obtain a user account with this permission.

WordPress is straightforward to use, and most nontechnical people can create compelling-looking content within its administration panel. For composing, a WYSIWYG (What You See Is What You Get) editor allows the user to type just as they would in a program like Microsoft Word. Through JavaScript, this is converted to HTML code. However, these kinds of HTML editors generally include a way to edit or add raw HTML code. Look for a `< >` symbol in WYSIWYG editors for this functionality.

If you want to edit the theme—that is, the header, footer, sidebar, and other page content, including CSS—first check out the theme customization options found under *Appearance* >> *Customize*. A graphical interface will guide you through making changes to the theme. For more complex changes that aren't supported by the theme's customize function, you can click *Appearance* >> *Theme Editor* to access a file manager that gives you the ability to edit style.css and other template files directly.

You can also edit the style sheet and theme files with FTP. Navigate to the `wp-content/themes/theme-name` folder (replace "theme-name" with the name of the theme). For complex edits to a theme, using FTP is easier because it allows you to use your favorite HTML editor.

Other CMS Systems

There are a lot of content management systems (CMSs) and website builders currently in use (Squarespace and Wix are among the most popular). Though we won't cover each of them extensively here, knowing some common terminology and workflow methods will help you adapt to any of these systems. Knowing HTML and CSS gives you a tremendous advantage when using these CMS platforms, as you'll be able to customize nearly every aspect of the site.

In most cases, other than choosing and customizing a theme, there will be three primary modes of input: adding pages or posts with a WYSIWYG editor, adding widgets (small blocks of functionality like an inline social media feed), and adding HTML code snippets. Instructions and capabilities vary considerably, so we'll focus on inserting raw HTML.

When inserting HTML into a content management system, you'll almost always want to omit the content in the head tag and any other page content that you don't intend to add. For example, if you want to add a bulleted list, only add the `<ul> </ul>` element and its containing `<li> </li>` elements.

Some content management systems (and some themes within these CMSs) will allow you to modify the CSS. If you cannot add or modify the CSS, you will need to use inline styles.

Chapter Recap

» A well-structured, consistent website design workflow is essential to efficient site creation and maintenance.

» Scaffolding and wireframing content helps to reserve space for other elements while facilitating site construction and editing.

» Frequent testing on a variety of devices, paired with a strategy to stage your updates for others to check before going live, helps reduce mistakes.

» Content management systems, like WordPress, allow for easy creation of content and can often be customized with raw HTML code.

| 16 |
Git

Chapter Overview

 » Git is a distributed version control system.
 » Git maintains version history and allows coders to collaborate.
 » GitHub provides free hosted git repositories.

Now that you've learned the basic workflow of website management, it's time to add another layer of knowledge to your website maintenance skills. Version control systems, like Git, allow you to not only produce versions of your work but easily collaborate with other designers and developers.

Git is an advanced topic, and some designers may not ever use this technology. Nevertheless, since Git is becoming quite popular, you'll have a leg up on future expansion should you decide to use this system.

What Is Git?

Git is a distributed version control system written by Linus Torvalds, the creator of the Linux kernel. "Version control system" sounds overly complex, so let's unpack the definition.

A version control system is a method of storing versions of your files. A version is simply an update to a previous version. Each time you add or edit content from a page, you're essentially creating a new version. A version control system keeps track of these changes by tracking the delta, or difference, between a file before and after you edit it.

Version control systems are usually centralized on a hosted server so users can check in and check out the content they're developing. In many centralized version control systems, the server maintains a series of locks, ensuring that two developers don't inadvertently work on the same file and make incompatible changes. This is a good arrangement but presents problems if developers need to work offline or if differences arise between individual developers' working copies.

The *distributed* nature of Git is what separates it from most version control systems. With decentralization technology, Git hosts the repository of version-controlled files on each developer's machine, not in any particular centralized location. Rather than relying on file locking, Git encourages the use of "branches" to separate individual developer efforts on specific features from the main branch and other developers' branches. When it's time to merge these branches, Git uses advanced algorithms to help reconcile and merge differences in files. When Git can't automatically merge the changes, it marks the conflicting files with a readable syntax, guiding developers to fix the issue manually.

Beyond these advantages, learning Git offers you a leg up on other web designers. Not only will you be able to work seamlessly with other programmers, you will also stand out in the eyes of prospective employers. They love to see these advanced technologies on a web designer's résumé.

Isn't Git overkill for a simple website? Possibly. If your website becomes a huge success and many people begin working on its code, you'll be glad you used it. But using Git from the beginning of a project provides benefits even if you never work with anyone else—mainly the ability to retain older versions of your files and revert to them if disaster strikes. On the other hand, it is fairly easy to import a site into a Git repository after it's been built, so this isn't a concern that should keep you up at night.

Downloading and Installing Git

You'll need to install Git on your machine. There are two primary methods of interfacing with Git—via command line and using a graphical user interface (GUI). The GUI approach is easier for new users, but the command line tools are more powerful.

» **GUI for Windows and macOS –GitHub Desktop**: www.desktop.github.com
» **GUI for Linux – GitKraken**: www.gitkraken.com
» **Command Line for Windows, macOS, and Linux**: www.git-scm.com

The instructions in this chapter will cover both the GUI and the command line. The GUI instructions will be somewhat too generic to account for the variation in software layouts and user interfaces. But no matter which you choose, the steps and workflow will be the same.

Accessing the Command Line

The command-line interface, or CLI for short, is a direct interface to the system that allows you to type commands instead of using a mouse or selecting icons and menu items. Many developers find the entering of commands preferable to a graphical user interface in certain situations. For more advanced development-related tasks, the CLI is often the only viable way to accomplish your goal.

While it's possible to use Git via a GUI, it's difficult to explain the steps involved, as each user interface is different. Skills learned in one GUI-based Git client may not translate well to another, and thus the command-line interface is the most stable and robust approach to using Git.

The command line may seem intimidating, but it's safer in some ways than using the GUI. A wrong click or inadvertent drag won't move files all over your drive. We will explore the process of starting a Git repository, adding files to it, updating, and pushing to a remote provider like GitHub. To get started, you'll need to install the Git command-line software.

Once Git is installed, you can launch a command-line (sometimes referred to as terminal) window and begin entering commands. On Windows, search for Command Prompt in the start menu or press WIN+R and type "cmd", then press ENTER to run the command prompt (figure 149). On Mac, run the terminal application. Linux terminal applications vary, but every distribution has one installed. On Ubuntu, for example, you can press CTRL+ALT+T to bring up a terminal, but your application list will undoubtedly show a terminal program.

fig. 149

The Command Prompt window on Windows

Starting a Website with Git

If you are just starting a new website on your hard drive, create the folder for your site in your home directory and call it `New-Website` (or some other meaningful name). Next, add some initial files (even if it's just an `index.html`), then "initialize" a Git repository in that folder.

Before you can create a Git repository, you must change to the directory of your website. To do this, run the change directory (`cd`) command:

Windows

```
cd %homepath%\New-Website
```

macOS and Linux

16-01
and
16-02

```
cd ~/New-Website
```

In the Windows example, `%homepath%` is substituted for your home directory, usually something like `C:\Users\YourName`. On macOS and Linux, the `~` is replaced with your home directory by the command prompt. If you use another folder name besides New-Website, be sure to change this.

Now it's time to start the repository. Once you've entered the folder of your website via the `cd` command, run:

```
git init
git add .
git commit -a -m "Initial commit."
```

16-03

In the `git add` command, we specify a period after the add to tell Git to add any files in the current directory. You can replace the dot with a specific file name if you only want to add one file. The `-a` option is to tell Git to stage all changes, and the `-m` option, followed by text in quotes, is to append a message to the commit. This message isn't shown on the site and doesn't modify the code, but instead provides a note to yourself or to others about the changes you made to this specific version. Since this is our first time committing a version of our site to the repository, our note states "Initial commit."

In a Git GUI, add the folder as a project, then initialize a Git repository. You'll also want to add any existing files you've created, then do an initial commit. You will be prompted for a message when committing.

Your commit was only to your local Git repository. If you want to add a remote repository and sync to it, such as with GitHub, you'll need to sign up for a GitHub account, create the repository on the website, then follow the instructions provided to add, commit, and sync. The GitHub Desktop GUI has integration with GitHub, so interfacing it with your GitHub account is easy.

Importing an Existing Website into Git

Importing an existing site is similar to starting a new one, except the `add` command will import all the existing files. The steps under "Starting a Website with Git" apply, but be sure to include your current HTML, CSS, and JavaScript files.

Also, keep in mind that version history will not be available until you make a commit. Git cannot track changes unless it has been added to a folder, so any changes made before adding Git are without history.

The Git Workflow

In the previous steps, we performed several operations: initializing (`init`), adding (`add`), and committing. In the `init` step, we added Git support to the folder. This is done only once for a repository. With the `add` command, we add files into Git to be tracked, then we commit the changes with the `commit` command.

The only step missing is the "push" (sometimes referred to as "sync" in GUI tools) command. Pushing allows you to sync your commits with another repository in another location. If you have added the repository to GitHub, you will push to GitHub.

We'll get into the nuances of pushing a repository later. For now, let's review the basic workflow. In figure 150, we create a new file called `new.html` and observe its life cycle within the Git paradigm.

fig. 150

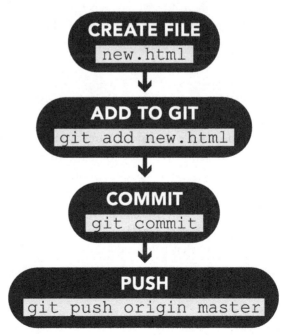

This workflow is repeated over and over, except the creation process is omitted if the file already exists. You can also skip the `add` part if you use the `-a` option on `git commit`, because it will include all changed files previously added (GUI programs will offer "include unstaged changes" or a similar option). With each commit, be sure to include a useful and meaningful message so you'll be able to refer to that change in the future, then push to GitHub if desired.

Git Branches

By default, your project has one branch, the *master* branch. For simple, single-developer projects, this may be all you need, but complex projects benefit significantly from multiple branches. Think of branches like diverging highways. You're still moving forward but in slightly different paths.

Branching your development allows you to work on new changes that might break your existing work, without disrupting your current site. Branches, when given meaningful names like "new_navigation_menu," are easily spotted in an online tool like GitHub and let you deviate from the existing code without affecting others.

To create a new branch, run...

16-04

```
git checkout -b new _ branch
```

...(where `new _ branch` is the name). GUI programs have buttons enabling the creation of new branches within your repository.

To switch branches, simply run:

16-05

```
git checkout master
```

In this case, you return to the master branch. Note the omission of the `-b` option, since the branch already exists.

When you're ready to merge your shiny new changes from `new _ branch` into `master`, you have two options. The easiest is to use GitHub to create a pull request between branches and then merge them using GitHub's online interface. This pull request allows you (or another coder) to review the changes before merging them into the master branch. This adds a layer of oversight that helps reduce mistakes in live websites. GUI tools have similar functionality, or you can use the command line.

```
git checkout master
git merge new_branch
```

If you want to delete the `new_branch` branch after merging, you can run:

```
git branch -d new_branch
```

A final note about branches: if your separate branch will be used for a long time, it's advisable to periodically pull changes from the master into the new branch so that you don't end up with a branch that is horrifically out of date. If you work in a large team, a merge can be disastrous if your code hasn't kept up with what's going on in the master and other branches.

Git Production Auto-Sync

In some web hosting control panels, you can configure an auto-pull from the master branch of a hosted repository on a provider like GitHub. This will automatically pull the contents of `master` from GitHub whenever you commit to `master`, providing a one-touch solution for deploying code to your website.

If you don't have this capability in your control panel, you can use your control panel to create a scheduled task (often called a "cron job") that runs the following code:

```
cd ~/public_html
git pull origin master
```

In the previous example, replace `public_html` with the path that contains your website files (if necessary) and `origin master` with the name of the remote Git repository and remote branch to pull. If you use GitHub, `origin master` will be the correct values.

Web hosts have a variety of control panels, and covering them all would be far beyond the scope of this book. However, the basic instructions, perhaps with the help of your web hosting technical support team to fill in any provider-specific values, should get you up and running.

GitHub and GitLab

Providers like GitHub and GitLab provide a centralized location to sync your Git repositories for easy collaboration with other developers.

You may have read that sentence and wondered why you would want a centralized location when Git touts itself as being a decentralized technology. Decentralization is indeed a powerful design feature of Git, but having a central repository with issue tracking, a wiki, and comment features amounts to a powerful suite of tools that will aid and enhance your team's collaborative efforts.

As you know by now, the ClydeBank Coffee Shop website and the source code for this entire book is stored on GitHub. You don't need an account to download or browse the code, but a free account is required for access to advanced features on GitHub, like forking and issue tracking.

Chapter Recap

» The version history and branch components of Git are powerful features for both stand-alone developers and those working on a team.

» GitHub is a popular provider of hosted Git repositories, but there are other providers. Most let you create and host repositories for free.

| 17 |
What's Next?

Chapter Overview

» PHP, Python, and other backend languages process data.
» Web design is a dynamic field that constantly changes.

The web is full of emergent technologies, and no book can hope to cover everything about even the most current tools and frameworks. Now that you've learned about HTML and CSS and common workflows, it's time to discuss a few specific technologies that are in use now and can empower you with resources and techniques to integrate new technologies as they are developed.

It's important to note that most of the topics covered in this chapter are related to HTML and CSS but are vast subjects, and thorough coverage of them is beyond the scope of this book.

WordPress

WordPress is a very popular and extremely powerful content management system. We've discussed it several times throughout the book, and in chapter 15 we covered the basics of how to add posts and pages and edit the template. Exploring the concepts and techniques of WordPress-centric web design is beyond the scope of this book, but you will likely use or at least encounter WordPress in your web design career, so it's essential to have a good familiarity with its functionality.

While most users can add pages and posts using the simple editor in the administration panel, web designers will be able to edit the HTML and CSS used in the pages' theme. WordPress themes have become expansive in their capabilities and customizations, but I've found that even in the most configurable themes, a few lines of CSS are still needed to achieve the look and feel I'm trying to achieve.

JavaScript and jQuery

JavaScript is a flexible and powerful programming language that your browser fully understands and can use to automate, process, and extend the functionality of HTML and CSS.

We've discussed where JavaScript lives in your overall website structure (usually in .js files in a `js` folder, or sometimes in an `assets` folder) and some of its capabilities. Like the other technologies in this chapter, we could easily fill several books covering JavaScript.

jQuery is a JavaScript framework that helps developers write clear, concise JavaScript code that works well on all major browsers. Before modern JavaScript frameworks, developers had to adjust for the variations in the implementation of JavaScript in each browser.

17-01.css
and
17-02.html

CSS

```
#sale { color: red; }
```

HTML

```
<p id="sale">SALE STARTS TODAY</p>
```

JavaScript

17-03.js

```
// Show the sale paragraph
$("sale").show();
// Or hide it!
$("sale").hide();
// Change it to blue text
$("sale").css("color", "blue");
```

This JavaScript code showcases a small sliver of functionality from jQuery. In each line, the paragraph with the id of sale is addressed as an object. An object is a programming term for an instance of a collection of related program variables and functions. Those functions related to that object (that is, show, hide, and css), allow you to show, hide, and change CSS elements of that paragraph.

Each of these lines of code can be bound to a particular event on the page. For example, jQuery can monitor when a user clicks a button.

17-04.html

HTML

```
<input id="toggle" type="button" name="toggle"
value="Toggle Sale">
```

JavaScript

```
$("#toggle").click(function() {
$("#sale").toggle();
});
```

In this example, when the user clicks the "Toggle Sale" button, the "toggle" function on the "sale" object is called, triggering the element to display if it is currently hidden and hide if it is presently shown.

Backend Languages Like PHP and Python

We've hinted at the power of backend languages like PHP and Python. Let's explore them in more detail.

PHP

For a long time, PHP was an extremely popular backend programming language. It still is, especially since it powers popular CMS software like WordPress. PHP lets WordPress process user input and retrieve content from a MySQL database.

PHP has a relatively straightforward syntax that can be easily mixed with HTML code, making it a popular choice for web designers. PHP code is contained within `<?php` and `?>` marks in a .php file, but HTML code can be used outside of those delimiters.

Form input fields can be accessed and used easily:

```
Your name is <?php echo $ _ REQUEST['name']; ?>.
```

If a contact form has a name input box and the action is set to a file with this code with a .php extension, the text "Your name is David" will appear (provided you enter "David" in the input box called "name."

Coding a form in this way requires PHP on the web server, but many web servers, especially Linux-based web servers, already have this installed.

Python

Python is a modern, object-oriented programming language. An object-oriented language uses special structures called *classes* (not to be confused with HTML/CSS classes). When we discussed jQuery, we referenced the sale paragraph as an object. In programming languages like Python and JavaScript, classes act like templates for objects, allowing developers to organize variables and functionality logically.

Python has a cleaner syntax and a wide assortment of modules that can be integrated into the language to extend its functionality. It also requires proper indentation in code, enforcing readable source.

Unlike PHP, Python requires a bit more than just a .py file in order to run on a web server. Special configuration is needed to either spawn the Python script when the visitor accesses the code or run the program and have it listen for requests from the web server. A web host specializing in Python will be able to configure this for you.

David's Perfect Cup

You have dramatically improved the ClydeBank Coffee Shop website over the course of this book.

As I may have mentioned a few chapters back, the hard work and dedication you have undoubtedly shown by learning HTML and CSS has motivated me to take a crack at redesigning the ClydeBank Coffee Shop website. I threw in some extra little bells and whistles that you can explore on your own time. I've put all of my web design files in a repository called "David's Perfect Cup." You can find it on our GitHub site here: www.github.com/clydebankmedia/davids-perfect-cup.

As a final exercise, why not brew your own perfect coffee shop website? You can use mine as a guide or let your creativity run wild and do something completely unique. The choice is yours.

We want to see your work. Please share your HTML and CSS creations with us on social media using the hashtag #CBM-HTML.

Chapter Recap

» Backend languages like PHP and Python help process data, interface with a database, and display dynamic content.

» Web design, like most topics in information technology, is an exciting field that encourages never-ending learning.

Conclusion

Throughout this book, you've been introduced to HTML, CSS, and several related technologies, and you've used your growing body of knowledge to edit the ClydeBank Coffee Shop website. You've learned how to stage your work, create an effective workflow, and collaborate with teams using source code management systems like Git. You've learned the languages (HTML and CSS) that define the underlying technology for nearly all the display systems in use today. You now hold a tremendous advantage—one you can leverage in your personal and professional life.

So the answer to the question "What's next?" largely depends on you. Will you take this information and build a website for a personal hobby? For your company? For your child's sports team? Perhaps you'll launch the web's next successful startup.

Learning never stops. This is especially true with HTML and CSS. Web design is truly an art that takes a few hours to learn and a lifetime to master, and part of that mastery is keeping up with changes and advancements in the field.

Congratulations on your achievement. We cannot wait to see what is next for you!

REMEMBER TO DOWNLOAD YOUR FREE DIGITAL ASSETS!

 HTML Starter Template

 All Source Code from Examples

 Online Resource Library

TWO WAYS TO ACCESS YOUR FREE DIGITAL ASSETS

Use the camera app on your mobile phone to take a picture of the QR code or visit the link below and instantly access your digital assets.

or

go.quickstartguides.com/htmlcss

 SCAN ME

VISIT URL

Appendix I

Web Hosting

At some point, you will need to find a server to host your site. There is a wide range of places, from free to full-fledged dedicated hosting companies. The pricing typically depends on features. If you are doing simple HTML hosting, then you won't need many resources, but it is worth doing some research to determine which hosts and plans will best suit your needs (figure 151).

fig. 151

A sample comparative feature list for a website hosting service

When choosing a web host, you will likely want to consider the following features:

» **Storage**: How much space is provided? Most HTML and CSS files are not large (they are just text files, after all), but if you have a site with many multimedia features or photos, you may need a lot of storage space.

» **Bandwidth**: Bandwidth refers to the amount of data that can be transferred from the servers hosting your site to the users requesting information from it. Typically, bandwidth is measured in one-billion-byte increments, called gigabytes (often abbreviated GB or GiB). Prices for bandwidth are given in tiers. Creating a website that receives a lot of traffic can end up being costly—especially if users are downloading large files beyond the simple graphics found on a basic web page (figure 152).

EXAMPLE OF BANDWIDTH

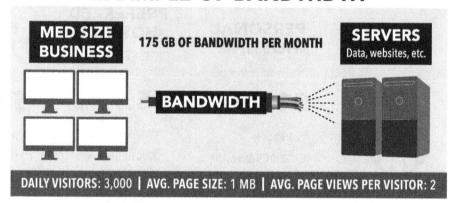

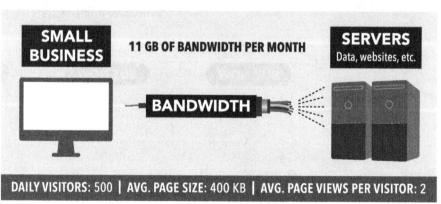

fig. 152

Source: https://tools.pingdom.com/

» **Uptime:** Will your website be available when people try to reach it? Web servers are far from infallible, and unforeseen circumstances like power outages, hardware failures, and denial-of-service (DoS) attacks are common problems with hosting. Even routine maintenance can take a server down for a small portion of each month. Web hosts usually calculate uptime as a percentage. A site with 99 percent uptime sounds like a great deal until you realize how much downtime that percentage is each month. Would a website that goes off-line fourteen minutes of every day be acceptable? What if the site had excellent daily uptime but went down for three days one year during a crucial time for your business? Both of those scenarios are possible within the limits of a 99 percent uptime guarantee (figure 153).

GRAPHIC

fig. 153

UPTIME GUARANTEE	DAILY MAX	WEEKLY MAX	MONTHLY MAX	YEARLY MAX
99%	14m 24.0s	1h 40m 48.0s	7h 18m 17.5s	3d 15h 39m 29.5s
99.5%	7m 12.0s	50m 24.0s	3h 39m 17.5s	1d 19h 49m 44.8s
99.9%	1m 26.4s	10m 4.8s	43m 49.7s	8h 45m 57.0s

» **Security:** If your website deals with the personal information of your customers, you will naturally be interested in security to keep that information safe. Website hosting companies offer a variety of safety and security features, which can include HTTPS, SSL certificates, content delivery networks (CDNs), firewalls, and attack protection.

» **Tech Support:** Good support is essential, especially for complex sites. You will need to be able to contact someone if something goes wrong or to find out if they have a solution that will meet a need.

» **Backup:** Does the host provide backup services that will preserve your website in the event of a server crash or other unanticipated incident?

Some hosting companies offer services beyond providing a platform for HTML, CSS, and image files. You may need dynamically loading content from a database, or you may wish to connect your website to an email server and allow visitors to send email from a contact form.

» **Database Support**: Can you create and use MySQL, PostgreSQL, or Microsoft SQL databases? WordPress requires one MySQL database. Some shared web hosting companies limit database size—something to keep in mind if you plan on building a large site with WordPress or a similar CMS.

» **SSH / Shell Access**: Can you do any command-line work on the server? This is helpful for Git and some PHP tools, such as Composer.

Appendix II
FTP

FTP, or file transfer protocol, is a method of sending and receiving files from remote servers. Once you understand the general workflow of FTP, it will seem much like copying files on your computer. However, understanding FTP involves defining a few terms and wading through an alphabet soup of acronyms so you'll recognize related terms.

It is important to note that FTP is an internet protocol (just like HTTP or HTTPS) and thus is not defined or controlled by a particular program. Various FTP programs exist, but they all provide a way for you to send and receive files to and from another computer.

Almost every web hosting company provides FTP access (see appendix I for details on web hosting). Nowadays, FTP is increasingly referred to by its more secure variant, SFTP, which stands for secure file transfer protocol. It encrypts the connection with SSL so that authentication information and file contents are kept from prying eyes and would-be attackers.

Sometimes SFTP is also called SCP, but this is a misnomer. SCP stands for Secure Copy, a protocol built upon SSH (Secure Shell), which is a method allowing users to access the command line of a server via a secure, encrypted tunnel. SCP lets the user transfer files in much the same way as with SFTP, so web hosting companies and software programs often reference SCP and SFTP in similar scenarios.

Now that the terms are out of the way, we'll need to discuss software. Almost every modern operating system includes a command-line client named `ftp`, but using it for anything but the most basic tasks is tedious at best. FTP uses commands like GET (retrieving files), PUT (sending files), and LIST (listing files), and, though typing is possible, you'll want an FTP program to present file listings and download/upload commands in an easy-to-use interface.

Common FTP Software Titles

As of this publication, some popular FTP clients include the following:

- » FileZilla (Windows, macOS, and Linux)
- » WinSCP (Windows)
- » Transmit (macOS)
- » ExpanDrive (Windows, macOS, and Linux)

FileZilla, WinSCP, and Transmit present, by default, a two-pane explorer. Files on the left-hand side are local to your computer, and files on the right-hand side are on the server. Dragging and dropping files from the local pane to the remote pane initiates a file transfer. In both windows, you can click on icons to navigate to folders, create new files and folders, and edit and delete data.

Programs like ExpanDrive represent the remote FTP server as a drive letter, allowing you to navigate, copy, edit, and delete files and folders as though they were on your local system. This can be very useful, but keep in mind that working directly on the server offers no easy backup route. For this reason, web designers may wish to either keep a local copy of their files or use a software package that features both local and remote panes to display files on their computer and files on the remote server.

Connecting to an FTP Server

All FTP clients will prompt you for information required to connect you to a remote FTP server. Necessary details include the following:

- » Server hostname or IP address
- » Username
- » Password
- » Remote path for files

Your web hosting company will provide the server hostname for FTP. This is sometimes named ftp.YourWebsite.com, but it may also be the name of the server. Or they may provide an IP address. Either will work. Unless you created a username and password in your web hosting control panel, your provider assigns these details.

The remote path isn't required, but knowing where your files are going will save you a lot of time digging through your web hosting account. On cPanel-based shared hosting servers, the remote directory is `public _ html`. On Plesk, it's `httpdocs`. Dedicated or virtual private Linux servers may use `/var/www/html`. If in doubt, check with your provider.

Some Final Notes on FTP

FTP provides an excellent way to back up an existing website. Simply connect to your FTP server and download all your files. Many FTP clients provide a "Download All" or "Synchronize" function to allow you to download everything from the remote server in one click.

FTP can be incompatible with Git, and using FTP to place files will likely break your Git workflow. If you're using Git to push your website files to your web server, you will only want to use FTP to back up your site, not to upload files.

Appendix III

Sizing Units

As discussed in chapter 7, CSS provides a great deal of flexibility in how we assign size, padding, margins, and positions to our elements. Several different units of measurement are available to determine the size of anything on a web page—font size, margins, spacing, padding, proportions of elements, and more. Units of measurement can be used independently or in conjunction with one another.

Pixels

Pixels, or px, are finite points in an image. They are the smallest element of an image and thus define the exact size of the target element.

An HTML coder wants to display an image at a specific size. He uses pixels to quantify his desired sizing specifications:

```
img {
    width: 400px;
    height: 600px;
}
```

A-01.css

Percent

Percent, designated by the % character, can be used to create flexible items, which will expand or shrink to fit the size of a container.

For instance, if we want to have an image that resizes automatically, we can set the width to be 100%. Setting the height to `auto` will ensure that the image remains correctly proportioned.

```
img {
    width: 100%;
    height: auto;
}
```

A-02.css

vw and vh

Since users view web pages on devices of varying size—laptop computers, tablets, smartphones—we often use "responsive design" sizing units, which will tailor their effects in response to the size of the viewport, or viewing area.

The viewport width (vw) and viewport height (vh) units are used to specify how an element will appear in relation to the device (the viewport). The easiest way to understand these units is to think of them as similar to "percent," but instead of being relative to a defined element, they are relative to the screen or viewport itself.

1 vw is equal to 1/100, or 1%, of the viewport's width. Similarly, 1 vh equals 1/100 of the viewport's height.

em/rem

As described in chapter 8, em is a type of relative formatting that specifies a font size in relation to the current font-size setting. The measurement is simply a multiple of the current size. For example, 1.5 em is equal to 1.5 times the current font size.

The rem unit is similar, but instead of being relative to the current font size, rem relates to the root (HTML) element, meaning that any setting of rem will be in relationship to the top level and not the current element.

Appendix IV

Open Graph / Metadata

The Open Graph protocol was created by Facebook to allow web designers to easily add their websites to Facebook's *social graph*, a model of the relationships between people, pages, businesses, and other entities on the web. Though initially started by Facebook, other providers, including Twitter, WordPress, Pinterest, Google, and others, use either the Open Graph protocol or subtle variations thereof.

Open Graph data provides hints to social media platforms of metadata that the system can use to better display and index your page. Absent this, most systems guess as to page title, description, and feature image. Presenting this data allows pages that link and reference your content to display to visitors the information you want them to see. These meta tags are added to the `<head></head>` element of your web page.

A-03.html

```
<meta property="og:title" content="ClydeBank Media">
<meta property="og:type" content="website">
<meta property="og:url" content="https://www.
clydebankmedia.com/">
<meta property="og:image" content="https://www.
clydebankmedia.com/wp-content/uploads/2020/06/3D_books_
display_2_1000.png">
<meta property="og:description" content="The official home
of ClydeBank Media, publisher of best-selling books and
digital courses. We make learning easy.">
```

Let's examine some of these specific properties in detail.

» `og:title`: The name, or title, of your content. In this case, we simply list the name of the page. If you're referring to a media file, you can provide the name of the content.

» `og:type`: The type of content. In this example, we are referring to a website, but there are several other "object types" recognized by the protocol. For an extensive listing visit ogp.me.

» `og:url`: The full URL of the content.

» `og:image`: The image you'd like the platform to use to represent your content. For a website linked in Facebook, this image would be used as the image of the post.

» `og:description`: A short description of the content.

The `og:title`, `og:type`, `og:image`, and `og:url` are required, but `og:description` is recommended. If you are referencing a page or article that isn't the main URL or isn't referring to a media file, the `og:site_name` property allows you to give a name to the site that may differ from the title of that specific page.

Appendix V

Coffee Shop Solutions

Downloading the Website from GitHub

To download the ClydeBank Coffee Shop website code, navigate in your browser to github.com/clydebankmedia/clydebank-coffee-shop.

Click on the green "↓ Code" button, then click "Download ZIP" to receive a ZIP file. Extract the ZIP file (usually by right-clicking the file in your file manager and clicking "Extract") (figure 154).

fig. 154

The GitHub code download dialog

Introduction: Adding an "About" Page

After you've extracted the website files from the ZIP file, open up the folder/directory. Copy (CTRL+C on a PC; CMD+C on a Mac) the `template.html` file, then paste the file (CTRL+V; CMD+V) back into the same directory. Select the newly created file (it might be named `template 2.html` or similar) and rename it to `about.html`. You're done.

Chapter 4: Adding a Description and Title

In chapter 4, we were tasked with adding a meta description tag in the header. Here's the completed code for your reference:

A-04.html

```html
<head>
    <meta charset="utf-8">
    <meta name="viewport" content="width=device-width,
initial-scale=1, shrink-to-fit=no">
    <title>ClydeBank Coffee Shop</title>
    <link rel="stylesheet" type="text/css" href="css/style.
css">
    <meta name="description" value="ClydeBank Coffee Shop
features premium coffee at an affordable price.">
</head>
```

Be sure to always save your changes in the code editor.

You can open your browser and view the source (usually Ctrl+u) to verify that the changes were made. The title tag will show in the name of the tab in your browser.

Chapter 5: About Page

In chapter 5 in the section called "ClydeBank Coffee Shop: About Page" we added content and changed the title of the About page.

Here's the completed code for your reference:

about.html: Main Content Portion

A-05.html

```html
<main>
    <div class="container">
<p> ClydeBank Coffee Shop welcomes you to our website. If
you're in the area, we kindly ask you to stop by and have a
cup with us.</p>
    </div>
</main>
```

about.html: Title

A-06.html

```html
<head>
    <meta charset="utf-8">
    <meta name="viewport" content="width=device-width,
```

```
initial-scale=1, shrink-to-fit=no">
      <title>About ClydeBank S</title>
      <link rel="stylesheet" type="text/css" href="css/style.
css">
   </head>
```

Chapter 5: Navigation

In the "ClydeBank Coffee Shop: Navigation" section, we fixed issues with the navigation. Here's the completed code for your reference:

index.html

A-07.html

```
<div class="container">
   <ul>
      <li class="active"><a href="index.html">Home</a></li>
      <li><a href="about.html">About</a></li>
      <li><a href="event.html">Event</a></li>
      <li><a href="contact.html">Contact</a></li>
   </ul>
</div>
```

contact.html

A-08.html

```
<div class="container">
   <ul>
      <li><a href="index.html">Home</a></li>
      <li><a href="about.html">About</a></li>
      <li><a href="event.html">Event</a></li>
      <li class="active"><a href="contact.html">Contact</a></li>
   </ul>
</div>
```

event.html

A-09.html

```
<div class="container">
   <ul>
      <li><a href="index.html">Home</a></li>
      <li><a href="about.html">About</a></li>
      <li class="active"><a href="event.html">Event</a></li>
      <li><a href="contact.html">Contact</a></li>
   </ul>
</div>
```

about.html

```
<div class="container">
    <ul>
        <li><a href="index.html">Home</a></li>
        <li class="active"><a href="about.html">About</a></li>
        <li><a href="event.html">Event</a></li>
        <li><a href="contact.html">Contact</a></li>
    </ul>
</div>
```

Chapter 8: Look and Feel

In chapter 8, we removed the gray background and replaced it with a more coffee-friendly color scheme. We did this by editing the style.css in the CSS folder.

Here is the previous code, and the code that replaces it. Please note that these items are not in the right order, but rather placed throughout the file.

```
header {
    background: #363F48;
    padding: 10px;
}

nav { background: #262d33; }

nav li a {
    color: #AFB2B6;
    display: inline-block;
    padding: 10px 10px;
}

footer {
    background: #333;
    color: #fff;
    padding: 10px;
    height: 100px;
}
```

The code should be changed to:

A-12.css

```css
header {
    background: sienna;
    padding: 10px;
}

nav { background: saddlebrown; }
nav li a {
    color: white;
    display: inline-block;
    padding: 10px 10px;
}

footer {
    background: saddlebrown;
    color: #fff;
    padding: 10px;
    height: 100px;
}
```

Chapter 9: Advertisement

In chapter 9, we added an advertisement for free delivery on orders of $15 or more.

CSS

A-13.css

```css
#top-announcement {
    position: relative;
    top: 0;
    right: 0;
    left: 0;
    background-color: yellow;
    text-align: center;
    padding-top: 3px;
    padding-bottom: 3px;
    color: black;
}
```

HTML

A-14.html

```html
    <div id="top-announcement">THIS MONTH ONLY: FREE delivery
on orders $15 or more!</div>
```

NOTE

If you use the word "ad" in the id of this element, an ad-blocker may hide the div.

Chapter 11: Contact Form

In chapter 11, we added a contact form to the site. Here is the code to add to the `contact.html` page.

SNIPPET

A-15.html

```html
<h1>Contact Us</h1>
<form action="contact.html" method="POST">
    <label for="name">Name</label><br>
    <input type="text" name="name" required><br><br>
    <label for="email">Email</label><br>
    <input type="email" name="email" required><br><br>
    <label for="message">Message</label><br>
    <textarea name="message" rows="5" cols="60"
maxlength="2000" required></textarea><br><br>
    <input type="submit" name="submit" value="Send
Message">
</form>
```

Chapter 12: Sprites

In chapter 12, we switched from separate image files to sprites. Included are the CSS modifications necessary to enable the sprite classes and changes to the HTML files necessary for their inclusion.

CSS

SNIPPET

A-16.css

```css
/* Sprites */

.sprite-palette {
    display: block;
    width: 40px;
    height: 40px;
    padding: 0;
    border: none;
    background: url('../images/sprite.png') 0 0;
}
```

```css
.sprite-guitar {
    display: block;
    width: 40px;
    height: 40px;
    padding: 0;
    border: none;
    background: url('../images/sprite.png') -40px 0;
}

.sprite-mask {
    display: block;
    width: 40px;
    height: 40px;
    padding: 0;
    border: none;
    background: url('../images/sprite.png') -80px 0;
}

.sprite-controller {
    display: block;
    width: 40px;
    height: 40px;
    padding: 0;
    border: none;
    background: url('../images/sprite.png') -120px 0;
}

.sprite-mic {
    display: block;
    width: 40px;
    height: 40px;
    padding: 0;
    border: none;
    background: url('../images/sprite.png') -160px 0;
}

.sprite-quill {
    display: block;
    width: 40px;
    height: 40px;
```

```
        padding: 0;
        border: none;
        background: url('../images/sprite.png') -200px 0;
    }

    .sprite-cup {
        display: block;
        width: 40px;
        height: 40px;
        padding: 0;
        border: none;
        background: url('../images/sprite.png') -240px 0;
    }

    .sprite-utensils {
        display: block;
        width: 40px;
        height: 40px;
        padding: 0;
        border: none;
        background: url('../images/sprite.png') -280px 0;
    }

    .sprite-milk {
        display: block;
        width: 40px;
        height: 40px;
        padding: 0;
        border: none;
        background: url('../images/sprite.png') -320px 0;
    }
```

HTML

Use these `span` elements in place of `img` elements to display the appropriate icon.

A-17.html

```
<span class="sprite-palette"></span>
<span class="sprite-guitar"></span>
<span class="sprite-mask"></span>
<span class="sprite-controller"></span>
<span class="sprite-mic"></span>
```

```
<span class="sprite-quill"></span>
<span class="sprite-cup"></span>
<span class="sprite-utensils"></span>
<span class="sprite-milk"></span>
<span class="sprite-clydebank"></span>
<span class="sprite-bigcup"></span>
```

Chapter 12: Gradients

In chapter 12, we added a gradient to the header. The color choice is up to you, but a gradient from `sienna` to `chocolate` is shown below in Snippet_A-19.css.

The header background was originally defined with the following code:

A-18.css

```
header {
    background: sienna;
    padding: 10px;
}
```

The CSS rule is now changed to:

A-19.css

```
header {
    background-image: linear-gradient(sienna, chocolate);
    padding: 10px;
}
```

Chapter 12: Keyframe Animation

In chapter 12 we added an animation to display a panoramic image. This sets the background position to "left" at the start and "right" at the end. We don't need any math, which makes it easier to swap images in the future. We have specified a longer duration so the image does not move frantically, and we've set the iterations to infinite so it will continue to move. Normally, I'd advise against a constantly moving animation, but this one is subtle and less distracting than most. To account for the changes in direction, we apply the `ease-in-out` animation-timing function, which has a smooth start and finish with a slightly faster speed during the middle of the animation.

A-20.css

CSS

```
#coffeehouse {
    background-image: url("https://otherfiles-cbm.s3-us-
```

```
west-2.amazonaws.com/CoffeeShopImage.jpg");
    background-size: cover;
    width: 100%;
    height: 250px;
    animation-name: background-pan;
    animation-duration: 10s;
    animation-timing-function: ease-in-out;
    animation-iteration-count: infinite;
    animation-direction: alternate;
}

@keyframes background-pan {
    from { background-position: left; }
    to { background-position: right; }
}
```

HTML

The main element already exists, so we'll just add id="coffeehouse" to it.

```
<main id="coffeehouse">
```

Chapter 13: Going Mobile

In chapter 13, we explored media queries and ended the chapter with an exercise to make the ClydeBank Coffee Shop website look good on both laptop/desktop screens and phones, with a minimum and maximum screen width of 375 and 750 pixels, respectively.

This solution will be a bit unique in that there isn't necessarily one way to accomplish this task. Making a website look good is an entirely subjective task, so ultimately you will be the judge of your code on this exercise.

CSS

```
@media only screen
and (min-device-width: 375px)
and (max-device-width: 750px) {

    /* Reduce padding in main element */
    main { padding: 5px; }

    /* Fix nav bar */
```

```
nav { height: 35px; }
nav ul { padding-top: 7px; }
nav li { display: inline; }
nav li a { color: white; }

/* Add extra spacing between menu items */
.menu-item {
    padding-top: 10px;
    padding-bottom: 10px;
}
.title-item h2 { font-size: 1em; }

/* Fix add on item */
.menu-item.additional-items h2 {
    padding-top: 10px;
    padding-bottom: 10px;
    width: 100%;
    float: none;
}

/* Reduce footer header size and add some padding */
footer h2 {
    font-size: 1.4em;
    padding-top: 3px;
    padding-bottom: 3px;
}

/* Reduce size of footer text to avoid awkward
wrapping */
    footer li { font-size: 0.85em; }

/* Add padding to bottom of footer */
    footer { padding-bottom: 5px; }
}
```

About the Author

DAVID DUROCHER

David DuRocher teaches web design and is a technical account manager at Adobe. A childhood love of video games helped fuel his passion to learn more about computers and programming languages. He attended the Rochester Institute of Technology and was later offered a teaching position at CUNY City College of Technology.

He enjoys teaching and developing web design curriculum, drawing great joy from seeing his students thrive with their newfound skills in HTML and CSS. His enthusiasm for education and a desire to share his knowledge led him to author this book.

When David isn't working or teaching, he enjoys exploring the outdoor beauty of New England and renovating his historic Victorian house. David lives with his wife in Northwest Connecticut.

About QuickStart Guides

QuickStart Guides are books for beginners, written by experts.

QuickStart Guides® are comprehensive learning companions tailored for the beginner experience. Our books are written by experts, subject matter authorities, and thought leaders within their respective areas of study.

For nearly a decade more than 850,000 readers have trusted QuickStart Guides® to help them get a handle on their finances, start their own business, invest in the stock market, find a new hobby, get a new job—the list is virtually endless.

The QuickStart Guides® series of books is published by ClydeBank Media, an independent publisher based in Albany, NY.

Connect with QuickStart Guides online at www.quickstartguides.com or follow us on Facebook, Instagram, and LinkedIn.

Follow us @quickstartguides

Glossary

Attribute
An additional option for an HTML element that modifies its behavior or appearance.

Breakpoint
The point at which CSS rules respond to the width of a device, "breaking" content from (usually) a horizontal to a vertical layout.

Code Editor
A text editor with specific features oriented toward developers. Code editing software typically includes syntax highlighting, automatic indentation, and multiple-file management.

Content Delivery Network (CDN)
A service that hosts CSS, JavaScript, images, and sometimes HTML code on a network of geographically dispersed servers for increased speed and reliability. Using a CDN frees the web server from having to serve all web page assets and leaves more processing power for serving HTML and dynamic pages.

Content Management System (CMS)
Software that allows web designers and content creators to easily add, edit, and organize a website with little to no knowledge of HTML, CSS, or related technologies. WordPress, Joomla, and Drupal are examples.

Cross-Site Scripting
The act of including or injecting code (usually JavaScript) from another page.

CSS (Cascading Style Sheets)
A coding system used to apply visual styles to HTML elements.

Deploying
The process of uploading website files to a web server.

Development Website (or Development Server)
A website used to develop new content or features. Development sites are generally not open to the public.

Element
A part of HTML code that instructs the browser to display content or adjust the functionality of a web page. Elements usually contain a start and end tag and can contain other elements.

Framework
In web design, a collection of CSS and JavaScript libraries that provide structure and utility to a website. Bootstrap is an example of a web design framework.

Hamburger Menu
A three-line vertically stacked icon that typically opens a menu for website navigation on a mobile device.

FTP (File Transfer Protocol)
A network protocol that facilitates file uploads and downloads to and from another computer. When referenced in the field of web design, FTP refers to the technology used to upload website HTML, CSS, and related files to a web server. FTP software uses this protocol to perform this transfer.

Full Stack Web Developer
A web designer who also codes JavaScript and works with backend languages like PHP and Python.

HTML (HyperText Markup Language)
A markup language that defines the appearance, behavior, and content of a web page.

Landscape Mode
A display orientation used with devices that are wider than they are tall. This mode is often used for movies, videos, and wide-screen photos.

Link (or Hyperlink)
An HTML element that, when clicked, takes the user to another URL.

Markup Language
A defined set of codes, symbols, and idioms that apply style or behavior to content.

Open-Source
Software that has its complete source code available for anyone to browse, use, alter, and distribute.

Portrait Mode
A display orientation used with devices that are taller than they are wide.

Production Website (or Live Website/Server)
A website that is currently online and available for public use, in contrast with development and staging websites.

Rendering Engine
The portion of a web browser that converts HTML and CSS code into a usable web page.

Responsive Design
A type of web design using media queries and related methods to adjust to various screen sizes and devices.

Shared Web Hosting
The process of hosting multiple websites from a single server. Shared web hosting dramatically lowers the cost of website hosting but can be limiting for sites with a lot of traffic.

Social Graph
A web-like network detailing links and connections between people, places, businesses, groups, and other organizations.

Source Code Management (SCM)
Software and systems that enable web designers and developers to manage updates and versions of source code. SCM systems usually facilitate collaboration between developers.

Staging Website (or Staging Server)
A website generally not open to the public that allows the web designer(s) to test out new code without breaking the production website. Once approved and tested, staging content is deployed to production.

Tag
A piece of HTML code that signifies the start or end of an HTML element. The term is sometimes used to describe an entire HTML element, especially if the element has no end tag.

URL (Universal Resource Locator)
An address of a website or other resource. May also be referred to as "uniform resource locator."

Web Designer (or Web Developer)
A person who writes HTML and CSS code for web pages. Some web designers also fulfill the role of graphic designer by creating or modifying photos or illustrations.

Web Browser
Software that allows a user to browse and interact with web pages.

Web Server
A computer that serves HTML web pages, CSS files, and other content to users via the internet.

References

DirtyMarkup. n.d. *10BestDesign*. Accessed February 24, 2020. https://www.10bestdesign.com/dirtymarkup/.

HTML: Living Standard. n.d. Accessed February 21, 2020. https://html.spec.whatwg.org.

Interactive Accessibility. n.d. *Accessibility Statistics*. Accessed February 14, 2020. https://www.interactiveaccessibility.com/accessibility-statistics.

Lemelson-MIT. n.d. "Linus Torvalds: Linux Operating System, Computing and Telecommunications." Accessed December 10, 2020. https://lemelson.mit.edu/resources/linus-torvalds.

Lippay, Laura. 2016. "What You Should Know About Accessibility + SEO, Part I: An Intro." *Moz*. March 30. https://moz.com/blog/accessibility-seo-1.

Otto, Mark. 2012. "Bootstrap in A List Apart No. 342." *Markdotto.com*. January 17. http://markdotto.com/2012/01/17/bootstrap-in-a-list-apart-342/.

Software Freedom Conservancy. n.d. *A Short History of Git*. Accessed June 10, 2020. https://git-scm.com/book/en/v2/Getting-Started-A-Short-History-of-Git.

United States Census Bureau. 2012. "Nearly 1 in 5 People Have a Disability in the U.S." News Release No. CB12-134. July 25. https://www.census.gov/newsroom/releases/archives/miscellaneous/cb12-134.html.

W3C. n.d. *Facts about W3C*. Accessed February 21, 2020. https://www.w3.org/Consortium/facts.

W3Techs. 2020. *W3Techs*. Accessed February 14, 2020. https://w3techs.com/technologies/details/cm-wordpress/all/all.

Wayner, Peter. 2011. "13 features that make each Web browser unique." *InfoWorld*. May 2. https://www.infoworld.com/article/2624020/13-features-that-make-each-web-browser-unique.html.

Weber, Jason. 2016. "Get More Out of Your Battery with Microsoft Edge." *Windows Experience Blog*, Microsoft. June 20. https://blogs.windows.com/windowsexperience/2016/06/20/more-battery-with-edge/.

Wikipedia. 2020. *Programming Languages Used in Most Popular Websites*. January 14. https://en.wikipedia.org/wiki/Programming_languages_used_in_most_popular_websites.

References

Index

WHAT DID YOU THINK?

We rely on reviews and reader feedback to help our authors reach more people, improve our books, and grow our business. We would really appreciate it if you took the time to help us out by providing feedback on your recent purchase.

It's really easy, it only takes a second, and it's a tremendous help!

NOT SURE WHAT TO SHARE?

Here are some ideas to get your review started...

- *What did you learn?*
- *Have you been able to put anything you learned into action?*
- *Would you recommend the book to other readers?*
- *Is the author clear and easy to understand?*

TWO WAYS TO LEAVE AN AMAZON REVIEW

Use the camera app on your mobile phone to scan the QR code or visit the link below to record your testimonial and get your free book.

SCAN ME

or

quickstartguides.review/html-css

VISIT URL

GET YOUR NEXT
QuickStart Guide®
FOR FREE

Leave us a quick video testimonial on our website and we will give you a **FREE *QuickStart Guide*** of your choice!

RECORD TESTIMONIAL　　　**SUBMIT TO OUR WEBSITE**　　　**GET A FREE BOOK**

SAVE 10% ON YOUR NEXT

QuickStart Guide®

USE CODE: QSG10

https://quickstartguides.shop/sql

https://quickstartguides.shop/business

https://quickstartguides.shop/investing

https://quickstartguides.shop/accounting

Use the camera app on your mobile phone to scan the QR code or visit the link below the cover to shop.

Get 10% off your entire order when you use code 'QSG10' at checkout at www.quickstartguides.com

LISTEN TO *QuickStart Guides* ON THE GO

NEW AUDIBLE MEMBERS
GET THEIR FIRST AUDIOBOOK

FREE!

DIGITAL MARKETING *QuickStart Guide*

FLIPPING HOUSES *QuickStart Guide*

INVESTING *QuickStart Guide*

FOREX TRADING *QuickStart Guide*

REAL ESTATE INVESTING *QuickStart Guide*

TWO WAYS TO SELECT A FREE AUDIOBOOK

Use the camera app on your mobile phone to scan the QR code or visit the link below to select your free audiobook from Audible.

or   www.quickstartguides.com/free-audiobook

📱 SCAN ME   🖥 VISIT URL

CLYDEBANK MEDIA

QuickStart Guides®

PROUDLY SUPPORT ONE TREE PLANTED

One Tree Planted is a 501(c)(3) nonprofit organization focused on global reforestation, with millions of trees planted every year. ClydeBank Media is proud to support One Tree Planted as a reforestation partner.

Every dollar donated plants one tree and every tree makes a difference!

Learn more at www.clydebankmedia.com/charitable-giving or make a contribution at onetreeplanted.org.

Made in the USA
Middletown, DE
28 October 2023

41414524R00197